From 'Good Order'
to Glorious Revolution

Salem, Massachusetts, 1628-1689

Studies in
American History and Culture, No. 19

Robert Berkhofer, Series Editor
Director of American Culture Programs
and Richard Hudson Research Professor of History
The University of Michigan

Other Titles in This Series

No. 13 *Migration in Early America:*
The Virginia Quaker Experience   Larry Dale Gragg

No. 14 *The Making of the Third Party System:*
Voters and Parties in Illinois, 1850-1876   Stephen L. Hansen

No. 15 *The Clergy and the Great*
Awakening in New England   David Harlan

No. 16 *Communities in Transition:*
Bedford and Lincoln, Massachusetts, 1729-1850   Richard Holmes

No. 17 *Freudian Theory and American*
Religious Journals, 1900-1965   Ann Elizabeth Rosenberg

No. 18 *French-Indian Relations on the*
Southern Frontier, 1699-1762   Patricia Dillon Woods

From 'Good Order' to Glorious Revolution

Salem, Massachusetts, 1628-1689

by
Christine Alice Young

umi
RESEARCH PRESS

Produced and distributed by
UMI Research Press
an imprint of
University Microfilms International
Ann Arbor, Michigan 48106

Library of Congress Cataloging in Publication Data

Young, Christine Alice, 1946-
   From 'good order' to glorious revolution.

   (Studies in American history and culture ; no. 19)
   Bibliography: p.
   Includes index.
   1. Salem, Mass.—History—Colonial period, ca. 1600-
1775.   I. Title. II. Series.

F74.S1Y68   974.4'5   80-20118
ISBN 0-8357-1101-3

Contents

Chapter One
Introduction: Salem as a Social Unit   *1*

Chapter Two
The Process of Accommodation: The Land to 1637   *9*

Chapter Three
The Limits of Accommodation: 1637-1650   *19*

Chapter Four
The First Generation of Local Government   *33*

Chapter Five
The Establishment of the Church   *53*

Chapter Six
Beyond the Limits of Accommodation   *61*

Chapter Seven
The Hegemony of the Merchants   *81*

Chapter Eight
The Context of Leadership in Colonial Salem   *95*

Chapter Nine
The Divisibility of Status in the Second Generation   *105*

Chapter Ten
The Consequences of Dispersion
and Differentiation, 1668-1684; The Church   *121*

vi   Contents

Chapter Eleven
The Consequences of Dispersion
and Differentiation, 1668-1684: The Town   *139*

Chapter Twelve
The Glorious Revolution: Salem in 1689   *167*

Notes   *193*

Appendix A: Occupations of Salem Heads of Households   *231*

Appendix B: Maps   *233*

Appendix C: Tables   *239*

Bibliography   *243*

Index   *249*

"Oh poor New-England, consider what thou wast, and what thou now art! Repent, and do thy first works, saith the Lord; so may thy peace yet be as a river, and thy righteousness as the waves of the sea."

Nathaniel Morton, New England's Memorial (1669), p. 84. From Isaiah 48:18–19.

Chapter One

Introduction: Salem as a Social Unit

Among recent historians of the colonial New England town several points of consensus have emerged within the past decade. Unlike its modern counterpart whose social, economic, political and religious boundaries rarely coincide, the seventeenth-century towns of Massachusetts Bay were characterized by tightly congruent patterns of organization in every sphere of community life. Not only were the basic needs of the townspeople met almost exclusively within the town's boundaries, but covariation among the attributes of leadership in local institutions was expected. Wealth accrued to the saints, who managed the political affairs of the town. Homogeneous, closed, corporate and cohesive, the pattern has been established and documented.[1]

Despite Salem's coastal location and consequent economic complexity relative to inland towns, and its function as a port of entry during the early years of its history, many aspects of life in the town justify its inclusion in this cluster of closed communities. Salem shared in the colony-wide practice of relative local autonomy from the central government. The allocation of land, assessment and collection of taxes, dispensation of social services, and commission of public works in the form of bridges, fences, roads, and the meetinghouse, were all the sole responsibility of the town. The decisions of the selectmen and the town meeting were of immediate consequence to Salem residents, while the deliberations of the General Court and the Governor were remote from their daily lives throughout most of the charter period. Generally, the business which was carried by the town's representatives beyond the boundaries of the town to the General Court concerned these boundaries themselves rather than the internal workings of Salem's institutions.[2]

Within these boundaries, the town controlled the allocation of land, and thereby the initial economic standing of its inhabitants. While adventurers in the common stock of the Massachusetts Bay Company had guarantees of specific amounts of land before they sailed, they had actually to take up residence in Salem to claim their allotments. Speculation by non-residents was limited by the condition of each grant made by the town that the land had to be improved within three years or forfeited back to the town.[3] During the three decades in which land grants were made, none were to non-residents. The intention to settle permanently was also a condition of these grants, as William Hathorne discovered when he was given 200 acres "where he hath built" on the "condition that he be dismissed from their church to ours of Salem."[4] While men who were not members of the Salem church were accommodated with land, those who were members of churches elsewhere had to establish a new tie with the local institution before their grants could be confirmed. After all of the land in the town had been allocated and men began to buy and sell among each other, the exchanges were no longer as controlled; yet fewer than 10% of all land transfers to 1689 involved a non-resident buyer.[5]

Admission to the town was effectively controlled by the decision to grant land during the first years of the town, since each new resident would need at least a small plot to use for subsistence farming. By the time the town's government was formally established by the General Court in 1636, admission had become a process controlled by the freemen, a power delegated to the selectmen for most of the period. Until 1637, admission carried a guarantee of a land grant according to an order of the General Court of 1634, but after that date land was allotted to new inhabitants at the discretion of the freemen or their representatives.[6]

This power to control access to the town was increasingly important after the cessation of land grants in 1659. The selectmen were able to attach conditions to their decisions to admit new residents, as in the case of Samuel Wakefield in 1677: "Samuel Wakefield is admitted an inhabitant and Henry Skerry and Samuel Archard are bound to save the town harmless from all charge that may accrue to the town by said Wakefield." The town's leaders could use the power to admit new residents to protect the town from potential expenses for indigent newcomers; this authority could also be used to assure that the town would consist of settled householders, as in the case of John Sampson who was admitted in 1660, "provided he take effectual course to bring his wife to him."[7] The social boundaries of the town were assured by the careful scrutiny of each new arrival throughout the charter period.

Not all newcomers were acceptable, and in a small community like Salem, strangers were both visible and unwelcome, as two unfortunate men discovered in 1665: "It is ordered that the currier and his man, to wit Henry Kirk, shall forthwith be warned by the constable to depart the town, and that a warrant be given to the constable to warn him to depart."[8] Perhaps the currier's character did not meet community standards, or possibly the selectmen felt the town was already well-supplied with curriers. In any event, this currier and his apprentice had to move on. At the same meeting, the selectmen were more hospitable to another man whom they agreed might "have leave to sojourn here until the weather break up, provided it exceed not two months."[9] The town could afford to act collectively as host for this man, as they did for a number of refugees during King Philip's War; but full admission to the town was another matter.

The town also controlled its social boundaries by requiring residents to cooperate in their protection. In 1657, a fine of 20s. per week was established for any inhabitant who "shall at any time after the date hereof receive or take in any foreigner upon any pretence whatever without approbation of the selectmen."[10] The immediate concern was the arrival of several Quakers in the colony; but the town was still concerned about incorporating any new members who could not become self-sufficient. Six months later, the selectmen took their first direct action concerning a "stranger." William Sergeant had moved his family to Salem "under pretence of some work he hath taken to do" and was ordered to leave or find some inhabitant to secure the town against any charges which might arise. Sergeant produced Henry Herrick, who on examination by the selectmen turned out to be in debt to the town himself; therefore, Sergeant's petition to stay in Salem was not accepted until Henry Herrick paid his account.[11] Those willing to take responsibility for visitors had to assure the selectmen that they could carry out their contract.

Prior to 1670, a Salem resident could take on a temporary servant or craftsman for a particular job by giving bond to the town in this manner that the visitor would both behave while in residence and depart at the appointed time.[12] By April of that year, however, the selectmen had become sufficiently concerned about the importation of temporary laborers to issue the following instructions: "It is ordered that if any housekeeper shall entertain any stranger to dwell as an inmate from any other parts above one week and not give notice to the selectmen in being, he shall forfeit twenty shillings per week for the time afterwards."[13] Despite the large size of the fine—more than would be paid to a Salem resident for eight full days of work on the town's highways—the selectmen did not trust completely in the efficacy of their threat, for they also chose Thomas Oliver "to go from house to house about the town once a month to inquire what strangers do come or have privily thrust themselves into the town."[14] Occasional notes in the selectmen's minutes about "warning out" are evidence of the failure of the town to maintain strictly its social boundaries, but these same references leave no doubt as to the ideal of a closed, self-selected community.

Within these controlled boundaries, the population of Salem was remarkably stable after the first decade, years in which the town served as a port of entry for immigrants who quickly settled further inland. Still nearly half of the first-generation heads of households in Salem between 1623 and 1689 (48%) had arrived in the first waves of immigration by 1640. Only one-fifth arrived in the next 20 years, and they were followed by the remaining third who arrived in the second wave of immigration after 1660.

Pattern of Immigration to Salem[15]

Date	Percentage of 1st generation household heads
1623-1635	16%
1636-1640	32
1641-1650	10
1651-1660	9
1661-1670	12
1671-1680	14
1681-1689	8
	100%

After the initial years, the retention rates for each group of new arrivals rose throughout the period. Many of the first immigrants banded together with other newcomers to petition for separate township grants further inland, and stayed only a year or two in Salem.[16] The later arrivals, an increasing proportion of whom were seamen, artisans and merchants, came to Salem for its location which was well-suited for trade, and stayed to help transform Salem into the bustling commercial center it had become by the end of the charter period.

Persistence

Dates of Arrival	Persistence Rate	Length of Persistence[17]
1623-1650	71.6%	at least four decades
1651-1660	90.2%	
1623-1650	74.9%	at least three decades
1661-1670	91.1%	
1623-1650	83.1%	at least two decades
1671-1680	92.8%	
1623-1650	94.3%	at least one decade
1681-1689	100.0%	

Even the earliest arrivals have a high persistence rate considering the opportunities they had to move on as new towns were formed in the richer farming areas to the west.

Another measure of the self-containment of Salem throughout the colonial period is the low frequency of marriages which created alliances across the town's boundaries. Of the 492 marriages noted in the Vital Records through 1689, only 17 (3.5%) involved a partner who was not a Salem resident. None of these marriages occurred prior to 1660, and 11 occurred after 1680. In only three cases did a Salem woman leave to marry a man from another town, while 14 men found wives elsewhere and brought them to Salem, all but two from adjoining towns.[18] While the economic interests of the mercantile segment of Salem extended far beyond the town borders by the end of the colonial period, the cementing of business ties among New England's merchants through marriages between their sons and daughters was a social invention of the provincial period.[19] Indeed, of the few marriages prior to 1689 which were not strictly intramural, no pattern of economic motivation can be found, and in only one case did a merchant's daughter marry into a prominent mercantile family of Boston.[20] This high rate of local intermarriage over a span of several generations inevitably created an extraordinarily intertwined kinship network coterminous with the town boundaries.[21] These family ties reinforced the sense of the boundaries of the town.

While the historical population of Salem consisted of 1529 heads of households who appeared in any of the public records of the colonial period to 1689, the total number within the town limits never exceeded 590.[22] The total population was thus small enough virtually to guarantee that every resident would at least recognize if not know the name of every other resident. Expecting to see only familiar faces, marrying almost exclusively within that group, exchanging land primarily with each other, and rarely witnessing the removal of an inhabitant except by death, the residents of Salem during the charter period must certainly have considered themselves to be a social unit, and we are therefore justified in studying their actions in that light. The screening of new entrants to the community together with the large measure of control exercised by the town's government over its own affairs could only reinforce the residents' sense of boundaries within which they created a closed, corporate community life.

In the wake of the many studies undertaken in the past decade of early American towns, some historians have begun to call for a sharpening of the conceptual bases on which further studies should proceed. It is now clear that patterns of life patiently reconstructed by one historian for one community do not always apply in a neighboring town; the variability of local arrangements is an accepted fact. At the same time, some similarities among the towns of seventeenth-century New England have been reconfirmed. In particular, we note John Higham's view that the decentralization of both church and state made ideology the central principle of organization in every town.[23] Uncovering the particularities of social organization in single communities of the New England landscape is a scholarly activity with deep and respectable roots in both the Boasian school of American anthropology and the "new" French history of the Annales school; but like the anthropologists from whom historians have borrowed many useful techniques to illuminate the social patterns of early American communities, we are now beginning to ask where, in the richness of all of the newly reconstructed local data, is the larger meaning. Further, some are asking whether our definitions of community are sufficiently strong to bear the weight of all of these recent, particularistic studies.[24]

At the risk of contributing to the further "balkanization" of early American history, this study is proffered as an explicit attempt to explore the definition and principles of community in seventeenth-century New England through an analysis of the actual operations of the institutions of Massachusetts Bay's earliest town and the interactions of its inhabitants throughout the charter period. This exploration has been guided by Robert Redfield's contributions to the definition of community—in particular his insistence that space and time are insufficient grounds for assuming that the population under scrutiny is a community, and must be augmented by analyses of both those collective actions and communications which hold a community together, and those communications which exceed the spatial definition of community to become the basis for external associations.[25] The diachronic dimension of Redfield's theory—that communities generally develop from units in which collective (horizontal) associations within their spatial boundaries are most important into more complex social organizations in which external (vertical) associations predominate—may need to be resisted in order to find the true evolution of Salem as a community, however.

Other historians have been led to overlook important factors in the history of community development by accepting uncritically the inevitability of Redfield's diachronic theory. For example, Richard Gildrie notes that the founding of Salem was a "complex event" but goes on to build a saga of the efforts to adapt Salem's covenants to encompass the externally-oriented commercial segment of the community within the original communal ideals.[26] The implication that a true "horizontal" community of the kind assumed by the early covenants can only exist within an undifferentiated peasant village is contrary to the facts of Salem's settlement, as will be seen in its land distribution schemes, which clearly reveal that Salem's earliest leaders—the designers of its covenants—believed otherwise. The overriding principle of accommodation of diversity which runs through each of the chapters which follow compels us to resist any interpretation of "community" which runs simply along the continuum from simple to complex, homogeneous to heterogeneous, horizontal to vertical. The merchants, far from destroying a fictitious organic unity, may actually have been the most significant unifying force for this early New England town.

Following Arensberg's definition of community as a social unit bounded by space, time, and the limits of a kinship system, the upsurge in marriages across the boundaries of Salem after the Glorious Revolution points to a shift in the definition of community in Salem beyond the limits of this study. Having established Salem as a relatively self-contained social unit before that time, however, it is possible to proceed with an analysis of the definition community received at the hands of its inhabitants during the charter period.

Chapter Two

The Process of Accommodation: The Land to 1637

Puritan social philosophy, derived from covenant theology, grew up in the closed, corporate agricultural towns of England. Its application in the new towns of Massachusetts was strongly influenced by prominent clergy from East Anglia, a region of homogeneous, open field farming communities.[1] Designed for small groups unified by a common religious purpose, the federal covenant assumed a similarity of economic goals as well. From its earliest years, however, Salem was not a homogenous community. Unlike the earlier settlement at Plymouth or some inland towns founded later by small groups of men of uniform farming traditions and religious impulse,[2] Salem throughout the first generation deliberately accommodated settlers of diverse backgrounds holding different assumptions concerning the ordering of church and society.

The original band of settlers were West Country fishermen who settled at Naumkeag in 1626 under the leadership of Roger Conant following the failure of the Dorchester Company venture at Cape Ann.[3] Most of the original company returned to England or followed the minister John Lyford to Virginia, but Conant and a small band of followers, intrigued by the possibilities for commercial farming to support the growing fishing trade along the New England coast, determined to stay and establish a permanent colony. They were encouraged by the promises of Reverend John White, a Puritan minister of Dorchester, England, to secure a patent for them.[4] They waited a year for word from White. When none came, Conant dispatched John Woodbury to England to promote the group's interests.

The situation Woodbury found in England must have both delighted and disappointed him. Reverend White, together with merchants in Dorchester and London, had indeed secured a new patent from the Dorchester Company for all the lands at Cape Ann and Naumkeag together with the rest of the Sheffield patent of 1620, but had also organized a new and larger group of settlers to send to Naumkeag under the governorship of one of the patentees, John Endicott.[5] He landed in September of 1628 with the new patent for the Massachusetts Bay Company and approximately 40 new settlers.[6] Conant was displaced as governor, but his desire to see the colony survive proved stronger than his dismay over the terms of the charter, and he persuaded his men to remain through the winter.

The following spring more ships were sent by the Company, and with their passengers a long letter of instruction was dispatched to John Endicott. The leaders of the Company were well aware that Conant and his men were apprehensive about their roles in the new colony, and so addressed a lengthy portion of the letter to these fears:

> And that it may appear, as well to all the world as to the old planters themselves, that we seek not to make them slaves, (as it seems by your letter some of them think themselves to be become by means of our patent,) we are content they shall be partakers of such privileges as we, from his majesty's especial grace, with great cost, favor personages of note, and much labor, have obtained, and that they shall be incorporated into this society, and enjoy, not only those lands which formerly they have manured, but such a further proportion as, by the advice and judgment of yourself and the rest of the council, shall be thought fit for them or any of them.[7]

The new Company thus recognized the existence of Conant's prior claims. 200 acres were granted to him and to each of the Old Planters, bountiful grants which cost "personages of note" recruited to the joint stock venture £50 to purchase.[8]

The Company might have assuaged Conant's fears by compensating him for his earlier efforts with these generous grants of land, but it intended an even closer alliance of the Old Planters with the new settlers if possible:

> And besides, it is still our purpose that they should have some benefit by the common stock, as was by your first commission directed and appointed, with this addition, that if it be held too much to take 30 percent and the freight of the goods for and in consideration of our adventure and disbursement of our monies . . . that you moderate the said rate as you, with the rest of the [council] shall think to be agreeable to equity and good conscience.[9]

"Conscience" required land grants and guided the rate of engagement in the common stock; but the Company was motivated in addition by the desire to amalgamate the Old Planters into the new chartered community as long as they were "peaceable men, and of honest life and conversation, and desirous to live amongst us, and conform themselves to good order and government."[10] This mutual accommodation of the two groups established a pattern which was to prevail in Salem: inclusion of different groups so long as they met very general standards of decent behavior.

Whatever fears and frictions might have existed between Conant and Endicott were erased by the orders from the Company. Having surpassed "the expectance of some dangerous jar," and in recognition of their new concord, they agreed to rename the little settlement Salem, "in remembrance of a peace."[11]

The Company continued to recruit new settlers, and approximately 300 arrived early in the summer of 1629. Endicott, together with the non-Separatist ministers who had arrived only a few months before, forged the group into a working community. While the Old Planters had been integrated fully, the greatest test of the policy of accommodation was yet to come. In gathering the large group of new Salem residents in 1629, the Company reached beyond the closed field farming communities of the west of England into the open field farming areas of East Anglia. One of the most significant social and economic divisions in all of England was thereby built into the tiny new settlement from the start.

The differences between the two groups of colonists extended beyond farming methods. The consistency of organization in all human affairs was assumed by seventeenth-century Englishmen; the compartmentalization of experience, the specialization of the personality into different roles for different settings, was unthinkable. Thus the organization of the church was linked inextricably to the conception of the community, which received formal expression in the federal covenant. The interrelation extended to the family, whose structure was analogous to the organization of the church, and Puritan metaphor emphasized this relation.[12] Major differences in farming methods were therefore not just a technical matter: they were related to differences in family governance, theology, and political organization. Partible inheritance, the encouragement of individual initiative, and the expectation of mobility were the regular features of enclosed field life. On the other hand, primogeniture was the rule in East Anglia, which stablized not only the transfer of land between generations but also the structure of the family and childrearing methods.[13] The emphasis on organic unity in the utopian Puritan community envisioned by the early ministers was in large part a product of their East Anglian provenance. This world view now had to be accommodated in Salem, where the earliest immigrants had been predominantly West Countrymen. Whatever new definition of communal unity was to be achieved in Salem could not rest on a single English background.

In amalgamating the Old Planters with the Endicott company, the officers of the Massachusetts Bay Company did not attempt to provide this new definition. Instead, they specified only that the Old Planters be "honest . . . desirous to live amongst us, and conform themselves to good order and government." As long as they were "peaceable men," they could be trusted to participate in whatever definition "good order" received in the wilderness.[14] Broad behavioral standards were supplied, and the principle of inclusion established, but the structure of the new community was not predetermined.

On the other hand, the Company gave a number of instructions to Endicott concerning land distribution, from which the town's early social structure would emerge. The names of the adventurers in the common stock and the amounts contributed were sent to Endicott, who was told to assign the appropriate acreage "by lot" in the proportion of 200 acres for £50 contributed.[15] In addition, "such others as are not adventurers, coming in person at their own charge, and the servants of adventurers sent over to reside upon the plantation, may have such a proportion of land allotted unto and for them as by our said order is appointed."[16] House lots were also distributed universally to the new colonists. Endicott was given 10 days to make assignments of these lots after the ships had landed; anyone who had not received a house lot within that period of time could choose his own, provided that it was not already occupied.[17] No one was left out of the process of land distribution; but those who had not supported the common stock, "which is to support the charge of fortifications, as also for the ministry and diverse affairs . . . should, by way of acknowledgement to such from whom they receive these lands, become liable to the performance of some service certain days in the year."[18] Labor and capital were interchangeable assets in the new colony. Each adult male would not only receive some accommodation of land, but also have it laid out according to his farming preferences:

> And whereas diverse of the company are desirous to have the lands lie together, we holding it fit herein to give them all accommodation, as tending to the furtherance of the plantation, do pray you to give way thereunto for such as shall desire the same, whether it be before a dividend be made according to our direction or at the time of the allotment to observe the same course.[19]

Servant and adventurer, East Anglian and West Countryman, all were to become full members of the new community. Uniformity was not seen as a requirement for achieving unity or "good order."

When Endicott was demoted from Governor to Magistrate in 1630 on the arrival of John Winthrop, he presumably retained the authority to allot lands in Salem. By 1634, however, the General Court reserved that right to itself.[20] Their idea of what "good order" meant relative to land distribution for those whose proportions were not specified by their contributions to the common stock was entered in the town record: "The least family shall have 10 acres, but greater families may have more according to their numbers."[21] While some men defined their relative social standing in the new town by their capital investment, the influx of others made careful assessments of their "worth" impossible during these years of heavy immigration. In dividing lands according to family size, the General Court was responding to the requirements for survival in the earliest towns of Massachusetts Bay.

Recognizing that they were not in the best position to make these assessments anyway, in 1636 the General Court authorized the freemen of individual towns to grant land.[22] By this time, Endicott and the General Court had established the general outlines of the town. The South Field of 600 acres had been laid out on a large peninsula across the South Harbor for the East Anglians, as well as the North Field of 480 acres across the North River.[23] The yeomen granted strips in these open fields travelled daily to and from their lands in long, rough canoes fashioned from pine trees; apparently this passage was not always smooth, for in 1636 the Quarterly Court ordered that these canoes be inspected regularly.[24] Larger tracts for the enclosed field farmers were laid out at Brooksby, Cedar Pond, and Skelton's Neck to the northwest and west of the town, and to the northeast at Cape Ann.[25] Despite their decision to settle on a rocky peninsula with a fine natural harbor, the early settlers had located their church inland, clustered their houses and shops around it, and turned their attention to the available farmland. By 1636, the town of Salem both resembled and operated like an English agricultural village. In 1636 the General Court confirmed the nucleated pattern of settlement by requiring that no house be built more than half a mile from the meetinghouse for security reasons.[26] While survival was still not a moot concern, the town of approximately 150 families was ready to turn from issues of subsistence to questions of settlement.

Given the freedom to do so by the General Court in 1636, the freemen of Salem were ready to make other decisions about land use. The Neck was reserved for grazing, more house lots were laid out near the church, parcels of land were allocated for shops, and there were many instructions concerning cartways.[27] Once established, there was great concern about boundaries; men were appointed to lay out bounds, and each inhabitant was instructed to mark the limits of his property with large stones or deep holes.[28] The earlier order concerning 10 acre lots was rescinded, and more grants of arable acreage were issued in the fields and among the farms surrounding the peninsula.[29] Anticipating the need for additional acreage, the town surveyed the rich farmlands of Jeffries Creek and Mackerel Cove.[30] Since marshland was desired by all regardless of particular calling, the town also surveyed the marshes around the main peninsula.[31] By the end of the year, the two common fields, some enclosed farms within the main peninsula, and a number of farms north and west of the town bridge and at Cape Ann were under cultivation. (See Appendix B, Map 4.)

This flurry of activity in 1636 prompted the town to take an account of the lands which had been distributed. Ralph Fogg was chosen to make a list of the families in Salem, noting the acreage allotted to each. Since every new household head to that date received a land grant according to the still standing orders of 1634, Fogg's list of 178 names is the first census for the town in the colonial period.[32] Although no land is recorded for 28 names, the principle of inclusiveness prevailed. Of the 28, the minister Hugh Peter received a large grant later that year when he actually settled in Salem, and a dozen others had received land from the town by 1640. Two single women were among those who received no land, while five women who were heads of households did share in the general allotment. The other 10 had just arrived in Salem in 1636; no clear explanation is available for the lack of grants to 7 of these men, but they may have been apprentices, or single men who used Salem only as a port of entry, since all of them had removed from the town by 1645. Of the remaining 3, one was only 18 in 1636; his father was among the grantees. Another was sent back to England in 1638 by the General Court because he hadn't brought his wife with him; the town of Salem in the meantime refrained from granting him any land.[33] The remaining one of the 10, and the only one who remained in Salem until his death, was freed from training in 1650 on account of "age and disability" and was given alms by the town in 1666.[34] There is no indication that any of these 10 men asked for or were refused land grants. Although the record is admittedly incomplete, the exclusion of these 10 people from the distribution of land in 1636 does not invalidate the general principle that all inhabitants would share Salem's natural resources.

While the method of land distribution in 1634 had been remarkably egalitarian—at least 10 acres for every household head and more for larger families—the settlement of the town recorded in 1636 was quite different. The average acreage per person was 63.5 acres, but half received 30 acres or less while 22 men were granted just over half the total allotted in amounts ranging from 150 to 300 acres each. [Appendix C, Table I.] The number of men in this "minimal majority"—those who held half of the land in Salem in 1636—is large in comparison with other New England towns, and is further proof that settlement to 1636 was based on the principle of generous accommodation. The criterion established by the Massachusetts Bay Company for receiving as much as 200 acres of land and the designation "adventurer" was the payment of £50 to the joint stock, yet only 6 of the 18 men who received farms of this size met this qualification.[35] Clearly Endicott, and subsequently the General Court, had not been motivated to hoard the land for future arrivals who could meet the price, but rather saw their task to be the reasonable distribution of sizable tracts to those men of worth who had settled in Salem by 1636.

This major accounting of land by Fogg, totalling over 9000 acres and including both previous grants and those made by the town that year, was intended to define both the ownership of virtually the entire topography of the peninsula and its immediate environs and the social standing of its inhabitants. Although some of the land reverted to the town as grantees moved elsewhere, there were no subsequent years of activity as intense as that in 1636 regarding the distribution of land.

While different farming methods had been accommodated, the fishermen posed a different problem. As early as 1635, Hugh Peter "moved the country to raise a stock for fishing, as the only means to free us from that oppression which the seamen and others hold us under."[36] The nature of that oppression, whether high prices or discordant behavior or both, was not specified. These men were clearly separated from the rest of the population, however, and most were given lots on a rocky peninsula beyond the South Field at first called Darby's Fort and later named Marblehead.[37] When more land was needed for fishermen, they were settled at the rocky eastern extremity of the Salem peninsula on Winter Harbor.[38] The full principles of accommodation were limited to those who tilled the land, whether as a fulltime occupation or as a supplement to their trades. To "avoid the inconvenience found by granting of land for fishermen to plow," the town ordered "a house lot and a garden lot or ground for the placing of flakes, according to the company belonging to their families, the greatest family not above two acres and the common of the woods near adjoining for their goats and their cattle."[39] While the town was busy parcelling out farmland according to their new ideas of settlement, the fishermen were being held to the subsistence standard of land use practiced earlier.

In December of 1637, a second population list was drawn up by Roger Conant to determine the division of meadow and salt marsh among the residents.[40] The turnover in population in just one year had been sufficient that these grants were made with the provision "that none shall sell away their proportions of meadow . . . nor lease them out to any above three years, unless they sell or lease out their houses with their meadow."[41] Despite the difficulty of accommodating a population in flux, the town was agreed that it would be a community of householders. Thirty-four of those on Fogg's list of the previous year do not appear on the Conant list, which contains the names of 52 new residents since 1636. Fully a quarter of the inhabitants in 1637 had arrived during the previous year, and over half of the residents had been in Salem less than two years. The policy of accommodation had successfully handled diversity; now the town leaders had to adjust their pattern of settlement to encompass new arrivals. The needs, preferences and worth of each would have to be judged and responded to with the appropriate allocation of land.[42]

Two characteristics of the more recent arrivals in Salem complicated the task of integrating them into the community. First, a decreasing proportion of the immigrants described themselves as primarily agricultural men. Of the 141 men on Conant's list whose occupation is known, only a fifth were farmers, yeomen or husbandmen, while nearly a third were seamen or pursued trades linked to the sea (for example, coopers and sailmakers); artisans were by far the largest segment of the population.

Arrival		Occupation		
	Agriculture	Sea and sea trades	Other artisans	Others
by 1630	28.6%	33.3%	23.8%	14.3%
1631-1635	23.5	29.4	38.2	8.8
1636	15.8	31.6	44.7	7.9
1637	13.9	27.8	41.1	8.3
Total to 1637:	19.4%	30.2%	41.1%	9.3%

Significantly, the proportion of farming men fell in each successive wave of immigration, while artisans moved into Salem at an increasing rate. Fully two-thirds of the artisans in Salem in 1637 had arrived in the previous two years. After a slowing of immigration to Salem between 1631 and 1635, the rate rose rapidly after 1636; the seacoast town was increasingly attractive to artisans, but less so to farmers and yeomen. Thus, 80% of Salem's population by 1637 required land for subsistence farming only, while they supplemented their farming to varying degrees through crafts and trades.

The second characteristic of the more recent arrivals which made their accommodation problematic was their marital status and family composition. Nearly half of the men who arrived in 1636 and 1637 were single, or married but childless, compared to 16% of those who came to Salem prior to 1636, most of whom were sons of the early settlers. The men who sailed with Endicott uprooted whole families to move to New England; half of this new group of immigrants came alone or with new wives. The impact of 30 unmarried men arriving among a total group of 114 immigrants in 1636-1637 must have been substantial in a town whose new land system, church, and social covenants were family-based. Not surprisingly, the persistence in Salem among these people was lower than among those who arrived earlier in the decade. There was a slight tendency for large families to remain, while men with small families or none

Arrival	Persistence
by 1630	52.0%
1631-1633	87.5%
1634	76.9%
1635	66.7%
1636	56.7%
1637	46.2%

at all were more likely to move on to other towns. The shifts in family composition and occupational base of the newest immigrants to Salem made the freemen's job of accommodating them all the more difficult.

These changes are also reflected in the acreage owned by the succeeding waves of immigrants to 1637. Only half of the men holding land grants had been in Salem since 1635 or earlier, yet this group held three-quarters of the land in 1637. The earliest arrivals held the clearest advantage; representing only 22% of the population in 1637, they held title to 40% of the allotted land. They were also more likely to have received large tracts from the town.

Arrival	Average Acreage	Number of owners
by 1630	101.5	31
1631-1635	64.8	42
1636-1637	30.2	68

Fully a third of the men who had arrived by 1630 owned more than 100 acres, while less than one-tenth of the subsequent immigrants were equally rewarded. This strong correlation between date of arrival and land ownership also held for those at the opposite end of the scale: none of the men who settled in Salem by 1630 were landless in 1637, while nearly a quarter of those who arrived in 1636 and 1637 had not yet received a town grant by the time Conant's list was compiled. These men would have to wait for their "accommodation" until the freemen had determined how to adjust their plans for the town to its newest arrivals, few of whom intended to earn a living from the land.

In a social economy in which land both reflected and determined status, the artisans were the least-favored group. A survey of those on Conant's list who had received some town land by 1637 reveals clear distinctions among occupational groups. The early merchants, who regarded land as capital, had received large tracts among the farms surrounding the peninsula, as had the ministers and elders, who constituted the "professional" class of the town at this date. Not far behind were the heavy artisans—men whose work required a relatively large capital investment and resulted in the production of heavy goods, such as fellmongers, blacksmiths, millers and wheelwrights. Yeomen, husbandmen and farmers had been granted 77.1 acres apiece on the average, far more than the seamen or any of the artisans.

Occupation[43]	Average Acreage
Merchants	164.0
Professionals	117.9
Heavy Artisans	100.0
Agricultural	77.1
Seamen	37.3
Building Trades	33.9
Sea Artisans	33.3
Light Artisans	26.4

Still, these differences fit the needs and capacities of Salem's early residents—subsistence farming for the seamen and artisans to supplement their trades, more substantial holdings for those who earned their livings entirely from the land, generous grants to those heavy artisans whose capital and talents were needed by the town, grants to the clergy which recognized their central importance, and the largest grants to the emerging merchants whose land was treated as a form of capital. The principle of accommodation was still intact.

Chapter Three

The Limits of Accommodation:
1637-1650

By the time the freemen of Salem were empowered to grant lands within the town bounds in 1636, both the principle of inclusiveness and the patterns of land use were well established. Although rapid immigration and changes in the characteristics of the newest residents tested the ability of the freemen and their new representatives, the selectmen, to assess the needs and worth of each new inhabitant and then make the proper accommodation in land grants, there was no question before 1637 that each new arrival would be incorporated into the little community.

Within the first year of their stewardship of Salem lands, however, the freemen made some important changes both in policy and in practice. In March of 1637, Richard Graves applied for admission to the town and was turned down; the consistent pattern of inclusion since 1629 was broken as the freemen began to sense the limits of Salem's ability to expand.[1] While the selectmen reversed this decision of the town meeting the next month, others were not as fortunate.[2] In April, "Robert Baker was rejected as an inhabitant here; but John Shipley and his wife were accepted."[3] Thenceforth, the admission of inhabitants became a routine entry in the selectmen's minutes. Their concern for controlling settlement in the town was shared by the General Court, which ordered in May that no strangers might linger in any of the towns of Massachusetts Bay more than three weeks without "due permission."[4] Offenders were to be reported to the Court of Assistants by the town constables.[5] While the freemen had no precise definition of the town's optimum size, they did have a sense of the broad behavioral standards which had been required of residents since 1629: being "peaceable men . . . of honest conversation, and desirous to live amongst us, and conform[able] to good order and government."[6] Settled households were part of that "good order," which may be why John Shipley was admitted while Robert Baker was not. The rising proportion of single men in recent waves of immigration was undoubtedly a matter of concern to Salem's leaders.

In another important departure from previous practice, the freemen did not universally accommodate new inhabitants with land. At the same meeting in January of 1637 where the selectmen decided not to grant any further arable land to Marblehead fishermen to "avoid the inconvenience we have found" thereby, they also rescinded the General Court order of 1634 concerning the basic subsistence allowance:

> It is generally agreed by us that the order which was formerly made, to grant a house lot and ten acre lot to every inhabitant shall be henceforward of no force or effect. But such lots are to be set out according to the discretion of the town.[7]

William Knight was received as an inhabitant at that meeting, "but no land appropriated unto him but a 10 acre lot, and common for his cattle grass and hay."[8] In a similar move, Sergeant Lockwood was "refused the house lot beyond his father Norman's."[9] These decisions were not intended to reverse the earlier pattern of accommodation, nor were they a sign that the town's supply of land had been exhausted. Far more men were granted land than not, and the reasons for rejection of requests which are noted in the records show that the new practice of considering each request for land was not intended to be exclusionary. Five acres were laid out for Benjamin Parminter, even "though he said he would follow his trade," while George Ropes' request was denied "because he hath a year to serve" as an apprentice.[10] Artisans were not by definition separated from the agricultural base of the town, and even an apprenticed boy had land-owning in his future.

Nor was the new policy based on the depletion of the town's land supply. Despite the all-inclusive land distribution strategies used prior to 1637, with no attempt to hold acreage in reserve, the town had sufficient land to continue its earlier policy. The acreage released by former inhabitants who left Salem in these years of high turnover would have been enough to practice a policy of universal accommodation for at least a few more years.[11]

The problem lay not in the total acreage available within the bounds of Salem, but in its location. By the end of 1637, only half of the arable acreage within the limits of the town had been allotted, but most of the farmland within commuting distance of the house lots on the peninsula was in individual hands. Moreover, the still-nucleated village did not have an inexhaustible supply of house lots. To accommodate the newest immigrants, most of whom were tradesmen and seamen rather than yeomen or farmers, the freemen would have to alter their earlier practice of allotting both a house lot and arable acreage to each new arrival—a practice well suited to a nucleated agricultural village of small size, but not to a growing population more and more of whom requested arable acreage for subsistence purposes only.

Several changes were evident by 1640. House lots, originally two acres each, had decreased to a quarter of an acre.[12] Even this drastic reduction from the initial size of two acres in 1629 was not enough to achieve universal accommodation: some had to be instructed to buy pieces of land to build on where they could find them.[13] Still, fully half of the grants made between 1636 and 1640 were of house lots. Most were clustered around the common, the pound and the meetinghouse in the center of town, but four were located at the western limits of the peninsula by the town bridge, and an equal number were laid out at the eastern extremity on Collins Cove. Only one of the grantees was described as a farmer; the others were all artisans and seamen. The density of the population on the peninsula increased and its composition changed, but even the more distant lots were less than half a mile from the meetinghouse, the limit advocated by the General Court in 1636. (See Appendix B, Map 5.)

Grants of other kinds of land during the same period indicate the increasing specialization of other areas of the town as well. Thirty-two fishing and shipbuilding lots were laid out on the Neck and at Winter Island, but two-thirds of the enclosed farms were located outside the peninsula and only one of the farmers with land located beyond the town bridge was also given a house lot. The pattern of 1637, when only 5 of 15 farmers of known location lived beyond the bridge, was thus reversed by 1640. Some grants of upland (open field) acreage were made to residents of the town center, but the enclosed field farmers could be expected to relieve the pressure for house lots on the peninsula by building on their farms outside. Although the location of only one-third of the grants from 1637 to 1640 is known with certainty, it appears both that all of the peninsula and most of the land west of the bridge, in the North and South Fields, and the lots on the Necks had been accounted for by that date, and that the peninsula had been designated for open field farmers and artisans.

Finally, the freemen recognized that the settlement of areas at the furthest reaches of the town bounds would require a different strategy. In 1637, a group of 11 West Countrymen were granted farms at Jeffries Creek, later renamed Manchester.[14] Four of them had arrived in Salem by 1630 and had received the usual house lot and 10 acre lot in the common fields; 3 of the later arrivals had received small plots at Winter Island. Eight of these men were members of the church, and two of the remaining three had just arrived in Salem. Faced with a godly group of men who wanted enclosed farms of the kind they had known in England, the selectmen sent them to Jeffries Creek en masse. Five others who arrived in 1636 joined this group of grantees between 1638 and 1643, giving up their house lots and common field acreage in the process. In 1645, these 16 men secured a town charter and with it the power to grant the remaining lands in the area themselves.[15]

An attempt was also made to gather a group at Wenham in 1638. Reverend John Phillips, an East Anglian minister, arrived in Salem that year with a dozen of his Wrentham parishioners, presenting two problems of accommodation for the Salem selectmen. The Salem church already had a minister in Hugh Peter, and the only open field farming areas in Salem had been completely allotted. A town meeting was held, and it was "agreed and voted that there should be a Village granted to Mr. Phillips and his company upon such conditions as the seven men appointed for the town affairs should agree on."[16] The only condition the selectmen attached to the agreement of the freemen to "plant a village" at Wenham was that the grantees actually live there and use the land. The village was not immediately successful. Reverend Phillips left for the church at Dedham, having failed to gather one at Wenham. At least four of the ten men granted Wenham lands and one of the widows did not adhere to the one condition set by the selectmen, for John Thurston went to Newbury in 1641, Hugh Stacy returned to Marblehead, Henry Chickering followed Reverend Phillips to Dedham, Thomas West was living in Salem again by 1644, and Mrs. Ames moved to Cambridge.[17] Therefore the General Court was not petitioned to establish Wenham as a separate town.

The matter rested for four years, but in 1642 the selectmen tried again. Twenty-one grants were made in Wenham to 18 men. Six of them had just arrived in Salem that year and could not be accommodated in the open fields there; two were sons of Salem yeomen who also desired land of their own; the remainder already had land in the enclosed farming areas of Salem, but wanted to exchange it for open field acreage in Wenham. John Fiske, formerly the assistant minister in Salem, "became helpful in preaching the Word to them when they were but few in number,"[18] and finally in 1644 a church was successfully gathered. The formal establishment of the town by the General Court preceded the gathering of the church by a year.

Yeomen in other New England towns faced with the depletion of the open fields, or planters who found no farms remaining for them, or either group on discovery of the primacy of the other within a given town, had to organize appeals to the General Court for new town grants, or to the selectmen for a new division of land. These appeals often led to bitter conflict which divided towns and sometimes even families.[19] In Salem, in contrast, the practice of accommodation was the central feature of life. The selectmen, backed by the freemen, took the lead in opening a new area for a godly group of West Countrymen who could not receive suf-

ficient farmland within Salem by founding Manchester in 1637; the next year, they tried to settle a group of open field yeomen with their minister in Wenham, and when their first efforts failed they tried again to accommodate this segment of the Salem population. Simultaneously, they moved to accommodate the new tide of artisans by reducing the size of house lots on the peninsula and encouraging the settlement of enclosed field farmers beyond the town bridge.

While these actions taken together clearly demonstrate that the town of Salem had moved to include and accommodate virtually all newcomers according to their needs and desires during the first five years in which the freemen managed the pattern of settlement, there were other signs that they had begun to reach the limits of accommodation by 1640. The nearly universal granting of land to new residents had rapidly depleted the supply of available acreage; by 1640, 80% of the arable land was in individual hands.

The accommodation of new arrivals was not, however, the major cause of the depletion of the town's lands. More than half of the arable acreage granted between 1636 and 1640 went to supplement previous grants. Men with already existing farms were granted 535 additional acres of enclosed fields, while new arrivals were granted only 360 acres. Similarly, 13 yeomen and artisans were given 469 acres in addition to their existing parcels of upland, while seven newcomers divided 300 acres of new upland grants.

	Farm	Open Field	Total
First grants	360	300	660
Additional acreage	535	469	1004
Total	895	769	1664

While the selectmen continued to accommodate both of the elsewhere competing farming methods, enlarging prior grants to alter status patterns established by 1636 was more important than including new residents in the land system by 1640.

This unarticulated but obvious shift in land policy was accompanied by another change of equal importance. The average grant to the yeomen was only 38.45 acres, while the farm grants averaged 127.9 acres each. Moreover, only one of the men who received a farm in this period called himself a farmer; the others were or became better known as merchants, ministers and artisans.[20] On the other hand, among those who received grants of upland whose occupations are known, ten were yeomen while seven used their common field allotments to supplement their trades as tailor, house carpenter, mariner and ironmonger. Commercial farming in

enclosed fields and open field yeomanry were in fact two different occupations, and the distribution of arable land in 1640 reflected not only
this divergence within the agricultural community but also a growing preference for the former.

Finally, the depletion of town lands was related to the concentration
of increasing amounts of acreage in the hands of a few men. "Good
order" in land distribution had always required the allocation of substantial tracts to adventurers and others of significant worth in the community,
but by 1640 these men had increased their holdings dramatically.

Minimal Majorities

	Number	% of Population	Acres Owned	Average Acreage
1636	23	15.6%	4670	203.0
1637	20	12.4%	4520	226.0
1640	23	14.3%	6245	271.5

The sheer size of the minimal majority—those men who held title to half
the land in Salem—had always been large relative to other towns, due to
the history of Salem's settlement. Five of the minimal majority of 1640—
Roger Conant and members of his original company—had received 200
acre grants at Cape Ann in 1629 on instructions from the New England
Company in recognition of the prior claims these men held to the territory.
Five others arrived in the earliest migrations under the Massachusetts Bay
Company charter between 1628 and 1630. All but 1 of these 10 men were
church members and active in town politics. Had there been only one
period of major migration to Salem, the size of this landed elite would
approximate that of other towns,[21] but the two groups headed by Conant
and Endicott were not left alone to perfect their amalgamation of 1629.
Ships arriving in Salem in the 1630s carried more men of wealth and
standing who held claims to equally large or larger tracts, and all were
accommodated. Sixteen of them appear in the minimal majority of 1640.
Their large farms were laid out beyond those of the earlier elite, in areas
that would become separate towns or precincts: Wenham, Marblehead,
and Salem Village. (See Appendix B, Map 3.)

In the meantime, the lower half of the population remained quite stable.
While the average allotment remained virtually unchanged, the share of

	Number	Total Acreage	Average Acreage	% of Total
1636	73	1500	20.5	16.1%
1637	72	1520	21.1	16.0%
1640	81	1722	21.3	13.6%

this segment of the population in the total resources of the town decreased. The accumulation of land by the minimal majority thus occurred at the "expense" of the middle range of landowners rather than the lower half. Upward mobility for the middling sort, those whose grants averaged 56.2 acres, was limited by the practice of maintaining all inhabitants at a level comfortably above subsistence, but those men who had already gained recognition as leaders were not under equal constraints. The large tracts laid out for these men, together with the granting of additional acreage to early arrivals at a greater rate than initial grants were made to new arrivals between 1637 and 1640, greatly reduced the ability of the selectmen to practice their policy of accommodation for newcomers after 1640.

The town of Salem in 1640 contained nearly 1000 people living in approximately 300 households.[22] While some farmers had moved to their fields at Cape Ann and beyond the town bridge, and others had been settled at Jeffries Creek, most of the populace lived on the main peninsula where they pursued their trades and commuted to their nearby fields. In the next 2 decades, only 135 new household heads are known to have arrived in Salem; during the same period, 119 left the town. Deaths were more than balanced by the number of sons reaching maturity between 1640 and 1660, but overall the growth of the town was slight in the generation after 1640. Eighty percent of the available land had already been allocated, and 58.9% of all town grants for the colonial period were already on the town's records. The grants made after 1640 would be primarily in outlying precincts and involve smaller amounts of land than had been the average prior to that date.

Grants of Known Location

	1637-40	After 1640	Total
Within Salem	48	24	72
Outlying precincts	64	54	118
	112	78	190

The settling of areas far from the Salem peninsula remained a task for the selectmen after 1640, but not one of the magnitude that distributing lands in Salem proper had been. With the exception of 1642 and 1649, years which deserve special scrutiny, the average number of grants made each year from 1641 to 1659 was only 11.7, a substantial decrease from the average of 91 per year from 1637 to 1640. The near cessation of migration from England and a greatly reduced rate of settlement in Salem coincided with a dramatic decrease in the land-granting activity of the Salem selectmen.

A closer look at the two years of greatest activity in the decade after 1640 reveals an acceleration of trends already apparent before that date: an increasing ratio of additional grants to initial grants, and the increasing distance of these plots from the peninsula.

The reason for the flurry of activity in 1642 is unclear; perhaps the second attempt to gather a new open-field community at Wenham spurred other residents of longer standing to press various claims as well. The grants made to the new Wenham residents ranged from 5 to 22 acres; the average was only 10.6 acres, and the total of 193 acres was less than a single Old Planter grant in neighboring Beverly. Still, from these small beginnings the new Wenham settlers were able to build a town. Their grants, though small, were not out of line with the 44 others made elsewhere that year, all but 10 of which were of 10 acres or less. Over half of these small grants were to accommodate new residents and other men who had not previously received any land from the town. Ten of the grantees had arrived in Salem after 1640, too late to receive a house lot and 10 acres automatically; 2 others were sons in the Gardner family who successfully appealed for a share of the town's land despite their father's earlier grants. The desire of the selectmen to accommodate new residents with land was still operative in 1642, even those who were new only to adulthood and not to the town.

The other small grants went to men who already had some land. The blacksmith John Cook received less than one acre of additional land in the North Field, probably allotted in adjustment by the town for a new cartway; other examples include Obadiah Holmes, who enlarged his house lot in Glass House Field, and Thomas Gardner Sr., who annexed an orchard to one of the four house lots he had already acquired for his large family. These small adjustments to the landscape accounted for nearly half of the grants of less than ten acres in 1642.

This ratio of new to additional grants was reversed in the 10 grants of 30 acres or more made in 1642: 8 went to men who already had substantial acreage, while only 2 were to new residents. The eight successful petitioners for additional land were all church members, had served in town offices, and had arrived in 1635 or earlier. The selectmen used what little land remained in Salem to adjust their original allotments to reflect the changed status of these men in the town since their arrival. Henry Bartholemew will serve as an example of this process: a merchant who arrived as a single man in 1635, he received only the usual house lot and 10 acres of upland in the original division of lands. By 1642 he had served in a number of town offices, had received 270 additional acres in 5 separate grants, and the next year (and many thereafter) was elected as a selectman. The development of the other men in the eyes of the town was similar, if less dramatic. These men, rather than the new arrivals, received the most generous allotments in 1642.

Although many more grants were made in 1642 than in the average year of the decade, the pattern still reflected at least partially the same purposes demonstrated by the town leaders in 1636. The open field farmers got their 10 acre grants in the common fields, and the larger, enclosed fields were laid out in Beverly among the other farms. Men who needed smaller parcels of land for special purposes—an orchard, an enlargement to a house lot, or a small parcel of saltmarsh—were also accommodated. Finally, a few men of great worth in the community received the more sizeable allotments. Portions of four general town meetings and seven meetings of the selectmen were devoted to the distribution of 836 acres in 1642, less than 9% of the acreage accounted for in 1636. Although little land remained to be granted, the town's concerns for its proper allocation remained both unaltered and unabated.

Again in 1649, a large number of grants appear in the town records; altogether, 1410 acres were parcelled out to 59 men. While nearly half of the grants in 1642 had been initial allocations, in 1649 only 10 of the grantees had not received land previously. Grants of accommodation represented only a small fraction (17%) of the activity of the selectmen in 1649.

While the variation in the sizes of the grants was not as great as in 1642, there is evidence that once again land was being used to adjust changes in status within the community.

Acreage Granted:

	Church member	Nonmember	Total
Town officer[23]	58.8	30.0	53.0
Not elected by 1649	36.0	39.9	39.0
Total	50.0	38.8	43.5

Both older residents and more recent arrivals, large landowners and those with little or no land from prior grants, received approximately equal parcels. However, there was a tendency for those who had joined the church or served in a town office to receive the larger allotments. In a town where church members were expected to become involved in the management of civil affairs and those chosen to serve the town were assumed to be godly men, those few who did not fit the pattern fared less well in 1649 than the men who were neither elect nor officers. Robert Moulton, a shipbuilder who arrived in the Endicott fleet in 1629, had been a church member and had served as deputy in 1634, 1635 and 1637, but was excommunicated from the Salem church in 1637 for his Antinomian heresy. While he was chosen as a jury member 6 times between 1637 and 1649, he did not receive further grants in that period and in 1649 was allotted one of the smaller parcels of 30 acres. A schismatic was not to be rewarded equally with those whose service to town and church was unblemished.

While there appears to have been a tendency to use land grants after 1640 to reward leading citizens, the pattern was by no means absolute. The two largest grants in 1649 went to men who fit the extremes of this model. Walter Price, a tailor by trade who became a successful merchant and frequent town officer, arrived in Salem in 1641 and had to purchase a house lot. The following year he was admitted as a freeman and joined the church. By 1649 he had served on three juries and as constable, and was given his first grant in that year. Between 1651 and his death in 1674, he purchased 14 more pieces of land and served as selectman 16 times. On the other hand, Philip Cromwell was a slaughterer who arrived in 1642 and also became a successful merchant but never joined the church and was not admitted as a freeman until 1665. His three terms on juries all occurred after 1663, and his 4 terms as selectman began in 1675 after he had established his standing in the town with a succession of 30 land purchases beginning in 1661. Only hindsight can reveal the similarities in the economic success of these two men. In 1649 they shared only their relatively late admission to the town and the fact that neither was a farmer. It is hard to interpret Price's grant as a reward for his church membership and involvement in the town when Cromwell received equal acreage.[24] Price fit the behavioral pattern of leaders in the first decade of the town, but Cromwell did not. Since land was one of the primary evidences of status, both men were ascribed the same degree of that elusive quantity in 1649, and both parlayed this advantage into further mercantile successes. Thus, the advantage of men who were church members and town officers in the land granting process should be interpreted as only a tendency, not a rule. The selectmen appear to have followed two different principles of land distribution throughout the 1640s, and neither was applied uniformly. Some newcomers received grants according to the old principle of accommodation, but it was no longer applied universally. Simultaneously, older residents received grants in recognition of their service to the town, but there were occasional grants which show that this practice had not become a fully articulated principle.

While the land records of 1642 and 1649 show a tendency to reward church membership and leadership the clearest examples of this practice occurred in 1648 and 1650. No very large grants had been made since 1638, when Allan Kenniston received his farm of 200 acres. No other men of great worth arrived after that date to swell the ranks of the minimal majority. However, by the late 1640s two earlier arrivals had risen to positions of leadership which made their earlier grants disconsonant with their actual status. The first was George Corwin, a tailor who arrived in Salem in 1638; he was granted 250 acres in 1648, ten years after both his arrival and the last previous large grant. Although Corwin was not registered as a freeman of the colony until 1665 and never joined the church, he served as selectman for 24 of the years between 1646 and 1676. Unlike Cromwell and Price who both served in lesser town offices before being elected as selectmen, Corwin never held any other posts in the town. During his first eight years in Salem he was granted no land and held no offices, but in 1646 he was chosen for the town's highest post. Two years later he received the largest land grant in a decade, a large farm "toward Ipswich River" in Salem Village.

The only other large grant after 1638 was made to William Brown in 1650. A "shopkeeper" when he arrived in 1636, he received the usual house lot, plus 20 acres of upland. As a young, recently married man with no children and no special claims on the joint stock, he was treated well enough, but certainly not as a man who would become one of the pillars of the community. In 1639 he was given an additional eighty acres, but still held only half as much land as those in the minimal majority of 1640. During the next 11 years he had 6 of his 9 children, became a freeman in 1641, and joined the church in 1648. In 1649 he served the first of his 8 sessions as juror, and the following year was elected to the first of his 14 terms as selectman between 1650 and 1668. His grant of 275 acres in Salem Village was his third but by far the largest.

After 1650, what had appeared to be a tendency became virtually a rule. Only 3 grants made in the next decade were to men who had no prior land: the farmers John Britt and Joseph Holton received farms of 30 and 60 acres when they were received as inhabitants in 1651 and 1652, and the mariner John Swazy who had lived in Salem since 1639 was granted a 40 acre farm in 1651. With the exception of these last three grants of accommodation, the land which remained at the disposal of the selectmen after 1650 was used to augment prior grants. Initially a universal practice, the accommodation of the residents had gradually given way to another principle: adjusting status patterns within the town through increases in the acreage of earlier residents. By 1642 only half of the grants were to men with no other land, a proportion which decreased to one-sixth by 1649; after 1650, it was clear that new residents could not depend on the selectmen to provide land.

While the selectmen changed their priorities during the 1640s, their ability to change status patterns through land grants was limited. Only two men joined the minimal majority of 1640 who had not been in that group in 1637 due to additional grants from the town.[25] In the next decade, only Brown and Corwin were granted enough land to be added to that group. Neither Cromwell nor Price, despite the large size of their grants relative to others of the decade, held enough land as a result to be considered among the major owners of 1650.

Very little land remained after that date. Only 480 acres were distributed during the 1650s, one-third as much as in 1649 alone. If the selectmen had less land to work with, their intentions concerning "good order" became clearer. They would tolerate a higher proportion of landless men in the community—already over 10% in 1650[26]—and they would use what acreage was left to bring land ownership, church membership and civic leadership into better alignment. By 1649, it had been clear that grantees who were church members and held an elective office tended to receive larger farms than the others; but only a quarter of the grantees held both these credentials while fully half were neither church members nor town officers either before or after receiving land from the selectmen. After 1650 the proportion of grantees who were both church members and had held town offices rose to one-half; only two men received land in the 1650s who were neither church members nor town officers. With little land remaining to be granted, the selectmen added it to the acreage of earlier residents who were participants in the major institutions of the town. These last, small grants were clearly intended as a final gesture to the desired covariation of godliness, leadership and wealth based on land by the selectmen who, farmers and merchants alike, exemplified that ideal.

The distribution of lands recorded on Ralph Fogg's list of 1636 was intended to define the patterns of land use and status for all time. In fact, these patterns were sustained with very little change for a generation, due to both decreased immigration after 1640 and the depletion of available acreage. After 1640, the conditions of grants became increasingly unclear. Nicholas Woodbury received 40 acres of closed field, 20 of which had been previously granted to and subsequently released by Mr. Thorndike, the other 20 of unspecified location. Unable to designate a particular plot to satisfy the second half of Woodbury's grant, the selectmen ordered that those 20 acres should be "laid out where it may be found most convenient."[27] Mr. Britt had received an even vaguer reply to his request for land presented at the previous meeting of the selectmen. He was granted 60 acres of upland "in the place he desireth it if it be there and not prejudicial to former grants."[28] His request for more acreage was deferred until grants to other men had been "made good," at which time Mr. Britt's request would be "further considered."[29] Unlike earlier grantees, Mr. Britt could have no idea what he had actually received at the hands of the selectmen until the surveyors did their work.

Occasionally the acreage available turned out to be less than expected or of unusable quality, which prompted new requests to the selectmen for additions to former grants, or for exchanges of rocky land for arable acreage.[30] The selectmen also handled many requests for small pieces of land to compensate for land lost due to the construction of a new path or cartway.[31] Most grants made after 1637 were laden with conditions, or involved a tiny amount of land, or both. Still, the business of making these fine adjustments to the landscape consumed much of the time of the selectmen for the next 20 years.

By 1649, nearly all of the land to the town boundaries, miles from the main peninsula, had been apportioned. In that year, the selectmen "agreed that those which have land granted to have it laid out towards the great [Ipswich] River as far as it will hold out, and those which cannot have it there to have it laid out on Cape Ann Side."[32] No additional accommodations for open field farmers had been made for several years, since their common fields would have to be located near the town center where they lived, and all of that land was long since parcelled out, but the enclosed field farmers were still eyeing the few undeveloped parcels at the furthest reaches of the town. The vast area referred to in the grants of 1649 as "toward Ipswich River," separately incorporated a century later as Salem Village, was nearly filled with individual farms; the selectmen could not assume that the grants they had made could all be laid out there. The farmers of Cape Ann Side, the second area designated, by this time had a sufficient sense of cohesion and community apart from the peninsula to resent the selectmen's granting of lands they had grown accustomed to using as commons for a decade or more, never fearing that the exhaustion of lands elsewhere would prompt the town to start surveying acreage which the farmers of this area considered their own. They reacted by converging on a general town meeting three weeks later, at which they succeeded in reserving the remainder of the common lands for the use of Cape Ann landowners.[33] The practice of accommodation by which different groups were all granted land had by 1650 led to the development of distinct neighborhood feelings, a sense of separateness from the town as a whole.

After 1650, the selectmen were reduced to giving new applicants land which had already been granted. The original grantee in one case had to show that he "needed" the land in order to retain it; otherwise it would be handed over to a man whose claims seemed more pressing.[34] In another case in 1658, the selectmen suspected that a particular parcel had already been allotted, but weren't sure; they followed the expedient course of granting the land again, giving the original grantee (if any) two years to press his claim.[35] Thomas [Oliver] successfully appealed to the selectmen for land in 1653, but was told that he must lay out his tract "in any place he can find it provided it come not within any former grant."[36] Others received grants contingent on the surveyors finding suitable and previously ungranted land anywhere within the town bounds.[37] After 1659, there were no further grants; there was simply no more land available.

The limits of Salem were filled before the end of the first generation. Instead of leaving vast tracts of wilderness undivided in reserve for the second and third generations, the early leaders of Salem practiced a policy of inclusion and accommodation which required the use of outlying areas for special groups—Marblehead and Winter Island for the fishermen, Salem Village for the enclosed field commercial farmers, the Bass River area for the Old Planters, and the open fields encircling the main peninsula for the East Anglian yeomen. While the legal status of these areas was not fully established for several generations, their character as distinct areas for different groups of people had been established by 1636. In the process of accommodation, Salem had incorporated diversity by design.

Chapter Four

The First Generation of
Local Government

Although the population of Salem after 1640 was remarkably stable, the years just prior to that date were a period of flux and change. Over half the men who received town grants recorded by Ralph Fogg in 1636 did not remain in Salem; those who did stay served as the pool for political leadership for the next generation. The period during which Salem served as a port of entry and temporary residence for many immigrants were also the years in which the church, the town government, and the land system were firmly established. Tracing the development of these institutions within the very years of greatest instability in the population is a difficult but not impossible task.

If the various relationships of Salem's inhabitants to the land described both economic diversity and geographic dispersion by 1650, the political leadership of the town had an inverse history. After the initial decade of formal town government, a small group of men with common mercantile interests emerged late in the 1640s as the town's leadership, and held nearly unrivalled sway over the management of Salem for the next 40 years. Whatever stability Salem had for the remainder of the charter period, decades in which the church and the economic order were transformed, must be due in large part to the combination of preeminence and longevity of these few men.

All were residents by 1640, but they did not immediately emerge as a political force. The deliberate inclusion and accommodation of immigrants with a variety of English backgrounds made the definition of clear attributes of leadership impossible in the early years. The pattern was set by the orders delivered to John Endicott from the New England Company in 1629:

> We are content the old planters that are now there within our plantation and limits thereof shall choose two of the discreetest and judicial men from amongst themselves to be of the government, that they may see we are not wanting to give them fitting respect, in that we would have their consent (if it may be) in making wholesome constitutions for government.[1]

While the Company itself had named seven persons to serve on the first "Council of Massachusetts Bay," and reserved to Endicott and these seven the right to choose "the other three which will be wanting to make up the full number of thirteen," they also clearly wished to amalgamate Roger Conant and the other Old Planters into their new society. Recognizing that additional ships would bring more men whose talents would be needed to "advance the general good of our plantation," the Company reminded Endicott to look over the newest arrivals when making choices to fill out the Council.[2] Inclusiveness was the goal.

Endicott carried this principle further by calling all of the new residents together to subscribe to "certain articles" which he had composed with the assistance of the minister. While the text has not been preserved, an eyewitness wrote later that the residents were asked to agree "that in all causes, as well ecclesiastical, as political, we should follow the rule of God's word."[3] The alternative to signing this civil contract, for Old Planters and new immigrants alike, was expulsion from the colony, but the intent—far from being exclusionary—was to provide the opportunity for public expression of a common cause.

No records remain of the deliberations of the Council of Massachusetts Bay in this first year of the new colony. The removal of the charter to Boston after the arrival of John Winthrop as the new governor in 1630 left Salem with no formal local government. Endicott, in his role as magistrate, apparently ran the town with whatever help he chose to call on from the freemen. When the General Court decreed in 1631 that none but church members could be freemen, Endicott was in effect left to manage Salem's internal affairs with the assistance of the church members.[4] For six years, the church was the only established local institution; Endicott in the meantime accommodated new immigrants with land, ordered public works as necessary, and established whatever rules for peaceful coexistence were required. If the freemen as a whole participated in these decisions, their contributions went unrecorded.

The emergence of leadership patterns can be seen in these years, however, from the freemen's elections of deputies to the General Court. Until 1634 the Governor, Deputy Governor, and Assistants were elected annually by the freemen and proceeded to manage the affairs of the colony. In violation of the charter, which specifically reserved legislative rights to the freemen, the Assistants assumed this power in 1632. By 1634 the freemen had organized sufficiently to force the Assistants to back down; they did so by creating a role for the freemen in the General Court: that of deputy.[5] Each town was empowered to elect two or three deputies to represent their interests in each session of the General Court. While the town records of Salem reveal only a few occasions during the seventeenth century when the freemen formally issued instructions to their elected deputies,[6] the revised form of the General Court after 1634 was seen as a victory for the freemen over "arbitrary" rule by the Governor and Assistants.[7]

In the first three years in which Salem elected deputies to the General Court, the freemen divided their votes evenly between the two major groups in the population at that time. Eleven terms were served by East Anglians, and a dozen by West Countrymen between 1634 and 1636. Despite the heavily West Country cast of the first immigrants—both Old Planters and the Endicott company—the tide of East Anglian immigration which started in 1633 quickly compensated for whatever advantage Endicott and his fellow West Countrymen held in local political life. In 1634, two Old Planters (Roger Conant and Francis Weston) were elected as deputies, but joining them were Robert Moulton and John Holgrave, recently arrived from East Anglian towns. That same year, Holgrave was also chosen as "overseer" of the town's supply of powder, shot, and other ammunition, one of the most prestigious local positions.[8]

Elections of Salem Deputies, 1634-1639[9]

Year	West Countrymen	East Anglians	Others	Total
1634	2	2	0	4
1635	4	2	1	7
1636	2	2	0	4
1637	2	2	3	7
1638	2	0	2	4
1639	3	1	1	5

None of the East Anglian deputies emerged as a preeminent leader of that faction, however; none were elected for more than three consecutive sessions of the eight held in these years. In the March and September sessions of 1636, two of the three deputies from Salem were East Anglians, but in none of the other 15 sessions of the General Court from 1634 to 1640 did they constitute a majority of the town's representatives. Robert Moulton's election in April of 1637 and Townsend Bishop's in November of that year were the last for East Anglians in this period. The banishment of Roger Williams in 1635—the spiritual leader of the East Anglians—and continued immigration to Salem by groups allied with neither East Anglians nor West Countrymen dissipated whatever modest claims the East Anglian deputies had to political power in Salem.

Among the West Country deputies, only William Trask stood out as a consistent early choice of the Salem freemen; he served seven consecutive terms in 1635-1637, but then virtually disappeared from this level of leadership.[10] His record of service was equalled in the next two years by William Hathorne, an immigrant from Berkshire,[11] who was associated with neither of the groups between whom Salem's voters had previously been evenly divided. Hathorne's political career, moreover, was of longer duration than that of any earlier deputies: he continued to be elected in all but three years to 1661, when he was elevated to the Court of Assistants. Another deputy unallied with either of the groups earlier jockeying for position in Salem was Edmund Batter; first elected in 1637, he served 16 additional terms over the next 45 years. The only East Anglian with a similar record was Henry Bartholemew, whose only service as deputy prior to 1645 consisted of being denied his seat by the General Court in 1635 due to his association with Roger Williams.[12] Only Hathorne and Batter among the deputies of the 1630s developed the history of leadership which might have been predicted on the basis of election as deputy in the earliest years of the colony; they were the compromise candidates for East Anglians and West Countrymen alike. Indeed, of the 18 men who served in the post prior to 1640, only 2 besides Hathorne and Batter were sent to the General Court as Salem's representatives after that year: West Countryman Jacob Barney for 2 terms in 1647 and 1653, and East Anglian Emanuel Downing in 1641, 1644 and 1648.

The 19 men chosen by the Salem freemen to represent them in the 18 General Court sessions of the 1630s were in fact, with the few exceptions noted, the choices of well-defined subgroups of the Salem electorate rather than of a unified town. The issues which divided East Anglians from West Countrymen ranged from the doctrine of the church to the distribution of land; the same issues which divided much of England in the sixteenth and seventeenth centuries were now encompassed within the boundaries of a single town.[13] Only the unallied merchants—William Hathorne and Edmund Batter, and, after a cooling off period of a decade, Henry Bartholemew—could draw support from the majority of the freemen on a consistent basis.

During these same years, a more formal system of government was beginning to take shape within the town of Salem. The initial form of government specified by Matthew Cradock's letter to John Endicott in 1629 was intended for the new colony, not a particular town. There is no evidence that the initial Council of Massachusetts Bay consisting of 13 men was perpetuated after John Winthrop arrived in 1630 and removed the center of government to Boston; if Endicott replaced this Council with another group of freemen of his own devising, this fact is not recorded.[14] The first extant notations in the Town Records were probably orders which emanated from the General Court, by that time located in Boston. In October of 1634 they decided, "On the 4th day seventhnight next the market at Salem [is to] begin, and to continue from 9 o'clock in the morning [until] 4 of the clock after noon."[15] The next entry, from January of 1635, like the first was an instruction from the General Court to the towns of the Bay, this time concerning the universal distribution of ten-acre lots.[16] That same year, the General Court ordered that only freemen were to vote in local elections for deputies, but no other specifications for town government were made.[17] Prior to 1636 it appears that the General Court created what legislation was necessary for the towns, while the magistrates who lived in each town assured that these orders were carried out and made other local decisions as required.

If the General Court and the magistrates of each town had been able to manage land distribution, the establishment of markets, and other affairs of the towns in the new colony until 1636, by that year it was clear that the increasing number of towns and the burgeoning populations within them made a larger degree of local decision making necessary. Accordingly, the General Court specified those questions it was willing to divest to the particular towns:

> Whereas particular towns have many things which concern only themselves, and the ordering of their own affairs, and disposing of business in their own town, it is therefore ordered, that the freemen of every town, or the major part of them, shall alone have power to dispose of their own lands, and woods, with all the privileges and appurtenances of the said towns, to grant lots, and make such orders as may concern the well ordering of their own towns, not repugnant to the laws and orders here established by the General Court.[18]

To manage this "business," the General Court authorized the freemen "to choose their own particular officers, as constables, surveyors for highways, and the like."[19] In order to concentrate on resolving the schisms and "popular" disturbances which had consumed the efforts of the Governor and Assistants during the middle years of the decade, Winthrop and others agreed "that trivial things, etc., should be ordered in towns, etc."[20] The entry of town representatives in the form of deputies to the General Court in 1634 must also have played some part in the willingness of the Governor and Assistants to relinquish some of their control over the towns.

The Salem freemen proceeded to elect 7 men to conduct the "trivial" business of the town in 1636; the following year they chose the maximum allowable number of 13, but in 1639 again reduced the size to 7, a number which was altered in only 3 of the remaining 50 years of the charter period.[21] Electing the selectmen during the first decade of formal town government was complicated both by the large number of men who received extensive land grants in the early years—men who would naturally be expected to emerge as leaders in the institutions of the town—and by the variety of their English backgrounds.

By 1640 there were 26 men with 200 acres or more in grants from the town. 15 others had at least 100 acres. The size of this group was remarkable compared to other New England towns in which a much smaller number of men held such large grants by this date.[22] If large land grants confirmed status, then Salem's social hierarchy was top-heavy. The number of large landowners was due to the unusual pattern of settlement in Salem. Five of the minimal majority in 1640 were Old Planters who had received 200 acre grants at Cape Ann on instructions from the New England Company in 1629 in an effort to merge their interests with those of Salem's earliest residents. All five of these men were church members, and all did serve in a variety of town offices. Five other men—William Clark, Richard Davenport, John Endicott, Francis Johnson, and Samuel Sharp—arrived in the first wave of migration under the new charter between 1628 and 1630, and were given 200 acres or more of land. All except Johnson and Sharp were active in town offices, and Sharp was unavailable due to his role as elder of the church. Had there been only one migration to Salem, the size of this landed elite would approximate that of other towns. These five men, plus the five Old Planters with their Cape Ann farms, would have jointly managed the affairs of the town, secure in their status as firstcomers and church members with sizable estates located outside the peninsula.

The two groups headed by Conant and Endicott, however, were not left alone to perfect their policies of accommodation. The ships arriving in Salem in the 1630s carried more men of wealth and standing who held claims to equally large or larger tracts of land. Sixteen of them appear in the minimal majority of 1640, with farms laid out beyond the lands of the earlier arrivals in areas which would become separate towns or precincts—Wenham, Marblehead, and Salem Village. All but two of these men joined the church and held various town offices, thereby maintaining the expected link between wealth, godliness and leadership.

Clear patterns of leadership and deference among such a large group of land-rich men would take time to emerge. Not all were equally known to the community, having arrived at various times in the 12 years preceding the establishment of town government. Several did not meet the test of accommodation: William Alford and Thomas Scruggs were disarmed in 1637 for their support of Anne Hutchinson.[23] Ten others left the town within its first decade of local government. The leaders among the town's landed men thus emerged at least in part through the default of those who removed from Salem. Only two men among the minimal majority of 1640 who remained in Salem were never elected to the town's highest office; one of them could not serve since he was an elder of the church, while the other was the Old Planter, William Trask, the man most frequently chosen as deputy in these years. The 14 men among the minimal majority of 1640 who settled permanently in Salem clearly assumed the civic roles expected of them.

While the process of winnowing the town's major leaders from an overlarge supply of potential candidates was simplified by the removal of nearly half of the major landowners of 1640, the diversity of English backgrounds represented in the Salem population was a complicating factor. Each of these groups brought different views of the good of the whole to the meetings of the selectmen. Only 8 of the 19 selectmen to 1646 were East Anglians. Seven of them held 10 of the selectmen's seats from 1636 to 1638, and after 4 years of total absence of East Anglians from the board of selectmen, Henry Bartholemew served the first of his 16 terms in 1643. The East Anglian segment of the population had been more successful, though briefly, in securing representation among the town's deputies than they were in electing their spokesmen to the local board of selectmen. The presence of these men among the selectmen in 1636 and 1637, the years in which the pattern of land distribution was well established, helped to assure that the principle of accommodation of men from different backgrounds than the dominant West Countrymen would prevail. Nevertheless, their influence quickly faded, to be replaced by other leaders whose service to the town was of longer duration.[24]

Elections of Salem Selectmen, 1636-1646

Year	West Countrymen	East Anglians	Others	Total
1636	2	4	1	7
1637	7	5	1	13
1638	7	1	1	9
1639	6	0	1	7
1640[25]	5	0	1	6
1641	4	0	0	4
1642	5	0	2	7
1643	5	1	1	7
1644	5	1	1	7
1645	5	1	1	7
1646	5	1	1	7

The second distinct group of early selectmen were six Old Planters, who served an average of 5.6 terms each during the decade. All of them except Thomas Gardner moved to their farms on Cape Ann Side during the 1640s after which their influence in the town decreased markedly. John Balch, John Woodbury and Roger Conant were not elected after

1641; Lawrence Leach's last term was in 1642, and Peter Palfrey disappeared from the board after 1646. Only Roger Conant among the Old Planters ever served as selectman again; he was reelected to the post in 1650 after a hiatus of nine years. In his first years as selectman he sat with his neighbors in the nucleated village, who included other Old Planters, East Anglian yeomen, and the rising young merchant John Hathorne. By the time he was returned to the board in nine of the years between 1650 and 1661 in what could be characterized as his "second career" as a selectman, he represented the minority interests of his Cape Ann neighbors in a group dominated by merchants of the main peninsula. Within 10 years of the institution of town government in 1636, and only 15 years after the accommodation reached between Conant and Endicott, the farmers of Cape Ann had virtually withdrawn as leaders of the town of Salem.

The third "group" of selectmen in the first decade were three men first elected in 1637 who stand out as the most prominent leaders of the period. John Endicott served every year until 1646, when his attention turned increasingly to colony-wide matters until his death in 1665.[26] His fellow West Countryman, Jeffrey Massey, was elected in nine years of the decade, and served an additional eight terms by 1656. Finally, William Hathorne, one of the mediating group of Midlands immigrants tied to neither East Anglian nor West Country interests, began his 32 term career in 1637 as well. Until 1646, however, the board of selectmen was characterized by rapid turnover among the 19 men elected to serve as the representatives of the freemen. Only the three major leaders of this period were elected almost continuously throughout the decade, while other men—Old Planters and East Anglians, large and small landowners—were rotated in and out of the town's highest office. Holding over 200 acres of land and originating from the western counties of England increased the chances that a man would be chosen to serve as selectman, but no single set of attributes were shared by all who were elected to the board. Its composition reflected instead the fluidity of the Salem population in these years.

Like its composition, the function of the board was unspecialized in the first decade. Just as the creation of the town meeting had been for the convenience of the General Court, the existence of a specially elected group of selectmen was for the convenience of the town—to reduce the number of gatherings of the whole. In the first four years of this new system of local government, the selectmen held twice as many meetings as the freemen in general. The distinction between the powers of the two groups was not clear, but it was at least easier to call the selectmen together than to follow the procedures for warning a town meeting.

Even when town meetings were held, it is not clear who attended. Apparently the participation of the townspeople in their collective meetings was not consistently general, for in 1639 the quorum was set at "above the number of six persons," provided that proper warning of the meeting, including its agenda, had been effected. Knowing the date and time of these meetings and the business to be done, a minimum of seven townsmen were empowered "to transact all such occasions and make such orders therein as they shall judge meet and the said orders and determinations to be as authentical as if the whole town met provided that the said persons have been together or have stayed an hour after the time first appointed," presumably to allow for unavoidable delays in the arrival of inhabitants who lived greater distances from the meeting place.[27]

Since attendance was not posted in the town record, the actual numbers who participated in these early town meetings cannot be determined, but the quorum of seven persons suggests that attendance was frequently, if not generally, very low. In effect, the selectmen alone could have constituted a quorum if all were present and proper warning had been given for a full town meeting. There was no functional imperative for attendance, since in these first years the powers of the elected representatives were undifferentiated from the authority of the freemen as a whole. Both groups could receive new inhabitants, grant land, raise local taxes, and make orders about fire ladders, livestock, fences, and the town bounds.

The emergence of the board of selectmen as the town's most active political organ in the first decade was undoubtedly due to its efficiency. Seven men could easily set the date for their next meeting before adjourning, while a town meeting had to be warned by the constables well in advance and its agenda agreed upon and posted on the meetinghouse door for all to study. The existence of a specially elected group of selectmen was a convenience for the freemen, who were called to general meetings only half as often as the selectmen met from 1637 to 1640. No specific powers were delegated to the selectmen which could explain the difference in their rate of meeting on grounds other than convenience for the larger body. Given no limits on their authority and no particular tasks which were not shared by the town as a whole, these early selectmen were in an ambiguous position.

Their undefined authority was open to challenges, which occurred as early as 1640. At a town meeting in January of that year the townspeople discussed the power of the selectmen to distribute land, and concluded that the grants already made which had sparked the debate "shall stand firm and this present town meeting do with one consent confirm them."[28] However, while the inhabitants decided not to limit the authority of their representatives, they moved to assure that one faction or another could not meet privately to make decisions which had the force of law. They established a quorum for the selectmen as they had done for the town as a whole the previous year. While the minumum for the town meeting was surprisingly low, the rules for selectmen's gatherings were strict: six of the seven men, or "four with the magistrate might do any thing or act, and had power so to do as if all were together."[29] With this high standard of attendance, together with the rapid turnover of the diversified leadership before 1647, the townspeople could be content that the meetings of the "few" would indeed be on behalf of the "many." Still, they wanted to be informed of the actions of the selectmen, and in September requested an audit of the town books "that the whole town may receive satisfaction therein."[30] Further, they approved a rate of £15 for necessary meetinghouse repairs and the keeping of a book of town records. All of the transactions of the selectmen would thus be open to the scrutiny of any inhabitant. After five years of resisting the specialization of the selectmen's function, the town assured that the actions of their representatives would reflect the good of the whole.

While the freemen did not specify the powers of their representatives, by 1640 other changes in the town altered both the role and the composition of the board of selectmen. Many of the early leaders moved to their farms beyond the peninsula, among them the Old Planters who had served as selectmen with great regularity between 1636 and 1641. Endicott, Hathorne, Massey and Gardner among the large landowners who had also been representatives remained in the town and continued to be elected, but the Old Planters virtually disappeared except to serve as surveyors of highways in their own Cape Ann precinct and occasionally as jurors. Their withdrawal coincided with a change in the function of the board, as the duty of office which had been the most time-consuming—the granting of land—was reduced to a fraction of the activity prior to 1640. The selectmen therefore met less frequently in the next few years. The town meeting banned further grants in the cattle common in 1640, and gave the residents of Marblehead the rights to the common there in 1641; except for the grants made in Wenham in 1642 in the second attempt by the selectmen to settle that area, the board was largely inactive, and the number of meetings held decreased.

In December of 1643, the town meeting instructed the selectmen to meet monthly "upon the penalty of ten shillings to be levied on the whole or upon such of them as are absent without just ground," thus indicating both that not enough meetings were being called to satisfy the town, and that those convened were not well-attended. The town meeting did not specify, however, what business of the town had been neglected thereby in the preceding three years of irregular and infrequent meeting.[31] Six of

7 selectmen attended the next 2 meetings;[32] they made 7 grants, and bound an 8 year old child as an apprentice for 12 years.[33] The February meeting was also attended by six selectmen who accommodated several residents with land, sent a "lazy, idle and loitering" woman to the Boston jail, and bound out an orphan.[34] These 3 months of compliance with the order of the town meeting were followed by 11 months of total inactivity during which time 6 town meetings were held; no mention of the lapse in the selectmen's meetings was recorded.

On the other hand, the middle three years of the decade were a busy period for the town. Six town meetings were held every year between 1644 and 1646, while the selectmen met less frequently. In 1645, the town agreed "that the rates and other particular occasions which were presented to the general town meeting shall be ordered by the seven men and they will stand to their order."[35] But in fact most of the "orders" in these years were issuing from the town meeting itself on subjects ranging from the gift of a cow for the relief of a poor resident to the authorization of a new bridge costing £100.[36] Lacking a definition of selectmen's authority as distinct from that of the town meeting, the inhabitants reassumed the primary burdens of decision making. The obverse was also true: the centrifugal forces which led by the early 1640s to the founding of Wenham and Manchester, the reservation of the Marblehead commons, the movement of the Old Planters to their farms on Cape Ann Side, the settlement of the Salem fishermen on Winter Island, and the settling of farmers "beyond the bridge" made the earlier agglomeration of leaders both impractical and unnecessary. Feeling the loss of unity, albeit a coalition of disparate men grounded in the principle of accommodation which existed before 1640, the Salem populace briefly reasserted their collective sense by managing the town in meetings of the whole between 1643 and 1646. Each decision to survey fences, levy a rate to collect firewood for the elders, or license an ordinary reaffirmed the sense of the participants that they shared a single, if dispersed, community.

At the same time, there were clear signs of a lack of common cause. By 1645, the regular quarterly contribution to the ministry fell short of the needs of the Salem pastor, so the town agreed to tax nonmembers for his maintenance.[37] The expectation that all residents would be in the meetinghouse on the Sabbath was also unmet, leading the town to establish a watch of two men "to walk forth in the time of God's worship, to take notice of such as either lie about the meetinghouse without attending to the word or ordinances, or that lie at home or in the fields, without giving good account thereof."[38] The resurgence of collective action in the town meeting was at least in part a response to the clear lack of universal support of the other focus of communal identity, the church.

In 1646 this exercise of communal consciousness reached its apex: in January the inhabitants agreed to meet weekly for the next month "to consider of the public good of the town." The agenda once again included the bridge at "townsend" over which the farmers passed in entering the town, a house of correction, a bridewell, the purchase of a "town stock of cotton wool," whether or not to sow hemp and flax, and the question of a town agent in Barbados.[39] Control of deviants, public works, and the economic development of the town as a whole were the issues of 1646. In the meantime, the selectmen were instructed "to survey all the fences and to fine such as are defective according to order."[40] Although other men had been appointed by the town prior to this date to perform this task, the selectmen seemed to have nothing better to do in 1646 as the town meeting assumed most of the responsibility for the management of the town.

While only the bridge was discussed at the meetings which followed, other issues appeared during the year which underscore the determination of the town to reassert its unity. The supply of gunpowder had been distributed to several different men for safekeeping, but now the inhabitants called it in to be stored in a central place. Private funerals were banned, and it was ordered "that there shall be no burial within the town but that there shall be notice given to the town thereof a little before the burial."[41] Since baptism and communion were rituals for church members only, and marriage was a private, civil ceremony, funerals were the only important public rituals of colonial New England, and the townsmen of Salem intended to keep them that way. All weights and measures were called in to be sealed, to assure the equity of economic exchanges among the inhabitants. Finally, concerned about the separation of the Cape Ann farmers and those of Jeffries Creek from the town center, a new ferry large enough to transport cattle and men on horseback was ordered, and the Beverly planters were told to repair the bridges along their route to the town.[42] Each of these decisions was an attempt to reinforce the centrality of the peninsula and the unity of the town.

The exercise of authority in the town meeting in the interests of the good of the whole was all-pervasive in 1646, touching on public safety, ritual, transportation, and the economic ordering of the community. The rate of church admissions had declined in the previous five years since Hugh Peter's departure for England, and the geographic dispersal of the population had accelerated in the same time, but in 1646 the town of Salem consciously set about the task of reasserting its unity. Their efforts were impressive but shortlived. Not until the Quaker crisis of 1658 would there be as many town meetings as in 1646, and in every year after that date the selectmen met more frequently than the town as a whole.

After choosing the selectmen in March of 1647, the town met only twice more that year and the business was of a different order: constables were elected, a grand jury appointed, and a doctor paid for attending a sick woman. On the other hand, the selectmen met six times, and made the decisions about the town's arsenal, the poor, and repairs to the meetinghouse. The town had taxed itself twice in 1646—once for the new bridge and again for the elders' firewood—but in 1647 the selectmen calculated the tax needed and called a town meeting to "approve" the work they had done. The seven men also appointed a jury of trials, a power previously reserved to the town as a whole. Other appointments besides the usual keepers of swine and cows were made by the selectmen: a new keeper of vital statistics, a marshall of the court, and the clerk of writs. While the constables' accounts had been reviewed by the town meeting in 1646, the following year the selectmen not only took over this responsibility but also called the deacons to account.

The marked change in the activity of the selectmen in 1647 was accompanied by a change in the membership of the board. Five of the seven men were new, the largest turnover since 1637. The merchant William Hathorne was retained, along with William Lord, a West Country ironmonger who served the last of his five terms in 1647, but five other earlier selectmen with years of experience behind them were not reelected: John Endicott, Jeffrey Massey, Thomas Gardner, Henry Bartholemew, and the Old Planter, Peter Palfrey, were swept out of office. In their places appeared five men with no previous experience in the town's highest office. The mariner, John Hardy, and house carpenter Samuel Archard were only elected once, and never served again in this or any other major office; however, the other three new selectmen all became major leaders in Salem—George Corwin and Edmund Batter who were rising merchants in the town, and the Village farmer John Porter. Together, these 3 men held the office for 62 terms. They joined William Hathorne in 1647, who had already served 9 terms and had 22 ahead of him. John Porter was the only farmer among the selectmen in 1647. The leading planter in Salem Village in 1650 in terms of total acreage held, Porter's commercial approach to farming tied him increasingly to the mercantile interests of the town.[43] He remained the only farmer among the small group of men who dominated the office of selectman after 1647.

The following year, Henry Bartholemew was returned to office. Refused his seat as deputy in 1634 due to his staunch defense of Roger Williams, Bartholemew disappeared from the town's leadership for nearly a decade. He finally was elected to the board of selectmen in 1643 for the first of his 16 terms, and in 1645 served the first of 19 terms as deputy. By this time the East Anglian conflict with West Countrymen, centering on Roger Williams' doctrinal tests and the method of land distribution in the middle years of the 1630s had subsided, and Bartholemew had emerged as one of the town's rising merchants. He and the ever popular William Hathorne, and the three new leaders of 1647, were joined on the board of selectmen by William Brown Sr. in 1650 and Walter Price in 1651. These seven men—six merchants and one commercial farmer—would serve over half of the available terms as selectmen and constitute a majority of the board in all but one of the years to 1668. Indeed, together with the sons of five of them, these seven men would be a controlling majority of the selectmen except for six years to 1683. While they occasionally differed on major issues confronting the town during the 37 years in which they dominated Salem's political structures, these 6 merchants and their ally John Porter agreed far more often than they disagreed. They constituted a highly visible and generally coherent interest group, holding similar views of the good of the town.

The reasons for their sudden emergence as the delegates for most of the authority of the town are various. Their performance in lesser offices had not marked them for the selectman's post, since they had not been prominent among the constabulary or the juries of the previous decade.[44] Walter Price, the last addition to the group in 1651, had served one year as constable in 1646, but none of the others held this onerous post. George Corwin had never served in any elective or appointive office prior to his election as selectman, while John Porter and William Brown had been called to jury duty once. Henry Bartholemew and Edmund Batter had been tested by the community somewhat more, as jurors five and six times respectively, but this degree of service hardly fits the definition of an apprenticeship for the town's highest office.

Again in contrast to the pattern in other towns, not all of these major leaders were large landowners at the time of their first election. Only William Hathorne and Edmund Batter were among the 26 largest owners in 1640, and these two men and Henry Bartholemew were the only ones of the group to receive all of their large grants prior to election as selectmen. William Brown, George Corwin and John Porter all were recipients of large tracts of over 200 acres in the first year they served as selectmen; all 3 grants were made by the board and not by the town meeting, so the rise of these men to landed eminence came as a result of their election, and by a decision in which they themselves participated. The major leaders of the first decade had gradually emerged from the oversized group of largest landowners, but land was used to confirm the status of the new leaders within the town in the second decade. These three and Walter Price were also highly active in the land market after 1650, while Hathorne, Bartholemew, and Batter were not.[45] The only three of these major leaders who were among the landed elite prior to election were thus the only ones who did not attempt to increase their holdings dramatically, either by purchase or by granting themselves land while they served as selectmen; the major leaders who came later to landed wealth were far more acquisitive.

What all seven men shared on election was wealth, whether or not it was expressed in land at that time. They were not only able to manage the financial affairs of the town with skill, but also to finance various projects personally and wait for reimbursement from the town later. Hathorne and Corwin paid for a bed and bolster for a poor woman, and for the cure of another woman for which they were to be repaid by the town in six months.[46] Edmund Batter covered the cost of two blackstaves for the constables, while Corwin and Hathorne bought the nails to cover the meetinghouse "speedily."[47] Nearly half the bills granted by the selectmen in 1647 from the constables' accounts were to repay the town's debts to themselves.[48]

While their ability and willingness to serve as bankers for the town may explain their sudden rise to political prominence, these same attributes produced an important change in the procedures for managing the affairs of the town. Audits of the constables' accounts were called for by the town meeting prior to 1647, after which the selectmen assumed this role, while increasing amounts of the town's money were committed privately by the selectmen. In 1658 George Corwin engaged "to satisfy the Treasurer [of the colony] the remainder of the rate that is behind of 1656 and Major Hathorne and Edmund Batter have promised to satisfy Mr. Corwin the same value again."[49] The previous year Corwin had paid £50 for a house for the minister which the town agreed to repay him by rate, and in 1659 George Corwin and William Brown spent £200 of their own money to build a house for the new minister, Mr. Higginson, according to the same arrangement.[50] Such extensions of personal assets for the use of the community confirmed the Puritan expectation that the few godly men raised to positions of leadership would act for the good of the whole.

While the financial prowess of the merchants which made such generosity possible was both the source of and the means for solidifying their influence in the town, the scope of the selectmen's powers was increased only in the area of accounting for the town's money prior to 1660. In addition to auditing the constables' accounts after 1647, the selectmen also approved disbursements on the highways and other public works, and then told the town meeting at the end of the year what accounts were due. These activities replaced the function which had been the most important during the first decade—the granting of land. After the spate of

grants made by the selectmen in 1649, residents of outlying areas moved
to halt the depletion of their remaining commons. The farmers of Cape
Ann Side returned Roger Conant to office, and after 1650 further grants
in that area required the permission of Conant or other Cape Ann representatives. In 1651, the residents of Ryal Side received similar rights to
their commons. The reservation of the various commons and the depletion
of remaining lands prompted the town meeting in 1653 to turn down a
petition from one resident for additional land, and only eight requests
received a positive answer from that body in the remainder of the decade.[51] The selectmen also slowed their activity, and the few grants made
were laden with restrictions or depended on the ability of the surveyors
to find appropriate acreage. Although the new leaders of Salem after 1647
were more prominent than their predecessors as individuals and more
active as a group, there was little they could do to alter the basic outlines
of the community established in the town's first decade which had a
lasting impact on its social structure.

Thus, the emergence of the merchants did not immediately transform
either the landscape or the function of the selectmen except in the management of finances. The board continued to make some appointments
to a variety of lesser offices, but the town meeting shared this authority.
Gradually the selectmen took over the responsibility for the arsenal, fences,
and swine, the town bounds and poor relief, but the town meeting consistently chose the members of both the jury of trials and the grandjury
after 1648, and named the commissioners for votes, small causes and
rates. Still, many appointments continued to be made by whichever group
was in session at the time the need arose: surveyors of highways and
bridges, and the town's cowkeep were appointed by the selectmen in
some years and the town meeting in others. Specialization of the selectmen's function was in a nascent stage.

The preeminence of the merchants by 1660 did not come about as a
result of conscious power-seeking on their part, but rather as a necessary
result of the further fragmentation of the town, in which the town meeting
actively participated. Marblehead was made a separate town in 1649,
although they did not have a fully covenanted church for another 35 years.
The reservation of the Cape Ann and Ryal Side commons in 1650 and
1651 also increased the sense of separation of residents of those areas
from the town's center. The selectmen's grants of 1649 had precipitated
the requests of these outlying groups for more control over their neighborhoods, but the town as a whole acquiesced. Other actions of the town
meeting confirm the sense that the areas beyond the bridge were viewed
as distinct precincts. In 1655 some men were allowed to hire their own
cowkeep, while the selectmen were asked to see to the provision for the

town herd.[52] That same year a second burial ground—a primary locus of community ritual—was approved, to be located among the farms of Salem Village.[53] Later that same year the rates for the Cape Ann planters were discussed separately at a town meeting, and within two years the three areas of Salem—Town, Village and Cape Ann—each had a constable. The town meeting further increased the separation of Cape Ann in 1658 by naming a surveyor of highways for that area.

Still, the withdrawal of the Cape Ann farmers continued. They delivered a petition to the General Court in the spring of 1659 "humbly desiring to be a township of themselves." The Court declared that "the petitioners should make their address to the town of Salem in reference to their requests," thereby reaffirming the authority of the Bay towns in matters concerning their own division, but revealed its views of the petition by ordering "the town of Salem to give the petitioners a speedy meeting to effect the same," and by declaring themselves "ready to answer their [the Cape Ann planters'] just desires in their petition."[54] In August the town meeting asked the selectmen, together with Henry Bartholemew and William Hathorne from the Town and Jeffrey Massey from the group of petitioners, "to meet with our brethren of Cape Ann Side the next second day to consider and draw up some positions to answer the desires of our brethren there."[55] The result, which fell short of the original request for township status, was an agreement that the planters might maintain their own minister, survey their own local highways, and provide for their own poor.[56] The decision of the townspeople of Salem to call Mr. Higginson to the Salem church that year, and to provide for him an annual salary equal to the total for the previous two ministers plus a house costing £200—four times as much as the previous parsonage—must certainly have contributed to the "desires" of the Cape Ann farmers.

Simultaneously, the town meeting concerned itself with the weakening of voluntarism among the populace. The assumption that free-will subjection to the central institutions of the town would flow naturally from the policy of accommodation was open to challenge, as church attendance had to be monitored as early as 1644, and nonmembers were rated for the support of the ministry the next year. Neither universal attendance nor voluntary contributions from the congregation could be assumed by the end of the first decade of the covenanted church. Similarly, incentives had to be provided for cooperation in public works. When the highway between Wenham and the head of Bass River needed repairs in 1644, the overseers of the work were authorized to offer the workers a choice: reduction in the amount of other work they would be called on to do, or abatement of their rates.[57] Even the freemen had to be reminded of their responsibilities; by 1654 the town ordered "that all those persons that shall not seasonably attend town meetings either by their persons or proxies for every offense or delinquency after due warning according to order shall pay eighteen pence to be levied by the constables."[58] The fine was small but the message was clear. An offender who wished to have his fine dismissed had to present his "excuse" to the selectmen within a week after his absence. The principle of accommodation had resulted in the creation of several new and independent or semi-independent towns by 1654, but the principle of unity required general attendance at town meetings by those who remained within the limits of Salem. Regular gatherings of the whole were seen as one important antidote for the social consequences of dispersion. The full participation of the townsmen in the meetings of 1646 had provided one model of unity; deference to the merchants, whose wealth by Puritan canons was a sign of grace, was another. Throughout the 1650s Salem tried to maintain both as supports for a fragile community, much weakened by dispersion which the town itself had encouraged from the earliest years. In the late 1650s the arrival of Quakers in Salem further threatened the cohesion of the town.

Quakers had appeared in Salem as early as 1657,[59] and by 1658 there were sufficient numbers to elect one of them, Joseph Boyce, as selectman.[60] Perhaps in an attempt to avoid this outcome, the town decided to elect only five selectmen instead of the usual seven that year, but the maneuver failed. Boyce served with Roger Conant and Thomas Lathrop, both Cape Ann planters, and with the older merchants Edmund Batter and William Hathorne. The Cape Ann representatives did not attend half the meetings, however, so Batter and Hathorne were left to contend with the Quaker yeoman from the farms west of the town bridge in 1658. Relationships among the three must have been less than smooth. Hathorne had already established strong credentials as an ardent prosecutor of Quakers through his representation to the General Court, and there is evidence that Batter's feelings were similar.[61] In September of 1658 when another Quaker attempted to speak in the meetinghouse, Batter "grabbed him by his long hair and pulled him backward, and furiously thrust a glove and a handkerchief into his mouth to gag him."[62] If there were similar incidents at the meetings of the selectmen, they were not recorded, but there is little doubt that the board of selectmen in 1658 could do little to promote the good of the town. Religious division within the town had infected the body politic.

As persecution of Quakers increased, the townspeople reacted in 1659 by sweeping all but Hathorne and Batter out of office and reelecting George Corwin, William Brown, and Walter Price. While the civil authorities in the courts harassed the Quakers in an attempt to quell their divisive influence in New England, the inhabitants of Salem responded to the Quaker threat by electing five non-Quaker merchants as selectmen in 1659.[63] Conant and Lathrop, who had absented themselves from three of six meetings in 1658, could be of little help in restoring a sense of common mission to Salem, and the town needed unification more than it desired representation from the outlying districts. The Cape Ann farmers, who by 1659 had secured the rights to their common and were geographically separated from the Quakers who had settled primarily among the farms west of the town bridge, could afford to view the Quaker incursion as the problem of another precinct and withdraw from active political participation in Salem's internal struggles.

The merchants, on the other hand, could be depended on to exert a centralizing control over town affairs. They all lived in the immediate area of the meetinghouse; all but George Corwin, whose wife was among the elect, were members of the church; and all were wealthy men with common mercantile interests. Thus, the response of the town to the geographic dispersal of the residents, compounded by the Quakers' destruction of the formal religious unity of the town, was to turn back to the merchants for leadership in 1659. To overcome religious conflict, the town looked to the merchants to restore order within the central political institution of the town. The resulting board of selectmen did not reflect the geographic dispersion or economic differentiation of the town, but it did represent the desire of the inhabitants for cohesion. The alternative of 1646—the resurgence of the town meeting—was out of the question since it would provide yet another public opportunity for the 10 to 15% of the population who were Quakers to be disruptive and divisive. The merchants were the only certain source of unification in 1659, and the town meeting turned to them to restore order through political cohesion and control in a community divided by religious schisms.

By 1660 the merchants had emerged as the only leaders powerful enough to command deference from all regions of the town in a time of stress. As magistrate and commissioner for Salem during the years of Quaker persecution, Hathorne and Batter established their credentials as men devoted to the ideal of a unified religious community.[64] They and their fellow merchants were also chosen to preserve political unity. The special financial talents of these men were thus translated into religious and civic leadership.

Once the burdens of leadership were delegated to these few merchants, their control over the civil affairs of the town provided opportunities to increase their own fortunes. Corwin, Brown and Price were able to build a large house for the new minister called to Salem at the height of the Quaker controversy in 1659, and at the same town meeting which approved this expenditure they received permission to build a corn mill on the South River over the objections of William Trask—the West Country-man most frequently selected as deputy in the first decade—whose North River mill would no longer be a monopoly enterprise in the town.[65] Elected due to their ability to finance public works, these men in turn received economic benefits at the hands of the townspeople which served to rein-force their position. Dispersion and differentiation within the community required the hegemony of the merchants in civic life, a preeminence concomitant with their economic standing and religious leadership.

Chapter Five

The Establishment of the Church

When John Endicott arrived in Salem in 1628 as the first governor of the Massachusetts Bay Company, he not only dashed the hopes of Roger Conant and the other Old Planters of receiving their own patent through the Dorchester Company for the land which they had inhabited for five years, but also brought with him new assumptions concerning the formation of a church. Conant had emigrated to Plymouth in 1623, where he was among the "Particulars" of that community. The Plymouth church consisted of the members of the original Leyden community and their children, and all others were considered to be outside the covenant. Conant and other West Countrymen found their marginal status in Plymouth repugnant not only on social grounds, but also for religious reasons. Neither Separatists nor Anglicans, Conant and others believed that the communities of the New World should be as inclusive as possible, and that their churches should be as concerned about the unregenerate as the saints. While the Leyden congregation based its church on doctrinal purity and excluded new arrivals to Plymouth, Conant and other West Countrymen in Plymouth in 1623 had hoped to find a more inclusive community. They apparently were sympathetic to the Pilgrims' reformist tendencies, but Conant and his followers agreed that "exclusion . . . was a painful last resort rather than an instinctive first reaction."[1] In 1624, Conant and a small band of other Particulars removed to Nantasket, and the following year to Cape Ann when Conant was invited by the Dorchester Company to become the governor of that struggling settlement.[2] They were joined by Reverend John Lyford, who had been expelled from Plymouth for his Episcopal tendencies.[3] He was probably relieved to have the opportunity to remove from the Pilgrims at Plymouth and Nantasket to join the non-Separatist group at Cape Ann. He preached among the fishermen there until the fall of 1626, when he left for Virginia.[4]

Conant and his small band had found no replacement for Lyford when Endicott arrived two years later with the charter of the newly formed and Puritan based Massachusetts Bay Company. While Endicott and his fellow passengers weathered the first winter in Salem, the company was preparing to send more colonists—among them three ministers who sailed at the Company's expense in the spring of 1629.[5] Francis Bright, Francis Higginson, and Samuel Skelton were all silenced Puritan ministers whose "faithful preaching, godly conversation, and exemplary life" recommended them to the Company.[6] While Matthew Cradock, on behalf of the Company, wrote to Endicott, "We doubt not but these gentlemen, your ministers, will agree lovingly together," he felt it necessary to add, "and for cherishing of love betwixt them, we pray you, carry yourself impartially to all."[7] While the behavior of all three was "exemplary," their views of church polity were quite distinct. Francis Bright had been a "Conformist" associated with John White, while Skelton had Separatist leanings; Higginson's views were at least initially indistinguishable from Skelton's.[8] Still, the Company clearly held the non-Separatist view that the church to be founded could rest on godly behavior or the Covenant of Works and include regenerate and unregenerate parishioners as well as ministers of different doctrinal persuasions. The anti-Separatist intentions of the Company were made clear in the case of Mr. Ralph Smith, a minister who paid his own passage. Suspecting him of being a staunch Separatist, the Company feared he might cause "distraction" and "siding" among the colonists and ordered "that unless he will be conformable to our government, you suffer him not to remain within the limits of [our] grant."[9] The Company had in mind a unified and inclusive community based on "faithful preaching, godly conversation, and exemplary life" rather than on any particular doctrinal tests, which would undoubtedly result in schisms and controversy.

By the time these three ministers arrived, Endicott had had an opportunity to learn more about the form of the covenanted church at Plymouth from Deacon Samuel Fuller who had treated several of Salem's colonists for scurvy during the long winter. The voluntary quality of the covenant idea appealed to Endicott, and he recognized in this form a useful tool for building a new society from waves of disparate immigrants. In forging new institutions in the wilderness, Endicott needed just such a mechanism for voluntary assumption of mutual obligations among the colonists. He wrote to Governor Bradford to let him know that they were in agreement "touching your judgments of the outward form of God's worship."[10] Endicott did not mention the use to which the covenanted church was put in Plymouth—the exclusion of all but the Leyden congregation—for he had another view of the utility of the covenant idea: the preservation of peace and unity. By engaging the new residents in the mutual bonds of a church covenant, Endicott hoped to recreate a purified form of the all-inclusive English parish.

In August of 1629 the church was gathered after a "solemn day of humiliation.''[11] Skelton was chosen as the pastor and Higginson as teacher, and thirty members agreed "that we covenant with the Lord and one with another, and do bind ourselves in the presence of God, to walk together in all his ways, according as He is pleased to reveal himself unto us in his blessed word of truth.''[12] No doctrinal tests were imposed. Indeed, according to eye-witness Nathaniel Morton, "The Confession of Faith and Covenant forementioned, was acknowledged only as a direction pointing unto that faith and covenant contained in the Holy Scripture, and therefore no man was confined unto that form of words, but only to the substance, end and scope of the matter contained therein.''[13] Each new communicant chose the form of his testimony according to his tastes and principles:

> And for the circumstantial manner of joining to the church, it was ordered according to the wisdom and faithfulness of the elders, together with the liberty and ability of any person. Hence it was, that some were admitted by expressing their consent to that written Confession of Faith and Covenant; others did answer to questions about the principles of religion that were publicly propounded to them; some did present their confessions in writing, which was read for them, and some that were able and willing did make their confession in their own words and way.[14]

Agreement to "walk together," the only stipulation of the covenant, did not require that everyone adopt the same gait. The different forms of joining the church used in 1629 would later characterize emphatically divergent doctrinal positions, but in the summer of 1629 the "truth" was not defined.

The Company officers should have been pleased with this church gathering, which met the stipulations of their letter to Endicott earlier that year:

> We have . . . good hope . . . of the love and unanimous agreement of our ministers, they having declared themselves to us to be of one judgment, and to be fully agreed on the manner how to exercise their ministry, which we hope will be by them accordingly performed. Yet, because it is often found that some busy persons (led more by their will than any good warrant out of God's word) take opportunity [of] moving needless questions to stir up strife, and by that [means] to beget a question, and bring men to declare some different judgment, (most commonly in things indifferent,) from which small beginnings great mischiefs have followed, we pray you and the rest of the council, that if any such disputes shall happen among you, that you suppress them, and be careful to maintain peace and unity.[15]

Francis Bright, the Conformist among the three ministers sent by the Company, saw the seeds of Separatism in the covenanted form of the new church and took the next ship returning to England, but if there were other residents who had "needless questions" concerning "things indifferent" they kept them to themselves in 1629. Among the new communicants was the fourteen year old son of Francis Higginson, who would remember this era of "peace and unity" and the absence of doctrinal tests when he returned to Salem thirty years later as minister.[16] The new covenanted church included Old Planters and new arrivals alike. The large number of initial communicants relative to other towns was an indication of the inclusiveness of the Salem church.[17]

The undefined inclusiveness of the fledgling church was soon tested. When Francis Higginson died in 1630, Samuel Skelton began to initiate various orders in the church which resembled Separatist practices. Women were forced to wear veils, and those who would not renounce their ties to the Church of England were refused communion.[18] When Winthrop arrived that summer, Skelton refused him communion on the grounds that Winthrop was not a member of a covenanted church, an action which prompted a strong rebuke from John Cotton.[19] The election of the ardent Separatist Roger Williams as Skelton's assistant was further indication of the inclinations of Skelton and at least some of the members in 1631. The objections of Roger Conant and of Boston's leading citizen, John Winthrop, prevented the Salem church from actually ordaining Williams, but their intentions were clear.[20] When the East Anglian (and heavily Separatist) tide of immigration started in earnest in 1633, Williams was again invited to the Salem church, and this time he was installed as Skelton's assistant.[21] For the next two years the Boston church and the General Court applied various kinds of pressures to encourage Williams to change his ways or leave.[22] In 1635 the General Court refused to seat two East Anglian deputies elected by the Salem freemen in a direct rebuke to Williams and his followers, who had written letters vilifying the magistrates and deputies.[23] The Court agreed that the East Anglian deputies could return if the majority of the freemen of Salem would repudiate the letters.[24] Further, the General Court "enjoined" the East Anglian elder of the Salem church, Samuel Sharp, "to appear at the next particular court, to answer for the letter that came from the church of Salem, as also to bring the names of those that will justify the same, or else to acknowledge his offense under his own hand for his own particular."[25] Worse yet, the Court refused a request for an extension of the town's territory.[26] Endicott, who had gone along with William's earlier policies, defected along with many other leading Salem residents. Williams and a few loyal Separatists departed for Rhode Island,[27] and the General Court confirmed Marblehead—the requested extension—to be part of Salem.[28]

For a year after Williams' departure the Salem church was unable to attract a new minister. Finally, in the fall of 1636 Hugh Peter agreed to accept the challenge of restoring unity to the divided congregation at

Salem. Recognizing that the original covenant, which had not specified either doctrine or organization, had failed to contain the communicants within the confines of non-Separatist practice, Hugh Peter added to the original statement nine injunctions. In reaffirming the covenant of 1629, each member had to agree:

> We whose names are here underwritten, members of the present Church of Christ in Salem, having found by sad experience how dangerous it is to sit loose to the covenant we make with our God: and how apt we are to wander into bypaths, even to the losing of our first aims in entering into Church fellowship: do therefore, solemnly in the presence of the eternal God both for our own comforts and those which shall or may be joined unto us renew that church covenant we find this church bound unto at their first beginning.[29]

If the first covenant was too "loose" then the new one had to be more specific. While the members of 1629 had merely agreed to "walk together," the members of 1636 had to promise "to walk with our brethren and sisters in the congregation with all watchfulness, and tenderness, avoiding all jealousies, suspicions, backbiting, conjuring, provokings, secret risings of spirit against them."[30] To avoid further schisms within the church, they agreed that "we will willingly do nothing to the offense of the church." Further, the church was to attempt to encompass all equally, whether members or not: "We bind ourselves to study the advancement of the Gospel in all truth and peace, both in regard of those that are within, or without." Even the Indians were mentioned as potential beneficiaries of the "advancement" of the church. Unlike the Separatist churches, the Salem church agreed in its new covenant to recognize "our sister churches . . . using their counsel as need shall be." Common agreement among the churches of the colony on points of theology and practice was one good way to avoid "bypaths" like the one travelled by Williams. Finally, the members had to "promise to carry ourselves in all lawful obedience, to those that are over us in church or commonweal, knowing how well pleasing it will be to the Lord, that they should have encouragement in their places, by our not grieving their spirits through our irregularities."[31] A combination of penitence and resolve, the language of the new covenant was designed to put the disunity of the Williams era behind the church of Salem, not by specifying fine points of doctrine, but by spelling out the behaviors required of a Massachusetts Bay Puritan: peaceful inclusion of all, and proper deference to one's superiors. These articles addressed themselves not to the quality of individual religiosity or behavior, but rather to the warp and weft of Puritan social theory: general accommodation, and a mutually understood hierarchy. Since West Countrymen and non-Separatists dominated both deputies' slots and the board of selectmen by 1636, the new covenant realigned the town's civic and religious leadership patterns as well.

A few of the East Anglian residents who had supported Williams refused to sign this more specific covenant, but all of the prominent West Countrymen attached their signatures. The 80 members of Salem's reconstituted church comprised about a fifth of Salem's adult male population in 1636, a proportion which was to rise dramatically during the next few years of Peter's leadership.[32] By the time Hugh Peter departed for England in 1641, nearly 100 additional men had joined the 47 male communicants on the list of 1636; roughly half of the male population of the town was within the church in 1641.[33]

The four and a half years of Hugh Peter's ministry in Salem were a period of growth and consolidation for the Salem church. By 1641, the Salem church had achieved peace, and Peter had acquired a reputation for skillful accommodation and leadership, which led the General Court to "intreat" the Salem church to release its minister for an ambassadorial assignment to England.[34] Upon Peter's departure, Edward Norris was elevated from teacher, a post he had assumed in 1640, to minister. During the 18 years of his ministry, the rate of admissions declined, due not only to the virtual cessation of immigration, but also to the new admission practices he enforced. Giving testimony about one's conversion experiences, first to the elders and minister, and then to the entire church, had become a standard practice in New England churches before Norris arrived in the Salem pulpit.[35] Hugh Peter had followed this procedure, but interpreted it leniently. Norris, however, was convinced of the value of cross-examination and close questioning, not only by the elders and himself, but also by the full church. In his last 2 years in Salem, Hugh Peter had accomplished the admission of 77 residents into full communion. Norris admitted only 59 in the next 6 years. Despite this decline in the rate of admission to the church, by 1650 slightly over one-half of Salem's families had at least one church member.[36] While this proportion is small relative to other towns, it was the high point of inclusiveness in Salem's ecclesiastical history.[37]

Hugh Peter had also been notably successful in suppressing dissension within the Salem church. Five Salem residents were presented to the Court in 1637 for their support of Anne Hutchinson and were consequently disarmed,[38] and Mary Oliver was committed to prison a year later "for disturbing the church of Salem,"[39] but after the Antinomian controversy in 1638—which bore a strong resemblance to Williams' brand of Separatism[40]—there were few doctrinal schisms to challenge the unity of the Salem church until the Quaker influx in the late 1650s. The covenant of 1636 had specifically enjoined church members to "watchfulness" over the congregation, and it appears that most deviations detected thereby were dealt with informally. Few were presented to the courts for unwillingness to give up schismatic ideas during these years, although Salem had its token representatives of Anabaptism, Gortonism, and Familiarism which resulted in presentments to the Quarterly Court.[41]

More telling were the notations in the town meeting minutes about lapses in observance of the Sabbath and difficulties in maintaining the minister's salary. During the summer of 1644 the town meeting "ordered that two be appointed every Lord's Day to walk forth in the time of God's worship, to take notice of such as either lie about the meetinghouse without attending to the word or ordinances, or that lie at home or in the fields, without giving good account thereof."[42] Inattention was as much a concern as failure to attend, and both were to be dealt with by turning over the culprits' names to a magistrate "whereby they may be accordingly proceeded against."[43] Inclusiveness now required enforcement.

Voluntarism was also at issue, when the town meeting "agreed that the nonmembers of this congregation shall be rated for the helping the supporting of some of the public ordinances in the church: as namely the preaching of the word."[44] This order, addressed to nearly half of Salem's families which did not contain any church members, and more specifically to over half of the adult male population who were not within the covenant, reflects a growing reluctance on the part of those who did not share in the full benefits of church membership to carry the financial burdens of maintaining the ministry.

Despite the greater stability of the Salem church after the first decade of rapid changes in leadership, doctrine, and polity, the greatest growth occurred during the early years of the Salem covenants. When Hugh Peter sailed for England in 1641, one half of the church admissions of the entire charter period had already occurred. Although the number of Salem men who were church members continued to increase slowly until 1652, the total by the end of the next decade was less than in 1641, and continued to decrease throughout the charter period as the total population rose. (See Appendix C, Table II.)

Although decreasing as a percentage of the total population, and after 1650 in absolute numbers as well, the membership of the church included all of Salem's major leaders and most of the largest landowners. The dominant principles of the Salem covenant—inclusiveness and voluntarism—thus continued to permeate the town even after they were no longer fully operational within the church itself.

Chapter Six

Beyond the Limits of Accommodation

From the first meeting of Conant and Endicott in 1629, the intention of Salem's leaders to include different and occasionally differing groups within the community was clear. Accommodation required the separation of dissimilar immigrants and the specialized use of land, but all were included in the new community. Fishermen were granted their own territories of Marblehead and Winter Island; the East Anglian yeomen tilled the North and South Fields, and when these were filled, the lands in Wenham; the Old Planters clustered at Cape Ann while other planters populated the farms beyond the town bridge in what would become Salem Village, and yet another group settled Manchester. The policy of accommodation also required recognition of "personages of note," who were granted larger tracts in anticipation (and later, in recognition) of their leadership in church and town. All of these arrangements were clear by 1636, by which time half of the town's acreage had been allotted. The social structure which is fully divulged in Fogg's list of landowners of that year was created deliberately and for all time.

This ordering of the town was subject to frequent amendments, but the twin principles of accommodation—universal inclusion and recognition of worth—were followed for over a decade, as each new inhabitant was matched with a parcel of land fitting both his occupation and his status. The men arriving between 1637 and 1640 who merited large farms of over 200 acres outnumbered those who had them by 1636, but these newcomers were accommodated. Others whose worth had been originally underestimated were granted more land, adding them to the group of men who held over 200 acres each in 1640—the minimal majority which owned half of the total acreage allotted. Even this new ordering did not stand firm: within a decade, two-thirds of the acreage held by the minimal majority of 1640 was in the hands of other men as the original owners left the town or died. Thus most of the confirmation of "worth" by land grants to 1640 was effectively undone by 1650. Still, the town tried to hold to the principles of accommodation. When a small number of rising merchants in the late 1640s upset the expected correlation among land, wealth, and service, the balance was righted by granting them the only large tracts of the decade. At the same time, the selectmen reinforced the position of the church in the community by showing some degree of preference for its members as the town's remaining lands were laid out. The rate of admissions to the church slowed markedly after 1641, but so did the rate of immigration; the covariation of godliness, leadership and wealth was maintained as the church contained all of the town's selectmen and most of the large landowners. The outlines of the "good order" hoped for in 1629 were still distinctly drawn.

By 1650, however, there were signs that the voluntarism which was expected to flow from universal inclusion and the leadership which was anticipated from men of worth were not consistently forthcoming. Both inattention in and absence from church services were noted in the town records, and the Old Planters had withdrawn from the leadership roles they had played earlier in both town and colony as they moved from the peninsula to their Cape Ann farms. There were also signs that the two tenets of accommodation—inclusion of all, and ascription of status—were no longer the rule. Many of the largest landowners had acquired land by purchase, not by grant, thus weakening the correlation between worth and wealth, while a number of residents had no land at all.

After the town rescinded the General Court order concerning universal distribution of house lots and subsistence farming plots in 1637, a small number of men in each new wave of immigrants was admitted to the town but granted no land. By 1650, there were 45 of these landless heads of households in Salem.[1] One quarter of them joined the church—a much lower proportion than the population as a whole in this period—and the same number were called on to serve in a variety of lesser posts in the town. After 1650, half of them purchased some land, but the remainder never owned property in Salem. Their eventual economic fortunes varied, despite their common landless beginnings in Salem.

Reuben Guppy was perhaps the sorriest of the group. A tailor who arrived in 1640, his children were "placed out" in other families in 1647 due to his inability to support them; he and his wife were given one pound and eight shillings for their own support as well.[2] Apparently this was a sufficient amount of relief, for Guppy did not need more help until 1669, when his town rates were abated due to his inability to pay.[3] The following year he was given work by the town: enforcement of the order that all swine pastured on the common be ringed properly. Guppy was "to have the benefit of the fines."[4] He refused the job the following year when the order was extended to include hogs, but continued in his role as enforcer of the swine ordinance until 1680.[5] He was given other duties by the town as well, as the price of his dependence on their charity. In 1675 he was asked to keep order during church services among the young boys assigned to seats on the stairs in the meetinghouse, and was "further ordered to keep the dogs out of the meetinghouse; and in consideration of that . . . he is allowed his whole rates for the year ensuing."[6] His misfortunes extended to the second generation, as his son John's rates were also forgiven in 1676, 1684, and 1685.[7] Reuben Guppy never succeeded in overcoming his landless origins.

At least eight of the landless men in 1650 were planters, none of whom ever joined the church and only one of whom became a freeman or held an office of any kind. These men farmed the lands of Salem Village which were owned by the merchants who remained in the town. Half of them eventually purchased some land of their own, and achieved a degree of respectability in the town. The most successful of these planters was Henry Kenny, who arrived in 1645 and spent the next 60 years developing a small estate and a reputation as a good workman. For his first 16 years in the town, during which he married and had five of his eight children, he owned no land. Finally, in 1661 he bought 60 acres of upland in Salem Village. The next year he approached the selectmen to ask for 30 or 40 more acres; his request was granted "if it be there and no way engaged to any other."[8] The land referred to was unquestionably "there," but it apparently belonged to someone else, so the grant was rescinded. The next year, Kenny went to the selectmen again to ask for some meadow land adjacent to John Putnam's. The selectmen this time decided to survey the parcel before making a grant, and the surveyors "having viewed it made this return that they find the meadow no more than of right belongeth to John Putnam."[9] There were no land grants made in Salem after 1659, and the reason is clear: even sharp-eyed Henry Kenny could not locate an unclaimed parcel by 1662. In 1668 he bought himself six acres of meadow, the second and last of his purchases.

Between 1668 and 1680, now established as a landowner, Kenny received frequent warrants to repair highways, the bridge at Beaver Dam, and the town's fortifications, for which he was paid two shillings per day.[10] Admitted as a colony freeman in 1677, he received his first town appointment in 1683, as tithingman for Constable Pope's ward in Salem Village.[11] His two largest appointments followed soon after: he was constable for the Farms in 1686 and overseer of highways there in 1687.[12] He was rated at the lower end of the tax scale in 1689, and then appears to have retired from active participation in town life until his death in 1705, for he does not appear again in the records. His first civic appointment came 48 years after his arrival in Salem, and was earned through his accumulation of a modest farm and a reputation for serving warrants for public works diligently and well. Never an outstanding inhabitant, Kenny was nevertheless the most successful of the planters who were landless in 1650.

Robert Starr's history is typical of the seamen who were among the landless inhabitants of these middle years of the century. He owned no land, served in no offices, was never called on to work on a public project, and died in 1677 without ever appearing in the town or church records. His widow did, however, appear in the town records in 1677 and 1678 as the recipient (along with eleven other widows and one man) of charity from the town.[13] Had he left a sufficient estate for his wife, nothing would be known of his 27 years of residence in Salem except that he arrived in 1649, was fined 20s. by the Quarterly Court for fighting with another mariner that year, lived in the east end of the town, and had a son who appears on the tax list of 1683.[14] Only 1 of the seamen ever purchased any land, 10 years after his arrival in Salem; the others lived decades in the town in rented houses, and none joined in the civil or ecclesiastical affairs of Salem.

All but one of the artisans on the other hand—by far the largest occupational group represented among the landless men of 1650—served as jury members several times, and half of them purchased land as well after 1650. Jeremiah Meachum's story will serve to illustrate the fate of this group. It was 20 years before he could purchase a house and lot in 1670 along the North River, during which time his method of earning a living for his family of seven children is unknown. After this purchase, however, he was chosen for the grandjury by the town meeting in 1677, and the next year served as inspector of families in Salem Village.[15] He had a fulling mill in Salem Village by 1675. In 1678 he served a warrant for work on the fortifications, and the next year was chosen again for the grandjury. His rates were abated in 1681 because he had been rated by mistake for a Salem Village farm he had previously rented, which may explain his means of livelihood during his first two decades in Salem.[16] By 1681, he apparently earned enough as a fuller and weaver to give up farming, but in 1686 his rates were abated again, this time due to his inability to pay.[17] That year he moved back to the main peninsula, where he set up a shop,[18] and by 1689 was able to pay his taxes which were slightly higher than Henry Kenny's, but still at the lower end of the scale. Meachum does not appear again in the records except to be assigned a seat behind the minister's in the meetinghouse in 1692 until his death in 1695.[19]

The 45 men who arrived after 1636 and had received no land from the town by 1650 put strains on the community which the principle of accommodation had in general held off until then. Nearly half were able after decades of hard work and raising families to buy land and to achieve a measure of respectability in the town, but altogether they acquired only 330 acres in their lifetimes, and none were ever far above the lowest rungs of the economic ladder. The town was still granting land to a few new-comers in the 1640s, but after 1650 only three new residents would be accommodated. When the granting of land ceased completely in 1659, and the new tides of immigration resumed from England, the numbers of landless men in the Salem population would rise dramatically: by 1689, half the heads of Salem households owned no land, and half were taxed at Jeremiah Meachum's level or less. The presence of 45 propertyless men in 1650—none of whom were called to any civic duty until they purchased land, and who joined the church at half the rate of other inhabitants to this date—was a harbinger of more changes to come.

The other group which strained the social structure established in Fogg's list of 1636 were those men who by 1650 had amassed large quan-tities of land by purchase, an achievement-oriented group which far sur-passed the town's ability to keep status patterns within the limits of ascription alone. After 1638, those who had received grants from the town began to sell them to others. Unimproved land reverted to the town ac-cording to the conditions of each grant, but land which had been cleared, cultivated or built on could be sold. The motivations of these sellers were, not surprisingly, quite unlike the intentions of the selectmen in their orig-inal distribution of acreage, and the result of these sales had a dramatic effect on the composition of the landed elite, which by 1650 bore little resemblance in either membership or ranking to the minimal majority of 1640. While the ratio of sales to grants was still low prior to 1650, the impact of these early deeds on the economic structure of the town was profound. Fourteen houses or improved house lots, 10 of which were on the main peninsula, were among the 54 exchanges of property between the inhabitants of Salem by 1650; but the major activity was the exchange of 2126 acres of arable land, only 28 acres of which were sold in small parcels. Henry Harwood and David Corwithen bought farms of 5 and 10 acres respectively in Marblehead, while William Hathorne acquired a Wenham farm of 13 acres. The remainder of the acreage was sold in

	Deeds[20]		Grants		Arrivals[21]	
	Number	%	Number	%	Number	%
1636-40	5	.3	439	66.4	370	46.7
1641-50	49	3.4	181	27.4	78	9.8
1651-60	271	18.6	41	6.2	71	9.0
1661-70	316	21.7	0	0.0	90	11.3
1671-80	487	33.4	0	0.0	110	13.9
1681-90	330	22.6	0	0.0	74	9.3
Totals	1458	100.0	661	100.0	793	100.0

amounts large enough to alter the social structure of the town.

Nine men by 1650 made 21 separate purchases; the total amounts of land acquired by these men ranged from 78 to 625 acres, the latter more than any single man had received in grants. Four of these 9 men by virtue of their purchases joined the elite land-owning group of those who owned more than 200 acres, while Daniel Ray, who had already been in the minimal majority of 1640, increased his holdings from 310 to 450 acres, and John Hathorne bought 140 acres to add to his previous 265 acres in town grants. In 21 purchases over 6 years from 1644 to 1650, these men succeeded in amassing 30% as much land as was distributed in the entire 1636 allocation. William Dodge's farm was in Beverly, but the remainder were among the farms of Salem Village. The sellers, including two widows, were leaving Salem: John Humphries, Salem's largest grantee, sold his 500 acre tract to John Porter and returned to England; John Pease sold his Beverly farm and moved to Marblehead; Elder Samuel Sharp sold his holdings in 1646 and died the next year; Townsend Bishop, Richard Davenport and William Haines all left Salem by 1650. Only two of the sellers (William Hathorne and Elias Stileman) remained in Salem; the former continued to buy and sell land in a process of consolidating his holdings, while the latter became an innkeeper and never again appears in the records of land transactions.

Buyers of Land to 1650

	Fogg grant	Add'l grants	Deeds to 1650	Total
Richard Hutchinson	60	—	625	685
Sgt. John Porter	20	—	500	520
Daniel Ray Sr.	160	150	140	450
John Hathorne Sr.	—	265	140	405
William Dodge Sr.	60	72	200	332
John Porter Jr.	—	—	200	200
Richard Ingersoll	80	32	75	187
John Putnam Sr.	—	—	140	140
Daniel King	30	—	78	108
	410	519	2098	3037

The bulk of the lands were thus transferred as the result of the departure of several of Salem's early leaders. Of the four men who joined the minimal majority of 1650 as a result, only John Porter Sr. ever served as selectman; Daniel Ray, twice the recipient of large town grants which he enlarged by purchase in 1647, had not been a selectman in the previous 10 years and would not be again. The connection between land and leadership, absolute among the minimal majority of 1640 who remained in

Salem permanently, was altered when acreage was exchanged not in the meetings of the selectmen but in the marketplace. All of these major buyers were church members except John Porter's son, but their involvement in that institution did not carry over to immersion in the civil affairs of the town.

After 1650 land would be sold in smaller lots to less wealthy men who simply wanted a few more acres of upland or a parcel of meadow, but there was little room for these buyers in the land market to 1650, which consisted almost exclusively of departing leaders of the first decade of the town and the few men who had accumulated enough capital to buy them out. The town selectmen had added three new merchants—William Brown, George Corwin, and Henry Bartholemew—to the landed elite of 1650, but four farmers bought their way into that group. These four did not owe their success to the selectmen; the assessment by the town of their worth had not resulted in large grants. After 1644, the buying power of these farmers surpassed the town's ability to reward its leaders, to realign the balance between land ownership and involvement in the political life of the town.[22] Simultaneously, the meaning of large estates changed. Acreage conferred by the town was a confirmation of high status, while the preeminence of the farmers was based on their own achievement; their purchases created their position.

Significantly, only three of the twelve men who had been granted more than 200 acres by 1650 made any purchases to that date.[23]

Owners of over 200 Acres of Land in 1650

	Average acreage granted by town	Average acreage bought	Average acreage owned
Old Merchants	299.3	21.9	318.4
New Merchants	302.0	0.0	302.0
Old Planters	203.0	0.0	203.0
New Farmers	104.4	333.0	439.4

An inverse relationship existed between buying land and receiving it by grant. Only Daniel Ray among the farmers of Salem Village had been granted more than 200 acres, which he enlarged by a purchase of 140 acres, while the two largest land owners in 1650 were Salem Village farmers who had been granted only 60 and 20 acres by the selectmen. The only purchasers of land other than the farmers by this date were the Hathornes, merchants who already owned substantial acreage and whose purchases were smaller than those of any of the new farmers. Those who thought of land grants as a natural result of preeminence did not rush to purchase more acreage when their peers left the town or died during the 1640s.

Distinctions within the landed elite of the town now had both an occupational and geographic basis. The merchants who lived on the peninsula were granted Salem Village farms which they leased for income, while the commercial farmers in the Village lived there among the tenants who used the land they had bought but could not personally till. The involvement of these two clearly defined and separated groups in the management of the town differed markedly.

Percentage of Terms Served as Selectman by Elite of 1650

	by 1650	after 1650
Old merchants	61.0%	63.5%
New merchants	6.8	16.5
Old Planters	20.3	8.2
Village farmers	11.9	11.8
	100.0%	100.0%

The primary beneficiaries of the decline in the Beverly planters' election to the town's highest office after 1650 were the new merchants, William Brown and George Corwin. Together with the merchants who were landed by 1640, they served four-fifths of the available terms in office. Only John Porter Sr. among the Salem Village farmers served as selectman after 1650, becoming the spokesman for that group, while Roger Conant played a similar role among the Old Planters. Clear sectional interests were operative in the board of selectmen by 1650, but the farmers of Cape Ann and Salem Village who served these interests were a minority among the merchants of the town.

The hegemony of the merchants in colony offices was even more complete:

Percentage of Terms Served as Deputy by Landed Elite of 1650

	by 1650	after 1650
Old merchants	76.9%	75.0%
New merchants	0.0	23.2
Old Planters	23.1	0.0
Village farmers	0.0	1.8
	100.0%	100.0%

John Putnam Sr. finally served in the General Court in 1677 and 1680, but was the only farmer among the large landowners in 1650 to be elected.

Again, the older merchants were firmly in control of the election of deputies, while the newer merchants were chosen instead of the Old Planters after 1650. William Brown and George Corwin, new to the landed merchant elite in 1650, and Edmund Batter, Henry Bartholemew and William Hathorne among the merchants of earlier date, served all but two of the terms among the large landowners of 1650. Only 8 other men who were not among the landed group of 1650 ever served as deputy, and altogether were in that office only 12 terms, none of them prior to 1665.

The control of Salem's voice in colonial affairs throughout the last 35 years of the charter period thus rested with 5 merchants, all of whom were at the same time substantial landowners. The wealthiest farmers, both Old Planters and the upstarts of Salem Village, were unrepresented except for John Porter Sr.'s term in 1668 and John Putnam's two terms in 1677 and 1680. Within the town's borders through the office of selectman, men with agricultural interests had more of a voice, but still were outnumbered on the board every year after 1650. All except George Corwin and John Porter Jr. who owned 200 acres or more in 1650 were church members, and with the exception of Porter all were freemen as well. Nearly universal formal participation in both church and federal covenants did not mean, however, that members of the different and clearly defined subgroups among the landed elite of 1650 would share equally in the exercise of power within either town or colony. "Accommodation" into the elite by 1650 meant adding a few merchants to those who already were dominant in the town, while the status of the farmers would have to depend on their own achievements which did not extend beyond the economic measures of success to include the exercise of substantial political influence in the community.[24]

By the end of the first generation in Salem, the town little resembled the community of 1636. From one nucleated village in which artisans, seamen, yeomen were settled in undifferentiated neighborhoods, a series of smaller villages at Wenham, Manchester and Marblehead had emerged.[25] Further, the lands encircling the peninsula from the Marblehead border to Manchester—including Brooksby, Salem Village and Cape Ann—by 1650 contained enclosed farms on which the owners lived. The yeomen of the North and South Fields continued to walk daily to their plots, but most of those with larger farms had by 1650 chosen the convenience of living on their lands, thereby increasing the proportion of artisans among the residents of the peninsula. Among the artisans and seamen on the peninsula were a number of men who had received no accommodation of land, and even among the farms there were a number of tenants. Within the clear sectional lines lived a few wealthy men, but the leadership of each precinct was attuned to a different model of success. A single church served the fishermen of Marblehead and the planters of Cape Ann and the Village together with the merchants, artisans and yeomen of the peninsula, and a single board of selectmen attempted to manage the affairs of the town for the good of the whole, but the economic diversity of the inhabitants was barely contained within the Puritan definition of unity—inclusion of all in a mutually understood hierarchy. In the next generation these separate interests would be heard and would change both the shape of the community and its standards for identifying its leaders.

Meanwhile, more men were arriving in the town each year, and had somehow to be included in a community whose old principles of accommodation had been eroded both by the failure of universal inclusion and by the emergence of a new breed of wealthy farmers whose land and church membership no longer served as either symbol or predictor of leadership. The arrival of these new residents served to intensify the distinctions emerging within the town of Salem.

By the midpoint of the seventeenth century, 460 household heads had been incorporated into the Salem settlements, and 90% of them had been accommodated with land. Not all were still in residence in 1650; some had died, while others moved on to inland towns or returned to England by that date, but most remained and lived out their particular callings in the various precincts of the town. During the next 20 years only 135 new inhabitants were admitted to the town, a number far smaller than the sons of earlier arrivals who came to maturity during this time. Since migration from England had nearly ceased after 1641, the new arrivals between 1650 and 1660 came to Salem primarily from other towns within Massachusetts Bay and the other New England colonies; after 1660 immigration from England resumed.

	1623-40	1641-50	1651-60	1661-70	1671-80	1681-89
Arrived in Salem[26]	371	78	57	78	110	53
Left Salem[27]	40	65	54	43	23	13
Net increase	331	13	3	35	77	40

As children of the earlier settlers grew to adulthood, the number of households in the town rose, but there was little new growth in the population during the middle decades of the century except by natural increase.

Those who were admitted to the town during the 1650s did not cause any discernable shift in the occupational distribution of the inhabitants. As farmers, seamen and artisans moved on to other towns, they were replaced by others of the same occupation. With the renewal of immigration from England after 1660, however, the pattern began to change. While 9 seamen left the town in the decade after 1660, more than from any other occupational group, 24 arrived; the trend for artisans was similar, but more farmers departed than arrived as new residents. The balance between agricultural and mercantile pursuits established in the first generation was to be revised again as artisans and seamen predominated in the waves of immigration.

Occupational Distribution of New Arrivals

	1651-1660	1661-1670
Agricultural	26.7%	8.1%
Seamen	31.0	40.0
Artisans	26.7	43.8
Other[28]	15.6	8.1
	100.0%	100.0%

The impact of the decrease in the rate of immigration by farmers was intensified in Salem by the departure of earlier farmers at a greater rate than they were replaced by new arrivals. What little new growth there was in the Salem population in these years occurred within its mercantile segment, that group which was already concentrated on the main peninsula.

The new inhabitants settled in ways which confirmed the distinctions established earlier between the farming precincts and the peninsula, and established new ones within the peninsula itself.[29]

Residence of new arrivals	1651-60	1661-70
South River districts	28%	58.1%
North River districts	32	23.3
Districts beyond town bridge	40	18.6
	100%	100.0%

The removal of the farmers from the peninsula to their tracts at Cape Ann and in Salem Village was virtually complete by 1650, and the new agricultural immigrants confirmed this pattern. None of them settled on the peninsula, but moved instead to the districts of Ryal Side and Salem Village. The new seamen, fishermen and mariners not only remained on the main peninsula, but all were located in its South River districts—two-thirds of them in the eastern portion of the town near the neck leading to Winter Island. This southeastern quadrant of the peninsula, sparsely settled by earlier residents, was clearly seen by the mariners who came to Salem after 1650 as their neighborhood: on the harbor, but set apart from the merchants and artisans who resided to the west around the meetinghouse. The artisans were not as clearly differentiated by residence; while they were concentrated within the peninsula,[30] they settled in all four of its quadrants. The mariners and the farmers set themselves apart more distinctly. (See Appendix B, Maps 4 and 5.)

In the 1630s when seamen and artisans represented a similarly high proportion of a wave of new immigrants, the town had responded by reducing the size of house lots and encouraging farmers to move to their fields beyond the bridge. After 1650, these measures would no longer work: the peninsula was filled, and the Village nearly so. Only two of the new arrivals after 1650 received accommodation from the town—two farmers who settled in Salem Village in 1651 and 1652. Thus the location of the residences of the others must be seen as a matter of their choice, subject only to the availability of property in the marketplace and the new residents' ability to buy or rent it. The clear separation of farmers and mariners into their own districts and the general concentration of artisans within the peninsula demonstrate that after 1650 there were distinct neighborhoods in the town. The small number of new farmers added to the Salem Village district were not conspicuous among their neighbors, but the seamen and artisans who settled along the South River formed a substantial percentage of the population of that area, a neighborhood in which most of the residents had not entered the town through the usual process of accommodation.[31]

The differentiation of these neighborhoods was also advanced by the choices these new immigrants made when they purchased land, as two-thirds of them eventually did. Eighteen of the mariners and artisans who were received as inhabitants in the 1650s bought houses and house lots on the peninsula, but only 8 of them purchased arable land in addition. Meanwhile, the farmers, the three artisans who settled in the Village, and the new Salem Village teacher bought only upland located beyond the town bridge, on which they presumably built houses. During the period of accommodation of new residents by the selectmen, most grants had included both a plot for residential use on the peninsula and some arable land elsewhere; these new residents, however, usually bought one or the other, but not both kinds of land. This tendency intensified among the new arrivals after 1660, when nearly twice as many artisans and seamen arrived and bought residential property in the town while only seven of them purchased additional upland. These men would earn a living exclusively through their trades and maritime occupations, not relying on farming as an adjunct activity—which further separated them from the agricultural interests of the residents outside the peninsula.

Even within the peninsula the mariners and artisans were distinguished from earlier immigrants who continued to practice subsistence agriculture. If any of these new inhabitants concentrated in the center of the town had hoped to keep a few animals for their own use, this possibility was closed off in 1660. Earlier residents, concerned about the size of the areas reserved as pens and common pasture for the use of all who received house lots and portions of the common fields, instructed Thomas Oliver to warn a meeting of the "commoners" to discuss incursions made by newcomers who had purchased houses and lots on the peninsula. While the selectmen forbade the meeting, the General Court that year legislated that new houses built on lots divided from earlier and larger house lots would not automatically have the privilege of commonage, except "such as already are in being or hereafter shall be erected by consent of the town."[32] New arrivals could buy a house, but they could not purchase access to the entire system of open-field landholding. Those residents of the peninsula who could eventually afford to buy more property chose warehouses, additional houses, and town lots instead.

Outstanding among this group was Thomas Maule, whose 25 purchases between 1661 and 1689 included only 3 acres of upland. His career is also illustrative of another characteristic of the most successful new residents: he never joined the church and did not participate in the political life of the community. Indeed, after 1670 he became a Quaker notorious for his disruption of Salem's civil and ecclesiastical institutions. This lack of synchrony in Maule's wealth and his worth to the town could not have happened earlier, when each resident's economic standing was based on and adjusted to his participation in the central institutions of the cove-nanted community, but Maule was free to achieve his own economic standing.

This same disjunction in the symbols of accommodation—property, church membership and service to the town—was apparent in the cases of the few other immigrants of these years who accumulated substantial amounts of land. Three men who arrived in the 1650s acquired nearly 200 acres of land each, and 4 men who came to Salem in the next decade surpassed this amount. Of these seven new additions to the major land-owners of the town, only one was a planter; the remainder were artisans and one seaman. None were church members or freemen, and only one ever served as selectman. The ranks of the major landowners now in-cluded a third distinct group; in addition to the merchants who were both church members and selectmen, and the farmers who bought large farms by 1650 and joined the church but did not enjoy full political participation in town affairs, there was now a new group of peninsula-based artisans who bought large farms but participated in neither of the two major in-stitutions of the town. The symbols of status were becoming increasingly separable.

These seven men who eventually purchased large tracts were not atyp-ical among the new inhabitants of 1650 to 1670 in their low rate of participation in the church or in the government of the town. As a group, these new residents contributed to the decline in church membership among the Salem population, and had minimal impact on the civic leadership patterns established prior to their arrival. Only four of the new arrivals between 1650 and 1670 ever served in the town's highest office. Daniel Andrews, the only large landowner among them, bought a 215-acre farm in Salem Village in 1677 from his brother-in-law Thomas Gardner, Jr.; the same year, he inherited a farm in the Village through his marriage into the Porter family. He was elected as selectman in 1684, although he was not a church member of a freeman and had never served in another town office. His major interests, like those of his in-laws, were in the Town, where he was a successful builder.[33] Daniel Weld, a physician who immigrated to Salem in 1669 was elected for one term in 1675, but never served in any other capacity or again as selectman after that date. He purchased four houses between 1675 and 1679, presumably for purposes of income, and in 1685 bought a house in Haverhill and moved there. The gunsmith Nicholas Manning bought four small parcels of arable land, served on two juries and as constable between 1666 and 1672, and in 1675 was elected to his only term as selectman; he left Salem before 1683. None of these three were freemen or church members, and only Andrews had the quantity of land previously associated with leadership. Timothy Lindall, who fit the earlier model except for his landowning history, was a merchant who arrived in 1660. He bought a house in the center of the town, joined the church in 1677, and was made a freeman in 1678; finally in 1686 and 1687 he was chosen as a selectman. His taxes in 1689 were among the highest in town, but he never owned large arable tracts—and unlike William Brown and George Corwin of the first generation, was not drawn immediately into the leadership of Salem despite his parallel (but later) economic success. None of these four men ever became major leaders, and none of them fit all parts of the first generation's prescription for leadership.

The only office filled by the men who arrived between 1650 and 1670 in proportion to their numbers was the constabulary, the position least likely to be filled by those earlier residents whose credentials as church members and freemen led them to dominate the more appealing offices and appointments. The principles of accommodation which had originally included all residents in the ownership of land according to their worth were no longer operative; having surpassed the limits of accommodation, the town also failed to include new inhabitants in its central institutions.

If these new arrivals did not fit the "good order" of the initial decades of settlement, neither did they immediately or directly challenge that order. The small number of farmers who moved to Salem Village augmented that hierarchy primarily at the lowest levels. Some remained tenants for life, while others bought farms much smaller than those of the area's leading residents. The average acreage accumulated by these new inhabitants was 25 acres, and only two bought more than 50 acres. Daniel Andrews began his life in Salem as a mason and ended up as a substantial landowner in Salem Village through marriage into the Porter family, but John Blevin was more typical of the newcomers. A yeoman who arrived in 1659, he purchased a house, barn, three acres of upland, and two of saltmarsh that year. Four other purchases occurred in the next 20 years, none larger than 11 acres. By 1679 he owned 29 acres and bought no more before his death 25 years later. Only Bray Wilkins among these new farmers was able to accumulate a large estate entirely through purchase; in 1673 he bought a 233-acre farm, and added a second one near the Topsfield line 8 years later. He alone challenged the leadership of the town, by urging repeatedly the separation of the Village from the town— a move which was successfully resisted by the Salem selectmen during the colonial period.[34] Even Wilkins' behavior fit well with that of his immediate surroundings, as he was joined in his views by the Putnam family of the Village.

Within the peninsula, the situation was much the same. Only one merchant was added to the population through immigration in these years, and he remained outside of both the church and political office for the first 17 years of his residency. Other wealthy men, primarily merchants, would arrive in Salem later in the colonial period and challenge the political and economic structures established since before 1650, but in the two decades after that date the increase in the numbers of seamen and artisans was to the advantage of the early merchants who had emerged as the primary leaders of both church and town. In their pursuit of their trades, the artisans and seamen created a round of secondary economic development from which the merchants profited.

Overall, the immigration of the middle decades did not alter the shape of the town substantially. The specialization of neighborhoods, already well-defined, was advanced by the new residents, but they generally ranked at the bottom of the economic scale in these areas. Few became church members or freemen, and only four served briefly—and all after 1675— in the town's highest office. The few new residents of the peninsula who amassed large farms in Salem Village but did not join the church or become freemen showed the increasing disjunction of the symbols of status within the community, but these symbols had not yet become associated with special and conflicting interests. The number of propertyless men doubled between 1650 and 1670, but tenant farmers were in demand, and the seamen and artisans of the peninsula settled into rented houses built for income purposes by better established artisans and merchants. The new residents of Salem in these decades adapted themselves to its landscape if not to its institutions, but for the time being at least they stood comfortably outside the latter.

There were, however, other strains on the "good order" of the town's first decades. The new immigrants had doubled the size of the landless group in Salem and added a few more men to the landed elite whose economic status did not covary with leadership and godliness, but the greatest changes came from the accelerated buying and selling of land among earlier residents between 1650 and 1670. The new arrivals, two-thirds of whom purchased some land, accounted for only 12.6% of the land transactions during these decades; the remainder of the buyers were men who had earlier received some accommodation from the town, but now sought to improve their lot.[35]

The ability of a man to pay for additional real estate would determine his status as a landowner after 1650 rather than a decision by a group of seven men about his worth and needs. Only four men entered the landed elite through their own achievement prior to 1650, but others followed. During the next decade, the selectmen dropped the first tenet of accommodation and did not attempt to include new residents in the division of land; they concentrated instead on the other half of the principle—that land should reflect a mutually understood hierarchy—and granted what acreage remained to men who had served in town offices and had joined the church. With little land remaining, however, it was clear that not even the worthiest resident of Salem could depend on the selectmen to build a large estate.

Earlier arrivals who could afford more land than the selectmen had granted them began to buy farms and town lots at a rate which far surpassed the land-granting capacity of the town. Salem Village farmer John Porter, selectman for 15 of the years between 1646 and 1661, was given 10 acres of upland in 1654, but bought over 1,500 acres more between 1646 and 1679. The other leading Salem Village farmer, Nathaniel Putnam, was granted 5 acres in 1651 to add to the 70 the selectmen had already given him, but he went on to buy 750 acres more between 1652 and 1682. Half of the men who received land grants in the 1650s bought additional land later; only Jeffrey Massey among the largest landholders of the group never added to his acreage by purchase.

Many of the men who quickly rose to landed wealth did not take on leadership roles assumed to be the due of large landowners. Porter and Putnam maintained the tie between land, church membership, and leadership, but most of the other large buyers did not. Initially the selectmen did what they could to resist the accumulation of large estates through purchase by men who did not fit the well-established definition of "good order." When Robert Goodale, a small planter in Salem since 1634, bought a total of 480 acres from 15 different Salem Village farmers in 1652, the selectmen rescinded his earlier (and only) grant of 40 acres. They agreed that Goodale "shall enjoy" his purchases, but at the expense of relinquishing the upland given him in 1638.[36] Earlier the selectmen had been able to adjust a man's acreage upward to reflect his status in church and town; now they were reduced to revoking earlier grants in a vain attempt to stem the rapid changes in economic stratification occurring among the inhabitants.

While the Porters, Putnams, and Robert Goodale among the farmers who arrived by 1640 accumulated vast estates, and even a late arrival like Bray Wilkins bought hundreds of arable acres, the availability of land for sale enabled other, smaller farmers to make similar if less spectacular gains. Giles Cory arrived in 1649 and was granted 20 acres of land; between 1652 and 1663 he added another 132 acres to his holdings in Salem Village. The sons of earlier farmers of Salem Village were the most active buyers in that area, but others were not closed out.

The consequence of not entering the land market was often landlessness for the second generation. The shipbuilder, William Jeggles, was a church member and freeman within a year of his arrival in 1636. He received a house lot and ten acres of arable land, but was never given more, nor did he buy land. His mariner sons and grandsons never owned land, and were assessed low rates in the tax lists of 1683 and 1689. While some early seamen and artisans acquired land and rose to levels of affluence not foreseen by the selectmen, in other families less lucrative callings were pursued through several generations.

During the 30 years in which grants were made, first by the Company, then by the General Court, and after 1636 by the town, over 300 men received acreage of different kinds in varying amounts according to the discretion of the freemen or their representatives. Many of these grants placed the owners in areas separated from Salem by 1650[37] or in precincts where little additional land was sought by the owners;[38] yet among the grantees who remained within the Salem bounds, 116 purchased additional acreage after 1650. They were joined by nearly four times as many other buyers in the remainder of the colonial period who had never received a town grant.[39] The patterns of settlement established by the selectmen in the first generation were thus subject to rapid and substantial change after 1650.

Each of these adjustments to the original "good order" was recorded in a deed; taken together, the deeds show the occupational specialization and mobility of Salem's inhabitants after 1650. Slightly over half of the exchanges were of arable acreage; the remainder were houses, town lots, and various kinds of commercial property. Thirty of the commercial lots were residential as well, as some of the sellers had built shops, warehouses and wharves on their house lots. The North and South Fields were the sites of 14.5% of the sales, while arable lands beyond the bridge totalled 38.9%, but 46.2% were on the main peninsula. More of the population was concentrated on the peninsula, but farmers were more likely to make multiple purchases.

Land encompassed within single original grants was partitioned and sold to make two house lots where there had been one before, or to adjust the boundary of a farm. As a result, the deeds on the average conveyed smaller parcels of land than had been granted initially by the selectmen.

	Deeds	Grants
Less than one acre	38.5%	13.8%
1-5 acres	25.9%	24.7%
6-10 acres	12.7%	17.2%
11-25 acres	10.1%	10.3%
26-50 acres	6.0%	17.4%
51-75 acres	3.0%	4.1%
76-100 acres	2.0%	4.3%
101-200 acres	1.9%	5.7%
over 200 acres	2.5%	2.4%

Artisans appear more often as sellers than buyers as they sold off their arable grants to the farmers; farmers appear with equal frequency as they bought and sold acreage to consolidate their holdings into convenient farms. Only the merchants were involved in more purchases than sales; they continued throughout the period to invest their capital in both arable acreage and town lots, and were thus the only occupational group to bridge the increasing gap between peninsula and Village.[40] Gradually these buyers and sellers were increasing the clarity of regional and occupational distinctions within the town, with only merchants maintaining ties across the entire landscape.

These transactions were usually made in cash, but occasionally other arrangements were made. Ninety-three sellers (6.4%) accepted cattle, a share of a ship, or part of a crop in lieu of money; 128 men deeded land to sons and daughters in exchange for "love and affection" and, presumably, care in their old age. Only 25 sellers (1.7%) agreed to accept payments over a period of time in a primitive form of mortgage arrangement; any profits to be made in the land market were primarily in the form of rents and appreciation of value, not in interest. While few men became creditors in the process of exchanging land, three times as many trans-

ferred land to satisfy their debts. In four-fifths of the transactions, however, the medium was money. Men had to have a cash crop or receive
money in exchange for goods and services in order to buy land in Salem.

These exchanges greatly increased the range of wealth expressed in
property by the end of the charter period. In the initial land division of
1636, the least inhabitant received 10 acres and a house lot while the
largest grants were 300 acres. By 1650 over 10% of the population held
no acreage while the largest landowner had amassed 685 acres through
grants and purchases.[41] By the time John Porter had put together an
estate of 1,500 acres in 1680, nearly half of the population owned no
property.[42] These men then lived as tenants of men who had acquired
property in excess of their personal needs as an investment. It took many
of the men who arrived in the middle decades of the seventeenth century
a full generation to accumulate enough capital to make their first purchase, but there were others who had large amounts of money to invest.
Only 27 of the original grantees in Salem received over 200 acres of land
from the town, an amount equivalent to a £50 contribution to the joint
stock in 1629, yet 263 purchases cost as much or more.[43] Large houses,
wharves, and other commercial property brought high prices, but there
were men in Salem who could afford to pay. Before 1650, only 14 houses
were sold in Salem, and only 9 men participated as buyers in the nascent
land market; in the next 2 decades there were nearly 600 separate sales,
and each one represented some adjustment to the "good order" of the
first generation.[44]

By some measures these middle decades should have been a period of
stability in Salem. The decrease in immigration, balanced by the number
of men who left the town in this period, resulted in little population growth
to strain the town's resources. The slow rate of population increase belies,
however, the dramatic reorganization of the town's resources that occurred in these years.

The distribution of land according to the principle of accommodation
had been the overriding preoccupation of the selectmen and town meeting
to 1650. Diversity had been tamed in a system where the wealth of merchants and farmers alike was expressed in land, and in which few served
as town leaders who were not both godly and wealthy. The granting of
land, admission to the church, and election to office were all collective
decisions made by men who themselves expressed the covariation of land,
religion and leadership. As the supply of land to be granted was exhausted
and the number of men who acquired wealth through their own achievements increased, the political and ecclesiastical symbols of unity in Salem
would have to change. While the membership of the board of selectmen

was not immediately altered and the merchants—whose economic base continued to be spread throughout the regions of the town—continued to be elected, the function of the selectmen was increasingly to oversee social services and public works, and to manage the town's financial accounts. The strains within the church became apparent as its membership declined and the townspeople became more diversified. The accommodation of diversity had been a success in the early decades, but the increased specialization and dispersion of subgroups within the population after 1650 threatened and eventually surpassed the capacity of the central institutions to maintain unity within the town of Salem.

Chapter Seven

The Hegemony of the Merchants

The continuing dispersion and differentiation of Salem's population after the rise of the six major merchant-selectmen along with John Porter to nearly unrivalled leadership in the town after 1647 confirmed their function as a focus for unity in the community. For the first decade in which they dominated the board of selectmen, their powers were undifferentiated from those of the freemen as a whole. Appointments, land grants, the care of the poor, and the setting of rates were handled by the group in session at the time a need arose. The selectmen met as often as seemed necessary to transact the business of the town.

By 1657, they began to establish a routine for the management of the town. Their duties had become numerous enough to require regular meetings, which they set for the second Monday of every month at 9:00 A.M.[1] In an act of self-regulation, they imposed a fine of two shillings on any of their number who did not attend the regular meetings, a much smaller penalty than had been imposed on the group by the town in 1643.[2] The fine reflected a desire to routinize their affairs rather than a need to coerce participation, since attendance was generally high.

Other routines were established as well. Appointments of fence surveyors for the year were regularly made at the first meeting in March, and the making and auditing of rates were done at intervals during the year. After more than a decade in office, Salem's major leaders were developing an orderly and efficient administrative style, embedded in an annual calendar of duties which they handled in their monthly meetings.

In addition to their responsibilities for making the town rates and appointing many of the lesser officials, the selectmen became the arbiters of an increasing number of requests from the residents. After 1657 they were given authorization "for ordering the seats in the meetinghouse to continue during the town's pleasure," an important annual task.[3] Anyone wishing to build a seat in the meetinghouse also had to gain the approval of the selectmen. In 1667 two groups successfully appealed for permission to build a gallery separated from the general seating; their request was granted on the condition that "it doth not annoy those that are seated under the gallery," and that "they take into them so many as the select-men think meet."[4] The selectmen also increased their share of the responsibility for other petitions which had formerly been referred to meetings of the whole town. While some men continued to be admitted as inhabitants by the town meeting, most went directly to the selectmen for approval. Again, there were frequently conditions attached, as in the cases of two men admitted to the town in 1662 "provided they bring a certificate from some magistrate that they are allowed inhabitants in the jurisdiction."[5] Others were warned out, while a few were given permission to stay for a few months on the security of settled residents.[6]

Still other new duties demonstrate the increased influence of the selectmen in Salem. Most cases of poor relief were decided by the selectmen rather than by the town as a whole, and the dispositions reached by the selectmen show their attention to detail and the personal character of the negotiations with various members of the community who agreed to maintain the poor in their homes. In 1662 the selectmen "agreed and covenanted" with Mrs. William Lord to keep Sarah Lambert for seven years, for £4 the first and £3 each year thereafter.[7] When this arrangement proved unsatisfactory, they moved her to Mrs. Cantlebury's house, and Henry Bartholemew personally provided the money for her keep until the town could reimburse him.[8] In another case, John Clifford was paid £5 for keeping Mrs. Goose "for the town." Rather than make him wait until the next town rate was made, the selectmen arranged with Widow Hollingworth, who had just been sold a house lot on the common for £5 by the selectmen, to pay that amount to Clifford instead of into the town's accounts.[9] Increasingly knowledgeable about all of the affairs of the town, the selectmen were able to arrange these complicated and highly personalized exchanges of land, money, and services. The selectmen also controlled the dispensation of the deacons' funds for the poor; in 1666 they ordered two of their number to join with the deacons in relieving a poor man with a gift of 20s.[10] By 1667, even this aspect of the selectmen's business was subjected to a new routine, when they appointed a subcommittee of two selectmen to handle cases of poor relief for that year.[11]

Other intrusions of the selectmen into the lives of the townspeople were increasingly common. In 1667 they ordered three of their group to settle the dispute between William King and "some of his relations and others." The subcommittee was empowered to "inquire into the matter and to settle all things in peace betwixt them."[12] The first abatements from town rates were also made that year; one man was judged "by reason of his deficiency to be freed by law," while John Norman was excused due to "great losses at sea being taken by the Dutch."[13] The mark of personal knowledge and involvement shows clearly in each of these decisions of the selectmen. In addition, the personal finances of the major leaders were entangled with those of the town; in most cases after deciding what work needed to be done in the town, they not only ordered it but paid the workmen directly.[14] Occasionally this practice created some risk to one or another of the selectmen. When the town approved a rate of £50 for meetinghouse repairs in 1657, they "agreed that Mr. William Brown shall have the sole managing of the repairs . . . and to have the rate paid to him and to disburse it . . . and the rate to be so levied that he . . . may be no loser in the disbursements."[15] Brown was willing to pay the workmen from his own assets, and to be compensated later. Occasionally the selectmen made these extensions of personal funds without the authorization of the town meeting. In 1663 Edmund Batter settled a town bill for £4 and was given that amount from the treasury. However, the town meeting had not approved that particular expenditure, so Batter took the money on the condition that if the town did not approve at their next meeting, he "hath promised to repay it the town again."[16] The wealthy merchant-selectmen were willing to take these risks, confident that the town would subsequently confirm the judgment of their elected leaders.

The townspeople apparently did not consider the increasing specialization of the selectmen's role and the decrease in their own involvement in the management of the town's affairs to be to their detriment, for these years were marked by no discernable conflict between the selectmen and the town meeting. Most of the meetings were called by the selectmen, who also set the agenda; elections were the most frequent item of business, but the selectmen also convened a town meeting "to examine the account of the town that they may consider of a town rate," and at another time the question of Higginson's maintenance "and other occasions" were specified.[17] But there were no "other occasions" at the next town meeting, and adjournment followed the election of selectmen and the establishment of a method of meeting the town's obligation to Higginson for the following year. Indeed, the selectmen had taken over so much of the town's business that in 1662 they decided to shed one of their duties, and noted in the minutes of their meeting to "remember to move it to the town to choose some others to lay out land."[18] They not only felt free to take on an increasing amount of the decision-making in the town, but also selectively eliminated earlier obligations which no longer seemed important.

The confidence of the selectmen in ordering the affairs of the town is revealed in their minutes, as for example, in 1660 when they ordered the running of one of the town's boundary lines "in the name of the town," a task formerly directed by the town in its meetings of the whole.[19] While

the town meeting received an audit of the deacons' accounts, the selectmen audited the constables' accounts between 1658 and 1668 as they had
in the years from 1647 to 1656.[20] Again, after 1662 two of the selectmen
were delegated this task by the rest of the group in yet another example
of the increasing use of subcommittees within the board of selectmen.[21]
Only once during the decade did the town directly receive an accounting
from a constable, and it was duly noted that the selectmen had already
reviewed and approved the delinquent constable's collection of the rates
assigned to him.[22] On only one other occasion, in 1661, do the town
meeting records reveal that the town as a whole was given an accounting
by the selectmen.[23] Throughout this period, the town approved rates
which were calculated by the selectmen, raised by the constables in
amounts assigned by the selectmen, and then audited and spent by the
selectmen, often to repay themselves.

While the town meeting annually elected an eighth man to join with
the selectmen after 1647 in the sensitive job of assigning the rates for each
of the householders, these men had no further duties and were not obliged
to report back to the town meeting.[24] Only one of these raters had ever
served as selectman, and none were ever prominent among the leaders
of the town. Their role was to give assistance in one of the most time
consuming jobs of the selectmen, rather than to represent any differing
viewpoints, since their impact would have been insignificant in the latter
case.[25] The relative worth of each of the inhabitants was thus determined
each year by the selectmen, together with the rater, in an exercise which
touched the life of every inhabitant.

Although the town meeting had to approve the rates, on several occasions the selectmen added to the authorized amount. In 1663 the town
received a specific list of expenses from the selectmen and voted a rate
to cover them, but by the next meeting of the selectmen that body had
discovered additional debts and needs, and simply added the necessary
amounts to the constables' accounts.[26] The following year, the town approved rates for their Beverly, Salem Village and Town constables to
satisfy the warrant of the colony treasurer, but the selectmen added a
town rate for the Salem Village and Town constables without consulting
the town meeting.[27] The country rate approved by the town was £74 8s.,
but the amount authorized solely by the selectmen was nearly as large—
£63 14s.—and represented a larger tax per householder in both Town
and Village since none of this amount was assigned to the Beverly constable. The Cape Ann farmers had secured the right to support their own
ministry, repair their own highways, and care for the poor of Beverly in
1659, thereby increasing the burdens of taxation on the other areas of
Salem.

Other tasks delegated by the town meeting to the selectmen also indicate that there was little if any friction between the two groups over the issues confronting the town of Salem. In 1662 the town asked the selectmen to run the Ipswich line, and "full power is given them fully to agree in all points for the issuing of all differences that may arise between them according to their discretion."[28] One of the most sensitive issues for any New England town, the exact limits of its boundaries and therefore its tax base, was delegated in complete confidence to a group of merchants who lived on the main peninsula, miles from the line in question.

The only general directives issued before 1668 were delivered by the town meeting a decade earlier in 1658, when the town meeting "agreed that the selectmen in being shall have full power to act in all prudential matters of the town of Salem as formerly until the town take further notice."[29] While the town meeting reserved the right to impose limitations in the future, they gave the selectmen free rein in 1658. In the next few years, the town meeting in fact delegated additional, specific tasks to the selectmen, who were told to hire a whipper, a cowkeep, and a bellringer, to lay out highways and lots for shops and wharves, to enforce the restrictions on the cutting of trees from the common, to organize the work of all townsmen on the fort, to relieve several of the poor, and "to petition the General Court for Pennycook as a plantation."[30] When the town appointed three commissioners of small causes in 1661, all were merchants serving as selectmen that year.[31] Clearly the small group of men who dominated the office of selectman during these years had the confidence of the town.

Did the delegation of an increasing amount of control of the affairs of the town to the selectmen violate the principle of widespread, indeed nearly universal, participation in civil affairs by the townspeople in their town meeting thought to be the quintessential expression of the federal covenant? Indeed not. The Puritan mind bound in uneasy coalition the "charms of volition" with the uncertainties of divine intervention, the voluntary and contractual submission of the many to the wisdom and godliness of the few, who were bound reciprocally to serve the good of the whole.[32] Civil polity was not to disintegrate to "mere democracy." To a seventeenth-century Puritan in Massachusetts, the opposite of one who submitted wholeheartedly and voluntarily to authority was a "fallen man."

By the 1660s, however, the "good of the whole" was not a subject of universal agreement, and the unity of the town expressed by their reelection year after year of the same godly, residentially centralized, wealthy men, was increasingly a fiction. The tensions between dispersion and unity created in Salem by 1668 resulted in a crisis in leadership, just as heterodoxy had temporarily suspended the hegemony of the merchants in 1659. The government of the many by the few depended on a correspondence between the intimate character of the selectmen's execution of their duties and the nearly universal incidence of primary, face-to-face relationships among the population, interactions characterized not only by frequency and directness, but also by mutuality of purpose. This connection was broken both by the Quakers and by the inevitable results of Salem's land policy of accommodation and dispersion along economic lines—two principles of land use which eventually had to conflict. By 1667 there were challenges to the godly authority of the selectmen which centered on two issues: disposal of land, and the support of the church.

In the earliest years of settlement, universal inclusion in the use of the land was an operational principle, one which was gradually changed in response to the perceived good not of the whole but rather of specialized subgroups. After 1637 not every new inhabitant automatically received a house lot and at least 10 acres of land, a concession to the earlier arrivals who held an interest as proprietors in the yet-undivided lands, and also in part in response to a directive of the General Court that land not be granted to those who did not at least show signs of eventually becoming church members.[33] In 1640 the town meeting stopped the granting of land on the cattle common, which some newcomers wanted for house lots.[34] In 1641 the residents of Marblehead, mostly fishermen among whom there were no church members even as late as 1649, were granted control over the disposal of their own commons, and the reservation of the control of the Beverly and Ryal Side commons to the residents of these two areas occurred in 1650 and 1651.[35]

No further restrictions were placed on the actions of the selectmen or of the town meeting until 1665, by which time the Village contingent had finally become numerous and cohesive enough to lobby for the same privileges previously granted to other precincts. Their reaction was in response to a series of events catalyzed by an order of the town meeting in 1661, that "all men that have any former grants of land from the town are to come to the selectmen and make their claim within one year after the day and date hereof or else to lose it forever."[36] Much of the land previously granted had not yet been laid out, either because the conditions of the grant were too vague, or because the grantee already had more land than he could reasonably farm by 1661. Faced with a small but persistent group of later arrivals who also desired land, the town decided to clear up its books before making further accommodations. The unavailability of land was made clear to new residents, as in the case of Matthew Price in 1662 who was accepted into the town "provided he purchase a house to live in."[37] The ideal was still to have a town of settled householders, but the town could no longer pursue that end by granting land.

As a result of the order of 1661, many residents appeared before the selectmen pressing former claims which could not be satisfied in the locations originally intended. The town meeting accordingly in 1664 "ordered that all the land undisposed from Mr. Humphries' hill to the Seven Men's Bounds and all on the other side of the river within the town's bounds be left to the selectmen to dispose of for making good former grants or to accommodate others as they should see occasion."[38] Areas in Brooksby and in Salem Village were affected, and in fact that year the selectmen confirmed former grants of 320 acres to a number of men near the Lynn line (Seven Men's Bounds); the next year they made good several former grants in the Salem Village area. Despite the willingness of the town meeting to consider new grants of accommodation, no new residents were granted land by the selectmen; they interpreted the orders of the town meeting conservatively, and merely made good former promises to earlier residents.[39]

The selectmen had not acted to affront the farmers of the Village. Indeed, the selectmen had for years followed the practice of appointing surveyors of fences and highways to work in the areas where they lived. Constables were always residents of the neighborhoods they served, and the boundaries of the areas in which they were to work were spelled out at the time of appointment by the selectmen; these natural boundaries coincided with economic subgroups of the town. On only one occasion during the 1660s were all men of Salem called to work on a single community project, the fort, and even then the warrants were served district by district. When the neighbors of one constable had performed their allotted work, those from another district were called on to serve.[40] For the same reason that the selectmen conducted their own business in highly personalized ways, they divided the work of the community so that it could be done within primary groups.

The selectmen were indeed immersed in their own "neighborhood"—the increasingly populated peninsula—and may therefore have recognized the natural differences and interests of the outlying residents; moreover, the Puritan concept of social organization demanded a network of primary contacts which could only mean that men must serve their own neighborhoods after the economic differentiation of the population along geographic lines was an obvious fact. The confirmation of grants in the Village area in 1664 was not a new incursion into that area, and it did not occur as a result of a decision of the selectmen but rather of the town meeting. The selectmen were not attempting to aggrandize their control over the land, but were instead responding in the most conservative way possible to an order of the town meeting.

Despite the caution of the selectmen, the Villagers reacted: in 1665 the town meeting ordered that the selectmen were to "dispose of no land."[41] When several exchanges of land were made by the selectmen in 1667, the town meeting made its meaning clearer by outlawing that activity as well.[42] Although the selectmen had carefully chosen two Salem Village men to view and lay out a grant in that area, the farmers wanted more control over their precinct.[43]

There were other indications that relations between the Town and the Village were increasingly strained during this period, but it would distort the record to blame the friction on any deliberate policy of the merchants. In 1664 the selectmen required that any man claiming his 50s. due for killing a wolf must present two witnesses. Since wolves were primarily a problem for the farmers beyond the town bridge, this new regulation could be evidence of some suspicion of the farmers by the townspeople, especially since the wolf bounty was in several years a major source of the town's debts.[44] Apparently the witnesses—most likely neighbors of the bounty claimants from the Farms—were not believed either, for in 1665 the selectmen required that the heads of any wolves killed be nailed to the meetinghouse door before the bounty would be paid.[45] Simultaneously, they reduced the bounty from 50s. to 40s. per head. Some measure of distrust, and some lack of appreciation for the danger posed by wolves in the outlying areas, were apparent in these decisions of the selectmen.

During the same few years in the middle of the decade, the farmers of the Village organized sufficiently to send one of their own to serve on the board of selectmen: Thomas Putnam, a young man when his father arrived in Salem in 1639, had joined the church and become a freeman in 1642, but was not elected as selectman until he was middle-aged. He joined a group of men in that office who were of roughly equivalent age, but they had decades of experience in managing the affairs of the town by 1665 when Thomas Putnam was elected. The next year he was replaced by his brother Nathaniel, whose credentials were similar. Both had served as constable, while only one of the leading merchants had held that thankless job, and had served on numerous juries. Nathaniel Putnam was reelected in 1667 and 1668, and in that last year was joined by yet another brother, John Putnam, who surpassed his siblings by serving seven terms in office. These men were elected by a newly coherent regional interest group to serve the same function Roger Conant had performed for his Beverly neighbors earlier: the protection and promotion of neighborhood interests. By 1667, Beverly had been incorporated as a separate town by the

General Court with the concurrence of the freemen of Salem. The Putnams undoubtedly hoped for a similar future for their precinct.

Another major source of evidence for the dissolution of voluntary, contractual subjection of Salem's inhabitants to the officers of their covenants was the difficulty the town had in raising the maintenance for the minister, Reverend Higginson. Even before his arrival in 1660, the town had experienced some difficulty in meeting the salary of his predecessor. In 1657 the town "voted and agreed . . . that they voluntarily yield up themselves to be rated by those whom they shall choose for the raising of maintenance for the ministry when need shall require."[46] The additional expenditure of £100 that year for a new parsonage and for repairs to the meetinghouse, paid for by town rates, probably did little to encourage the "voluntary yielding" urged.[47] The next year a new method was tried: subscription. Two men were appointed at the town meeting for each of the constables' districts "to take care for the subscription for minister's maintenance and to perfect it between this and the next town meeting and then to bring it to the next meeting."[48] These men were also to "endeavor" to raise the elders' maintenance at the same time by the same method.[49] Two months later it was clear that the experiment had failed. Voluntary contributions were not sufficient, and even a house-to-house subscription had not elicited enough to pay the clerical salaries for the year. The town agreed to the only alternative: "It is ordered that all those persons that will not subscribe nor contribute towards the maintenance of the ministry shall be rated and the selectmen to rate them."[50] Certainly the Quakers were not "yielding," but the frequency of town meetings called during the 1660s concerning the ministers' maintenance suggest that the voluntarism which lay at the heart of covenant theology and social polity was in a more general decline among the inhabitants.

When the town discovered in March of 1659 that the previous year's rates still had not been collected, they fined two constables two shillings sixpence each for "not appearing at meeting and not making return of their warrants," and ordered another rate.[51] Still, they were reluctant to give up the principle that the townsmen would of their own free will support the ministry, and in November they ordered "that the ministry for the next year shall be by voluntary contribution into the drawing box." Facing the reality of their prospects for successfully maintaining the ministry in this way, they added, "and those that will not so contribute to be rated by the selectmen."[52] The same method was presumably employed with adequate results for the next five years, as no further discussion of the subject appears in the minutes of the town meeting.

In the meantime, the cost per household of the ministry increased. In December of 1659, the residents of Cape Ann Side successfully appealed for permission to maintain their own ministry; three months later Reverend Higginson was engaged as the new Salem minister at an annual salary nearly double that of his predecessor, and was given a house costing two hundred pounds—four times the value of the previous parsonage.[53] Thus, rapidly increasing costs fell on a smaller number of contributors. In addition to the minister's maintenance, one-quarter of the usual, annual town rates were for church-related expenses in 1660: repairs to the meetinghouse, a pension for the widow of a former elder, and wood for the existing elders.[54] The church was clearly the single most expensive service in the town.

Meeting the financial obligations of church and minister after 1660 would be increasingly difficult. Until 1667, those making voluntary contributions went to the minister's house at a specified time in the first weeks of July and January; the deacons kept these accounts, and presented them to the town meeting, which then instructed the selectmen to rate those who had not appeared.[55] The church officials had to depend on voluntarism; when that failed, they could turn to the officers of the town. A new procedure was initiated in 1667 which may have served to increase the number of voluntary contributions by making them more public. At the first town meeting of the year, after electing selectmen, the inhabitants "voted that trial be made by voluntary contribution for the maintenance of the ministry and those present at the meeting to subscribe what they will give for this year beginning the first week of the eleventh month past, and the selectmen are desired to go to all the rest of the inhabitants and take their subscription and make return at the next town meeting . . . where the town is agreed further to treat for the best settling of Mr. Higginson's maintenance for time to come."[56] Even this attempt to increase subscriptions by conducting the collection in a public forum, followed up by personal visits to noncontributors by the selectmen themselves, was not sufficient. Six weeks later the town meeting gave up all pretense of voluntarism and voted "a rate of two hundred pounds . . . for Mr. Higginson . . . to pay forty pounds that we are short for the three years past, and one hundred fifty pounds for this present year." Still the selectmen did not immediately act to apportion and collect the money, for six months later the request was reiterated—but with an important amendment: the selectmen were to act "speedily," but were to omit Quakers from the rate.[57] The total to be raised was more than the sum of the country, town and county rates for 1667, and more than the total taxes in any previous year except 1659, yet again the tax base was narrowed. The town finally acknowledged its religious disunity, and agreed to exempt the Quakers who had contributed significantly to the difficulty of raising Higginson's maintenance in the previous eight years.

By 1668 the diminution of voluntarism took yet another form: resistance to paying taxes. No centralized public works were authorized by the town during the 1660s other than repairs to the meetinghouse and work on the fort which might have intensified the reluctance of residents of outlying areas to yield to taxation as they had done in the past. Nevertheless, there was increasing resistance to pay taxes calculated and spent by the merchant-selectmen. In 1667 the town meeting took the initiative and ordered the selectmen to raise a rate for the repair of the church and the care of the poor, where formerly they had agreed to rate themselves for expenses presented by the selectmen.[58] In addition, the town meeting assigned the various portions of the rates to the constables instead of leaving this sensitive task to the selectmen.

The narrowing of the tax base through the exemption of Beverly from the minister's maintenance in 1659, and the removal of the remainder of the income from Beverly together with the exemption of the Quakers from the support of the ministry in 1667, may have contributed to the growing unease about the taxes levied among the remainder of the townspeople. While each of the decisions which had narrowed the tax base had been made by the town meeting and not by the selectmen alone, the townsmen reacted in 1668 by sweeping three of the merchants (Walter Price, William Hathorne and Henry Bartholemew) out of office, retaining only three of the major leaders of the previous two decades: two merchants—Edmund Batter and William Brown—and the farmer, John Porter. Thus, after the removal of the support of the Old Planters, the seven men who had held a majority of the selectmen's seats in every year but one since 1647 were reduced to a minority of three. They were joined by two of the Putnam brothers of the Village, and two second-generation farmers from the town.[59] To this group fell the responsibility for collecting back taxes and dealing with the newly recalcitrant constables who had also failed to maintain the proper town watch mandated by the General Court.

After electing seven selectmen who were more representative of Salem's geographic and economic differentiation than the previous boards, the townspeople agreed to meet again "to attend some motions of several of our brethren and neighbors about several pieces and parcels of land and other matters of that nature suitable for so solemn a meeting."[60] Few of the town meetings in the previous decade had been called by the town meeting itself; instead they had responded to meetings warned by the constables on the orders of the selectmen, who had also prepared the agenda. Clearly the town meeting of 1668 had its own agenda in mind.

At the next "solemn" town meeting, the selectmen were issued for the first time a set of specific powers and limitations.[61] Unlike the infrequent and general orders given previously by the town, the list of five orders in

1668 is a summary of the breakdown of the universal voluntary spirit among the population. On their face, the orders appear to limit the powers of the selectmen, but taken in context of recent events in Salem they are better understood as acknowledgments by the townspeople of their inability to submit freely to authority, a necessity of Puritan social organization which even though not fully practiced was still beyond dispute.[62]

First, the selectmen were to "be careful to observe all those things that are enjoined you by the country laws that so the town may not suffer for your neglect therein." For the first time in its history, Salem had not met its colony tax warrants; Higginson was not alone in having to wait for the reluctant residents to pay. Further, the town had been fined for failure to provide the stipulated constables' watch, yet the selectmen had duly ordered the watch each year. The difficulty lay in the residents' unwillingness to respond to the constables' warrants either for taxes or for service to the town.

Second, the selectmen were told not to "give, sell or exchange any land belonging to the town," yet in fact that group had made no outright grants since 1660, while on seven occasions since that date the town meeting itself had made various accommodations. In 1662 and 1663 the selectmen had exchanged two parcels of land and sold four house lots on the common, while the town meeting had been more active. The order of the town meeting cannot be seen as the result of dissatisfaction with the activities of the previous selectmen, since their actions had been lesser in extent but similar in kind to those of the town as a whole. Instead, the order signalled the attempt to close the town to newcomers, increasing in numbers again after 1660 as immigration from England resumed. Different in both economic and religious orientation from the earlier waves of immigrants, the newcomers were admitted with great unease into a town already well aware that it was not the cohesive, godly community originally envisioned. Thus, the town did nothing to accommodate these newcomers, and used the powers it had reserved to itself concerning the dispensation of land only twice in the next five years: once to grant two acres of swamp in exchange for land owned by an older resident taken up by a new highway in 1669, and again to grant half an acre for a sheep pen in 1672.[63] New residents had to purchase land from earlier residents willing to sell, or rent from those landowners who had built or acquired houses for this purpose and who had farmland to lease. The restriction on the dispensation of town lands was to the advantage of those who had real estate in excess of their own personal needs, a group which certainly included all of the previous merchant-selectmen. The order about land included in the instructions to the selectmen in 1668 therefore cannot be seen either as a rebuke for previous excesses or as an attempt to curb the power of the merchants.

The next two orders like the first concerned taxes:

> You shall raise no money nor town rate without the vote of the town.
>
> You shall no way engage the town so as to bring them into debt except in case of necessity of the poor, etc., wherein we desire God to encourage you.[64]

The bulk of the taxes levied on Salem residents in the previous years had been for the maintenance of the ministry, rates which they had been unable to meet year after year, while the colony rates over which the Salem residents had little control were second in size. Since the selectmen had calculated, allocated and spent the third category of taxes—the town rate—the inhabitants were perhaps not aware that the bulk of these expenses were for highways, the poor, and the maintenance of public property (primarily the church). While the orders of the town appear to limit the powers of the selectmen, they are better read as an acknowledgment that the collection of taxes of all kinds had become a problem for the town.

The final order was to "take care of the herd and the bulls," a task which the previous selectmen had performed faithfully as part of their routine annual business. Keepers of the herd were appointed at the first meeting of the year, and only once in the previous decade had an appointee been negligent. When in 1661 the performance of the hogreeve was unsatisfactory, the selectmen reacted swiftly and harshly: the unfortunate hogreeve was fined 20s. for neglect of duty, and was forced in addition to serve again the following year "or else to pay the sum of five pounds instead of twenty shillings."[65] Again, the difficulty lay in compliance with the orders of the selectmen, not in the nature of those orders.

If Puritan social theory required voluntary subjection by "the many" to the "few" who expressed the universal good of the whole, by 1668 there were signs that the whole was sufficiently subdivided that no common basis existed for defining its collective "good." The result was a decline in voluntarism of all kinds, which by transference caused the removal from office that year of the selectmen who had been a symbol of unity for two decades. Far from being a new "covenant" between a resurgent and unified town meeting and a newly-limited group of economically and geographically specialized selectmen, the orders of the town in 1668 were a systematic admission that the old social covenant grounded in voluntarism was in serious decline, regardless of which subgroups of the population were in the town's highest office.

Thus, the new instructions to the selectmen from the town meeting in

1668 were neither a progressive accommodation to changed social conditions nor the harbinger of a new social theory. Rather, the orders reflect nostalgia for the voluntary support of a unified church and town remembered from the previous generation. The orders were a resolution to try harder. The election of the Putnams to the board of selectmen after 1665 was a clear sign that there were sectional interests in Salem, and other men would be elected after 1668 who also represented differentiated subgroups of the population, but it would be another generation before a new federalist social theory emerged which made sense of the actual practices of Salem's voters. The centrally located merchants who had dominated the board in the middle decades of the seventeenth century would be returned to office after 1668, but they served with leading men of the particular sub-regions of the town.

In retrospect, the decade of the 1660s was a relatively peaceful time in Salem. While decentralization accelerated, the only official division within the town—the separation of the Beverly farmers—was accomplished quietly and without rancor in 1667. Although signs of disunity appeared in the difficulty of maintaining the ministry, and finally the Quakers had to be exempted completely, the full-scale tax revolts of the next generation were unknown in the middle decades of the charter period. After 1668 the leadership of Salem had to face more serious divisions within the church, public and protracted struggles of the Village farmers for more autonomy, and the financial and personal drains of King Phillip's War, but the new men elected to the board of selectmen after 1668 were less experienced and more divided among themselves than at any time during the previous generation.

Chapter Eight

The Context of Leadership
in Colonial Salem

The major leaders in Salem in the generation prior to 1668 had incorporated in their personal lives the tensions between the covenant of grace and the covenant of works which Puritan theology kept in delicate balance, avoiding the extremes of strict Calvinist predestination on one side and Arminianism on the other. Civil obedience and Christian worship were two parts of the same contract binding God to man according to the Puritan mind, and Salem's leaders during the middle decades of the colonial period were exemplars of both kinds of service required by the God the Puritans created. According to Perry Miller, "The Puritan state was seen by Puritans as an incarnation of their collective will; it was driven by an energy they had acquired in their conversion, it was the embodied image of their power, of their resolution, of their idea."[1] The major leaders not only entered into the civil contract with God by becoming freemen of the colony, but also became the interpreters and exponents of that contract for the town of Salem. In addition, they were with one exception all churchmen, their "personal covenant with God . . . impaled on the same axis as the social, like a small circle within a larger."[2] The balance was not easy to maintain. Economic opportunities available to the merchants could be interpreted as obligations to contribute to the development of the godly state, but the conditions necessary for the advancement of commerce were often antithetical to those required to maintain the closed, corporate Puritan utopia. Somehow the merchant-leaders of the middle decades managed to lead civic lives which encompassed the poles of works and grace.

As in other American colonies of the seventeenth century, there was a "fundamental relationship between social structure and political authority" with the result that "superiority was indivisible" in Salem until 1670.[3] All of the major leaders among the selectmen were among the "minimal majority" of landowners by 1650, that group of 26 men who owned half of the available acreage; all except George Corwin were members of the church, and even he used his personal assets for its support;[4] finally, all were freemen of the colony. This overlapping of the signs of status was shared by lesser officials as well.

While over three-quarters of the historical population of Salem in the colonial period were neither church members nor freemen, only slightly more than half of the constables, one-third of the jurors, and one-fifth of the selectmen were drawn from this group; since this segment of the population was both larger and more apt to be elected or appointed to office after 1670, the hegemony of the men who lived under the seals of the church and federal covenants before that date was even greater than the figures for the colonial period as a whole divulge:

	Freemen-Church Members	Church Member Only	Freeman Only	Neither
% of selectmen	42.7%	16.0%	18.6%	22.7%
% of grand jurors	40.6	9.0	17.7	34.1
% of jurors of trials	34.2	12.9	16.3	35.2
% of constables	21.0	13.5	7.5	57.9
Entire population:	10.3%	7.4%	5.4%	76.9%

Men who were church members or freemen or both were also more likely to be reelected, thereby accounting for an even higher proportion of the total number of terms available than the above figures would suggest:

	% of Available Terms		Average # of Terms		
	Church Member	Non Member	Church Member	Non Member	Total
Selectmen					
Freemen	51.4%	17.4%	5.7	4.4	5.3
Nonfree	20.0	11.2	5.1	2.9	3.8
			5.4	3.6	4.7
Grand Jury					
Freemen	52.2%	9.1%	4.0	2.2	3.5
Nonfree	8.8	29.9	3.8	2.4	2.7
			3.9	2.3	3.1
Jury of Trials					
Freemen	54.1%	13.4%	5.1	2.4	4.2
Nonfree	9.8	22.7	2.5	2.1	2.2
			4.4	2.2	3.2

Thus, while freemen who were also church members were only 10.3% of the population, they constituted 42.7% of the colonial selectmen and served 51.4% of all available terms in office between 1636 and 1689. Conversely, 22.7% of the colonial selectmen were neither freemen nor church members, but this group accounted for only 11.2% of the available terms, despite the fact that men who stood outside these formal covenants constituted 76.9% of the total population. Only in the least desirable post, the constabulary, did this latter group approach a level of participation in local politics consistent with their numbers.[5]

The seven men who dominated the board of selectmen from 1647 to 1668 were not only freemen and, with one exception, churchmembers, but also ranked among the wealthiest men in the town; all were large landowners in 1650, and those who lived until 1683 when the earliest surviving colonial tax lists were compiled were among the largest taxpayers that year as well. This covariation of church membership, freemanship, and wealth also extended to other, less prominent town officers. Only 13.9% of the 590 men on the tax lists of 1689 paid more than 8s. in tax, yet 37.1% of the former constables and 77.8% of all former selectmen still alive by that date were taxed at this level.

Finally, the town officers of Salem throughout the colonial period were generally drawn from the families who arrived prior to 1640. Men deposited by later waves of immigration were under-represented in Salem's civic life:

Officers	Arrived by 1640	Born in Salem	Arrived after 1640
Selectmen	52.7%	31.9%	15.4%
Grand jurors	58.0	25.0	17.0
Trial jurors	44.4	34.3	21.3
Constables	22.0	47.5	32.5
Total population:	31.0%	37.2%	31.8%

Again, only as constables did later arrivals serve in proportion to their numbers in the population as a whole. Since more settled residents did not covet the position of constable, newcomers were frequently asked to serve. In 1665 the town meeting agreed that no one who had lived in Salem less than two years should be required to serve; similar protections were unnecessary for other town offices.[6] Sons of early immigrants carried their share of the burdens of town office, particularly as constables, but the men who landed by 1640 dominated both the board of selectmen and the grand jury in colonial Salem.

This predominance of the town's earliest residents reinforced the covariation of leadership with church membership and freemanship, since both of these attributes were very strongly associated with the date of immigration. Fewer men in each successive wave ever joined the church or took the freemen's oath. Thus, 58.3% of the churchmen and 64.2% of the freemen of the entire charter period, but only 30.2% of the historical

Arrival	% who Became Freemen	% who Became Church Members
1623-35	50.8	47.6
1636-40	36.8	40.1
1641-50	25.6	25.6
1651-60	11.3	9.9
1661-70	6.7	8.9
1671-80	3.6	5.5
1681-89	1.7	3.4
Average for period:	15.7%	17.7%

population of known arrival date, were living within Salem's borders by 1640, as were a majority of the colonial selectmen and grand jurors.

Church membership, wealth, freemanship, and early immigration all contributed to increase the likelihood that any particular resident would be elected to office in Salem. The seven major leaders carried all of these signs of preeminence, but they were different only in degree from less active officers. Always a minority of the Salem population even in the earliest years, those men who were church members, freemen, wealthy, and among the earliest arrivals bore the brunt of the responsibility for managing the affairs of the town until 1670, and still predominate when their participation is viewed in the context of the entire charter period. Fewer than 100 men were both freemen and church members by 1640 among a total historical population for the charter period 15 times as large, and fewer still were within the wealthiest segment of the population, yet this small group of men were clearly the chosen few—chosen over and over again by their fellow townsmen to fill offices in which they made decisions on behalf of the town.

Rate of Election to Town Offices

Office	Freemen	Nonfreemen
Selectmen	19.2%	4.9%
Jury of trials	40.4	7.0
Grand jury	29.2	4.1
Constables	15.8	7.4

Similar results occur when comparing those who joined the church to the men who remained outside the covenant of grace. More likely to be elected to every office than nonmembers, those who had joined the church were also more apt to be called to service in more than one office. For example, while 38 of the 65 selectmen were also members of juries, 27 of those who served in both posts were church members; thus, while 58.7% of the selectmen were members of the church, 71.1% of those who served as jurors in addition were within the covenant of the church.

Service on Juries by Selectmen, 1636-1689

Church Status	Elected to Board Before 1670	After 1670	Ave. Terms
Member	21	6	11.4
Nonmember	1	10	2.8

Similar patterns hold for the overlapping of other offices as well, and show the frequency of election to office among a small group of men; in addition, the clear change in patterns of office-holding before and after 1670 begins to emerge from these figures.

Despite changes in the criteria for leadership after 1670, the men who held the town's highest office before that date fit the Puritan ideal, both the 7 major leaders and the 14 men chosen after 1646 to serve with them. Five of the seven most active selectmen served an average of 16.2 terms as jurors in addition. The major and minor leaders of the middle decades were not distinguishable from each other in their degree of service in other offices, nor in their espousal of Salem's covenants. All were free-men, and only one man in each category did not join the church.

The differences between the major and minor leaders of Salem in these years were to be found in their degrees of wealth, places of residence, occupations, and ages, rather than in their degree of submission to the canons of Puritan social theory. All of the major leaders were among the major landowners of 1650, while only two of the farmers among the minor leaders—Roger Conant of Beverly and Nathaniel Putnam of Salem Village—held similarly large tracts. All of the seven also lived in the west end of the Town in the area near the meetinghouse, while eight of the lesser leaders whose place of residence is known lived elsewhere: two at Cape Ann, two in the Village, three in the eastern end of the peninsula, one in Glass House Field beyond the bridge, and one on the North Neck. While all of the major leaders except John Porter were merchants, and his ties to the mercantile community were strong, the selectmen from Cape Ann, the Village and the North Neck were farmers, while those who lived in the eastern sector of the peninsula and those whose place of residence is unknown included an attorney, a mariner, a house car-penter, two tailors, a tavernkeeper, and only one merchant. Except for the underrepresentation of mariners and fishermen, the men who occu-pied the second rung of Salem's political hierarchy were a good cross-section of its geographically dispersed and economically diversified population.

The final but important difference between the two groups—the seven major leaders and others who served with them—was the age at which they were elected. The merchant-selectmen were in their mid-30s when the town first singled them out for service; their average age at the date of first election was 33.3 years. On the other hand, the lesser leaders were older before election, with an average starting age of 46.7 years. Less wealthy and living further from the town center than the major leaders, it took these men longer to command sufficient deference from the community to be elected to the town's highest office. The prestige of the merchants descended as well to their sons, whose average age at first election was 34 years. When the second generation began to appear on the board of selectmen after 1657, most were middle-aged, yet John Corwin was chosen in 1669 at the age of 25, and William Brown Jr. joined him the following year at the age of 31.

The changes in patterns of leadership after 1670 were not caused by new immigrants. All of the terms on the board of selectmen prior to 1685 save two were served by men who had arrived in Salem by 1642, or by their sons. After 1685 a new generation of merchants who immigrated to Salem during the Restoration period began to exert their influence in the town, but Nicholas Manning and Dr. Weld—both of whom served their single term in office in 1675 during the height of King Philip's War, and both of whom left the town within a decade—were the only members of the board not drawn from the families of the earliest arrivals before that date.

Despite the control of the town's highest office by early immigrants and their sons throughout the charter period, after 1670 the composition of the board of selectmen changed quite noticeably. All but two of the selectmen between 1638 and 1668 were both church members and freemen; the mariner John Hardy served one term in 1647 but never joined the church, while George Corwin was elected 23 times despite the fact that he never joined the church and did not become a colony freeman until 1665. Still, these two exceptions did not seriously compromise the general expectation that leadership was reserved to those who bore the seals of the covenants before 1668:

Number of Terms Served as Selectman

Seals of Covenants	1638-1668	1669-1689
Both freeman and church member	176	58
Freeman only	18	55
Church member only	6	12
Neither	0	21

The pattern changed markedly after that date. Only 14 men who were both freemen and church members were elected as selectmen, and 10 of them were ending political careers begun prior to 1668; on the other hand, among the 25 who were freemen only, church members only, or neither, all but 2 were elected for the first time after 1668. Previously indivisible symbols of status became increasingly disjunct, with freemanship the clearly preferred route of access to leadership.

Moreover, after 1668 the close correlation between church membership and freemanship and the probability of reelection no longer held. The 11 freemen elected after 1668 who were not members of the church served an average of 5 terms each, but the 14 men formally bound in both the church and federal covenants held the office of selectman an average of only 4.1 terms apiece. None of the selectmen elected for the first time after 1668 ever served as long as the major leaders of the middle decades; 3 sons of the former major leaders held office for 10 to 12 terms each, a record of service which fell far short of the political careers of their fathers, while the remainder of the new additions to Salem's roster of selectmen held the office from 1 to 7 years. No new group of highly visible leaders emerged to take the place of the seven men who had dominated the office of selectman for two decades prior to 1668 as these leaders died or retired from that office. Their preeminence had rested on the indivisibility of status, the most salient feature of Salem's early social system and the bedrock of its social theory. The men coming to maturity and rising to positions of leadership after 1668 laid claim to one or another of the signs of status but usually not both, thereby changing the means by which the population had previously recognized its leaders. Only 26 men were needed to fill the board of selectmen in the 3 decades prior to 1668 due to the repeated service by a small number, but 36 men were elected in the next 20 years. The division of the signs of status created a larger pool of potential leaders, none of whom could elicit sufficient deference on a consistent basis from the entire community to build a record of service which approached the careers of the major leaders of the previous generation.

An important difference between the major and lesser leaders before 1668 had been their average age at first election, the latter group being 13 years older than the former at the time they first sat on the board. While the sons of the major leaders could not inherit the full power of their fathers since it rested on signs of status no longer universally recognized in the community, they did become selectmen at the same early age as their fathers had before them. However, just as there was little difference between the length of service of these sons and that of the other members of the second generation with whom they served in office, so too was there less of a difference in the age at which these other men were elected:

Age at election	to 1668	1669-1689
Leaders and their sons	33.3	34.0
Other selectmen	46.7	38.2

A gap of 13 years was reduced to four. Before 1668 it took longer for lesser leaders, who were also less wealthy and lived elsewhere than the town center, to accumulate sufficient deference for election; after that date, there was little difference in age between the sons of the former leaders and their colleagues on the board of selectmen.

The distinctions between the wealth of the seven major leaders and the assets of the men who served with them before 1668 had been clear-cut: all seven of the most active selectmen were among the minimal majority of 1650, that small group of men who owned half the land in Salem at that date, while only two of the lesser leaders were among this group. The difference in wealth between the sons of the major leaders and the men who served as selectmen with them after 1668 is not as sharp. All of the six sons who lived to be taxed in 1683—the date of the first extant colonial tax list—were among the wealthiest residents at that date. Only 13% of the inhabitants paid more than 5s. that year, yet all of the offspring of the major leaders who became selectmen were taxed at least 6s., and William Brown Jr. paid the munificent sum of 18s. John and Jonathan Corwin were each assessed 6s., but their father was still alive and paid the second-highest tax in the town: £1 6s. John Price, John Hathorne and Israel Porter each paid 10s. Of the 19 other men who served as selectmen after 1668 and appear on the 1683 tax list, however, a similar pattern holds. Only two selectmen paid less than 5s.: Joseph Grafton Sr., a mariner from the east end of the Town, and William Trask, the miller located just west of the town bridge whose monopoly had been destroyed by the permission given to two new merchant-selectmen in 1651 to build a second mill on the South River; two farmers in Trask's neighborhood were assessed 5s. each, but the remaining 14 men paid more. While the sons of Salem's leaders in the middle decades of the seventeenth century were still among the wealthiest men in town at the end of this period, they served as selectmen with men of similar economic advantage.

Likewise, the earlier leaders had been the only representatives of the Town center, occasionally joined by men from Cape Ann, the east end of the peninsula, or the Village; while their sons (except Israel Porter, who was taxed in the Village district) continued to live in the area near the meetinghouse, there were nine other men elected from that neighborhood after 1668 in addition to six men from the east end and five who lived west of the bridge. Living in the eastern end of the peninsula or among the farms was no longer a clear disadvantage for election. The seven major leaders before 1668 had spoken for the town, occasionally serving with men from outlying districts who represented clear minority interests—first Roger Conant and Thomas Lathrop of Cape Ann, and then the Putnams of the Village and the Gardners of the east end—but their sons were a minority among the selectmen from their own neighborhood. The mere fact of their residence could not serve as a focus for the unification of the town, as their fathers' central location had done in the past.

Finally, the clear occupational differences between the major and minor leaders in the middle decades began to blur after 1668. No longer were the merchants from the west end of the peninsula the core group on a board which included farmers from Cape Ann, the Village and the North Neck, in addition to a variety of artisans and an occasional mariner from the eastern sector of the peninsula. Three of the new selectmen from the west end were indeed merchants—John Ruck who had been born in Salem, and two more recent immigrants, Timothy Lindall and William Hirst—but the other four whose occupations are known were a farmer, a slaughterer, a physician, and a ship carpenter. Meanwhile, the eastern end of the peninsula housed three rising young merchants in addition to a baker, a ship carpenter, and one seaman, all of whom served as selectman after 1668. The area west of the bridge produced not only four farmers, but also one miller and a mason for the board of selectmen. As the various precincts of Salem continued to develop economically, a hierarchy of occupations developed within each; the leaders of each ward shared a roughly equal economic status, and no longer looked to a small group of wealthy merchants concentrated in the western end of the peninsula for leadership.

Until 1668, Salem's leaders were almost without exception subscribers to the major covenants of the town. They were freemen and church members, and the distinctions between the most active political figures and the marginal participants were based on wealth, occupation, residence, age at election, and experience. The seven dominant figures of the middle decades undoubtedly expected this consistency in the symbols of status to be transferable to the next generation, despite the increasing economic complexity of the town, which they themselves had helped to create, and the general decline in voluntarism which they had witnessed in their years as selectmen. Walter Price was the only major leader to die in office; he was 55 years old at his death, and had been a selectman in 15 of the previous 24 years. His son John began his 10 years as selectman in 1676, 2 years after his father's death; his political world was not the one his father had intended to bequeath to him, however. Three of the other major leaders who had sons to succeed them retired from office in their late 50s and lived another 10 to 15 years after their last terms as selectmen. William Brown's son was elected as selectman in 1670, two years before his father's last term, while George Corwin held the office for the last time in 1676—which was also his son John's first year of seven as selectman. John Porter did not wait for the election of one of his sons to occur before he stepped out of the running, and left a lapse of six years between 1662 and 1668 before the first of his two sons to hold that office was elected. The only major leaders who continued to serve as selectmen after their sixtieth year were Edmund Batter, Henry Bartholemew, and William Hathorne. Neither of the first two had sons who succeeded them in the office; therefore they continued to be elected until the ages of 63 and 68 respectively. William Hathorne finally left office in 1675 after 33 terms at the age of 65, and his son John began the first of his 6 terms in the colonial period 4 years later in 1679 at the age of 40. John Hathorne was by far the oldest at the time of first election among the sons of the early leaders, which may explain his father's relatively late departure date. All except Walter Price clearly expected their sons to carry on the task of unifying the community, since the others could have continued to serve themselves had they harbored any doubts. An historian one century later would bemoan the deaths of these major leaders, declaring "a more unhappy time could not have been found, when a town was deprived of all its fathers, who had governed it for half a century, with unbounded confidence,"[7] but in fact their hegemony was broken prior to their deaths, and the unity of the town was a fiction long before they were interred.

The indivisibility of status was the most salient feature of the social system over which these men presided for decades. Wealthy, godly and politically powerful, they embodied the ideal of seventeenth-century Puritan society. Despite their efforts, the next generation fell short of this ideal. Few of the men coming to maturity after 1650—including the sons of the major leaders—followed in their fathers' footsteps. Increasingly the particular signs of status which had marked a coherent, unitary system in the early decades became associated with particular subgroups of the population, and the social landscape was accordingly transformed. The resulting differences among the new leaders of Salem were not along lines of occupation, wealth, residence and experience, but instead concerned the covenants themselves, the sources of Salem's cohesion to 1668.

Chapter Nine

The Divisibility of Status in the Second Generation

The early leaders of the Massachusetts Bay Colony used their distance from the mother country and its laws to create communities in which the godly would not only be the core of the church but also control the civil institutions of both colony and town. In 1635, the General Court ordered that "none but freemen shall have any vote in any town, in any action of authority, or necessity, or that which belongs to them by virtue of their freedom, as receiving of inhabitants, and laying out of lots."[1] Since the General Court had four years earlier decreed that "no man shall be admitted to the freedom of this body politic, but such as are members of some of the churches within the limits of the same," the ruling of 1635 effectively limited the exercise of power to the minority of men in Massachusetts who had joined a church and then gone on to take the freeman's oath.[2] While it is impossible to know with any certainty how restrictive these orders were in fact, one historian estimates that the freemen, including those who took the oath before it was reserved for church members in 1631, numbered "at best a few hundreds in a total of twenty thousand inhabitants" in 1634.[3] In Salem there were 19 freemen by 1641, and 50 by the end of 1634. In 1637, when Roger Conant drew up a census for the purpose of dividing meadow lands among the population, 74 freemen were among the 229 persons on the list.[4]

The colony-wide restrictions on the franchise were intended to reinforce the conviction of the leaders that Massachusetts Bay would be a godly state. Sermons preached by the early ministers concerned questions of commercial ethics, and in turn the General Court of 1646 promulgated a moral code for the colonists.[5] The elders of the churches were prohibited from holding civil office, but their advice was sought on a wide range of non-ecclesiastical affairs, and the selectmen felt equally free to enact laws which affected the church—such as the enforcement of attendance on the Sabbath.[6] An eighteenth-century historian of the Bay Colony declared that "the liberties of the freemen of this commonwealth are such, as require men of faithful integrity to God and the state, to preserve the same."[7] In order to assure that the church and the state "may be close and compact, and coordinate one to another, and yet not confounded," the elect of the first institution were to control the second.[8]

Salem's early leaders fit this pattern. All but four of the selectmen in the first decade of town government were both freemen and church members; two of them were made freemen in 1634 and 1635 but do not appear in the church records. In addition, Robert Moulton was elected for one term in 1637 although he was neither a freeman nor a church member, and William Lord was elected for six terms between 1642 and 1647 after joining the church in 1639, but he never became a freeman.[9] Nevertheless these exceptions do not disprove the general rule that Salem's leaders in the first decade were both church members and freemen in accordance with the laws of the colony. Even after the transformation of leadership in 1647, this pattern held until 1670 with the sole exception of George Corwin, whose wife was a member of the church.

Although there were enough godly freemen in Salem to fill the town's highest office until 1646, by that date there was a shortage of qualified men for this and other offices both in Salem and elsewhere in the colony. The General Court reluctantly permitted justices of the Quarterly Court to have cases heard before a jury of 6 men if 12 could not be found.[10] In 1647 the Court took two additional actions to relieve the burdens on those men in the various towns who bore the seals of both covenants. First, they ordered that those church members who did not present themselves to take the freeman's oath in order to avoid public service would be obliged to hold office anyway.[11] Few of Salem's church members were affected by this remonstrance, however, as nearly all who remained in Salem more than a few years after admission to the church had become freemen as expected; only William Lord among the early selectmen joined the church without adding the second of the Puritan seals. The second order of the Court brought more relief to the overburdened elect: non-freemen over the age of 24 could serve as jurymen and vote in local elections, subject to several important restrictions. Even after a man had been examined and judged to be not guilty of any "evil carriages" and had been administered the oath of fidelity by a magistrate, he had to be accepted as a voter by the freemen of the town itself. Specifically, the law stated that "henceforth it shall and may be lawful for the freemen within any of the said towns to make choice of such inhabitants, though non-freemen . . . to have their vote in the choice of the selectmen for the town affairs, assessment of rates, and other prudentials."[12] Some towns needed this flexibility more than others, and the General Court expected the law to be used only when necessary. Even before 1647, the inhabitants of Marblehead had to choose a nonfreeman as constable since none of the residents of that rocky peninsula were official subscribers to the federal covenant.[13] While the General Court agreed that nonfreemen could also be elected as selectmen after 1647, they added that such men could not constitute a majority of the board.

It appears that Salem interpreted the new franchise laws of 1647 conservatively. While George Corwin was chosen as selectman that year, he was the only nonfreeman elected to that office until 1670. Since no records were preserved of the men who actually voted in town elections in these years, it is not possible to determine if nonfreemen were actually granted the franchise. William Hathorne received 116 votes in 1659, by far the highest number in the only recorded ballot before 1680. There were 186 men made freemen in Salem by 1659, but 42 of them are known to have left the town by that date, and others had died, making the votes cast for Hathorne roughly equivalent to the total number of freemen who could have voted. Hathorne was the most frequently reelected of the merchant-selectmen, so it is conceivable that the support of the voters was nearly unanimous for him—particularly in 1659, the year in which the electorate turned back to the merchants to reestablish order in the face of the Quaker crisis—in which case there were few if any nonfreemen authorized to vote in Salem's elections by that date. On the other hand, attendance at the town meetings was a problem as early as 1654, prompting those present to agree to a fine of 6d. for those who did not "seasonably" attend.[14] If attendance was poor at the meeting in which Hathorne received 116 votes, then it is indeed probable that the franchise had been broadened in Salem by that date. While it seems likely that attendance was good, given the concern of the town about the Quaker incursion, no discussion of the issue appears in the minutes of the town meetings or in the notes recorded from the meetings of the freemen, so the question of Salem's franchise cannot be answered with assurance.

The new franchise laws of 1647 also reversed the decision of the General Court from the previous year enabling judges to empanel juries of only 6 men if 12 freemen could not be located. Instead, they permitted nonfreemen to serve on juries when necessary, as long as they did not constitute a majority.[15] In fact, five men—all church members who had not taken the oath of freemanship—had already been selected for jury service from Salem by 1647, but 91.9% of the men who served on the jury of trials and 93.8% of the grand jurors were freemen of the colony at the time of appointment. Between 1648 and 1654 the town records do not show lists of men chosen as jurors, but the impact of the new legislation of 1647 may be gauged by the appointments made after 1654. While over half of the new members of the jury of trials between 1654 and 1659 were freemen, together with the jurors who had served prior to 1648 these men held 68.9% of the seats on the jury of trials in the five-year period; although nonfreemen were chosen to serve 31.1% of the jury terms in the same period they were less likely to return for additional terms. Non-freemen had even less impact on the grand jury; only a third of the men appointed to the post between 1654 and 1659 had not taken the freemen's oath, and they served only 29% of the terms in the five-year period. Perhaps these same men were given the franchise, but it is doubtful that it was extended more widely, since the freemen of the town continued to hold a disproportionate share of the offices filled at the town meeting. The decline in church admissions after 1640 made some adjustment in the colonial laws necessary by 1647, but the extension of both the franchise and the obligation to serve in office was made conservatively in Salem. Those freemen who were also members of the church continued to dom-inate all of the public offices, despite the fact that they constituted only a third of the population in 1637, a proportion which increased to a high of just under half in 1641 under the leadership of Hugh Peter, but declined to less than one-tenth by the end of the charter period in 1683.

By 1663 the freemen of Salem were sufficiently concerned about their diminishing numbers to instruct the Salem deputies to vote for the exten-sion of freemanship to men who had not joined the church.[16] Only 37 men had been added to the list of Salem freemen in the twenty years since 1643, and only 9 of those in the decade prior to 1663. The great majority of Salem freemen in 1663 had acquired this status by 1642; they were in their mid-40s or more by 1663, and few younger men were rising to take the place of those first-generation men who died. As a result, although the merchant-selectmen continued to dominate the office of se-lectman, the proportion of men who were neither church members nor freemen in the other town offices was rising. Rather than settle for a system in which the elect and free became a minority not only among the general population but also among the leadership of the town, the freemen urged the separation between the seals of the covenants of grace and works. The indivisibility of godliness and leadership defined and defended by Winthrop and others of his generation was being challenged out of necessity.

While the General Court did not enact the change recommended by the Salem freemen in 1663, another group of colonial leaders was con-sidering the other aspect of the same problem: access to church mem-bership. The issue which aroused the greatest concern within the church after 1660 was the small percentage of children of the covenant who were becoming "visible saints"[17] and members in full communion.[18] Unable to halt those changes in the community which dramatically altered the position of the church within the town, the leaders of the church turned their attention to the social unit which seemed most stable: the godly family. Within a year of his arrival in 1660, John Higginson took several steps designed to resolve, or at least to confront, the dilemma posed by unsaved children of saints. The responsibility for preparing children for church membership had been the sole responsibility of the parents, a charge which they received at the time their child was baptized. Since this method of bringing children into the church had proven ineffective, Higginson and the elders of the church in 1661 set aside one afternoon each week for "any that should come to them in a preparative way," and promised to hold additional meetings "if there should be need."[19]

Several months later, Higginson presented a list of "propositions concerning the state of the children of members."[20] They were declared to be "under the watch and care of the Elders," and to have "a right of claim to all the ordinances as they are capable of enjoying them in an orderly way."[21] The church was still charged with the judgment of "their fitness for full communion," but the very parents who were exhorted to do better in instructing their children, to "prepare them for and bring them to the trial," would be sitting as the judges of that fitness.[22]

Moreover, by the 1660s many of these children themselves had children whom they wished to have baptized; indeed, this question had been raised by Higginson's predecessor Nicholas Noyes as early as 1652.[23] A synod of the New England churches in 1662 was called to discuss this issue, which naturally arose when so few of the sons and daughters of the saints experienced a "work of grace" which met Puritan standards of conversion morphology.

The Salem church was at first reluctant to accept the result of this synod, the Half-Way Covenant, a measure which protected the high standards of all church admission by extending the biological coverage of the covenant through the sacrament of baptism to grandchildren of the saints, but retained the requirement of visible sainthood for their sons and daughters. The Salem congregation was initially unwilling to extend the privilege of baptism to the children of parents who, though baptized themselves, had not experienced a work of grace sufficient for full membership in the church. John Higginson was an advocate of the measure, however, and finally after three years of debate he staked his reputation on an attempt to convince his congregation that they should allow baptism of grandchildren of church members. He argued "that he apprehended it as one of the great sins of the country that so many of the children of the covenant were unbaptized, and that he would not that the sin would lie any longer at his door."[24] Conversion could not be coerced to increase the numbers of church members, but baptism—which was viewed as one of the essential preparations for conversion—could safely be extended to the third generation without diluting the purity of the fully covenanted church.

When the issue was put to a vote, only two members dissented. The following Sunday, four children of the covenant "having been privately examined by the Pastor did publicly profess their taking hold of the covenant after which their children were baptized."[25] Not only had Higginson assumed a role in the "preparation" of proposed members, but in the case of halfway members had assumed the sole responsibility for testing their fitness. While "owning" the covenant through public testimony about the experience of grace was still required for full membership in a church based on visible sainthood, "taking hold" of the covenant was sufficient testimony for baptized but unregenerate children of the saints to secure the rite of baptism for their own children.

Within three months Higginson proposed eliminating this distinction by extending the procedure used for baptizing the children of the children of the covenant to admission of the children of the covenant themselves. He prepared a "writing" for the "help" of the church, in which he outlined his "directive for a public profession after private examination by the elders." As Higginson noted, this was the procedure by which he joined the Salem church in 1629 at the age of 15 when his father was minister, prior to Massachusetts Bay's creation of the unique church polity based on visible sainthood.[26] That same day, Bartholemew Gedney, one of the four who only three months earlier had been admitted to halfway membership, "propounded his desire of partaking of the Lord's Supper, saying he had submitted unto examination of the Pastor and publicly professed his faith and owning of the covenant he saw not that anything more was required of him from Scripture."[27] The church, which had hesitated for three years at allowing half-way parents to promote children for baptism with no more extensive testing than this, succumbed to Gedney's request for full admission. Although it was duly noted that Gedney was a special case—perhaps because he had become one of the most visible leaders in the town, and was wealthy in addition—within three months the exception had become the rule.

In January, four children of the covenant requested admission. Higginson defended their presentation:

> The Pastor expressed that after his examination of them he did approve them as able to examine themselves and discern of the Lord's body and that they bring not under any church censure, he knew not of any church bar according to the Scripture that might hinder them from partaking of the Lord's Supper.

Only two church members expressed dissent, but "would not oppose."[28]

No "declaration of their experiences of a work of grace" followed by cross-examination by the members was required.[29] From this time, the Salem church was to elect new members not by collectively approving an applicant's testimony after questioning, but rather by not disapproving either of the minister's judgment of the applicant's worthiness and faith, or of the applicant's behavior before or during the month that he stood propounded for membership. Finally the procedure became standardized:

> It belongs to the Elders' duty to examine them [children of the covenant] of their knowledge with application to themselves . . . The Elders making known to the church their desire for full communion the parties are in a church meeting to express their own desire, their owning their parents' covenant . . . And if there be no just exception against them in a month's time they are to be received into full communion to enjoy and use their right in the Lord's Supper, and in votes as other members do.[30]

Among the last of the New England churches to adopt the test of the visibility of sainthood in the 1630s, the Salem church appears to have taken the lead in dropping this requirement, the unique feature of New England Puritanism.[31] Within six months of its adoption by the Salem church, the Half-Way Covenant had become obsolete. No children of the covenant applied for half-way membership after Bartholemew Gedney's full admission, since the latter was available on the same terms. Just as the General Court had agreed that any who had not been convicted of "evil carriages" and agreed to swear before a magistrate to uphold the laws of the colony could hold town offices and vote in local elections, the church of Salem agreed that private confession of faith to the minister and general good behavior, at least for one month, were sufficient for admission to the church.

The changes in polity affected only the descendants of the saints, and not the increasing number of Salem residents who were outside the covenant. Between 1655 and 1664, 20 men and 30 women, at least 15 of whom were children of the covenant, were admitted to the church. In the decade after 1665, the same number of men, 12 of whom were children of the covenant, were admitted; admissions of women rose to 45, 25 of whom had been baptized in the church. The most striking change was thus not in numbers of people admitted, but rather in the increased percentage of those admitted who were children of the covenant. Among those admitted to the church between 1655 and 1664, 30% were children of church members; this percentage rose to 57% between 1665 and 1674. While the increase may be partially due to larger numbers of children reaching maturity during that later period, the fact remains that the numbers of those joining the church who were not children of the covenant did not increase. The result of the change in polity was the addition of only a few more men to the minority of the population who carried the seals of both covenants. While 2 mariners from the eastern end of the peninsula joined the church without claiming freemanship, the other 11 men admitted to full communion in the year after Gedney's reception also became freemen of the colony. Still, the number of the children of saints admitted to the church after the change in polity of 1664 was never large, and decreased after the initial spate of admissions in 1665 and 1666. Higginson was able to continue to extend his principle of accommodation to the baptism of older as well as younger children in 1666, and the following year convinced his congregation to include adopted children in the new provisions, but his attempts to recreate the godly community his own father had known in Salem were never successful.[32]

While Higginson attempted to prevent church membership from sinking to low, sectarian levels, many among his congregation were pulling away to form new churches in their own precincts. Although the first fully covenanted church did not break away from Salem until 1667, both Cape Ann and Marblehead had meetinghouses by 1650 and church services earlier. While this arrangement reduced the interaction among residents of different precincts, it did not eliminate contact between those who attended different meetinghouses within the formal limits of Salem. William Walton was the teacher in the Marblehead church for 30 years after 1638, but the few who were church members in his congregation travelled to Salem for monthly services which included the sacraments since the Marblehead meetinghouse could not offer them. This arrangement continued for 46 years, until the Marblehead church was established in 1684, with 54 members of the Salem church joining in the new covenant.[33]

The residents of Marblehead seemed content for nearly half a century to have a meetinghouse but not a church; residents of other precincts had hopes for the greater separation of their ecclesiastical institutions. In 1666, church members from both Salem Village and Cape Ann requested permission from the Salem church to form their own covenanted congregations. The Salem Village petition, signed by only six members, "did acquaint the rest of the church and people living at the town, that by reason of their distance from the meetinghouse they found many inconveniences, that they and their families could not so comfortably attend the church assembly for the worship of God on the Lord's day as they desired, and therefore made a motion to the rest that either they would help them to a minister or leave them to their liberty to procure one themselves."[34] Two months later they had their answer, in the negative, from the Salem church. The six applicants from the Farms had acted hastily. They had not located a suitable or "competent" preacher, and they had not obtained the unanimous support of their neighbors, some of whom wrote to the church "desiring that they might not be engaged in that design."[35] Six years passed before the question was raised again.

The applicants from Cape Ann fared better. They offered Mr. Hale, who had been preaching there for several years, as their proposed minister, and agreed to observe "a day of solemn fasting and prayer to seek unto God for his direction and presence in such a weighty matter."[36] The answer was not immediately forthcoming. Several months later, the applicants submitted a new proposal, again offering Mr. Hale's name, signed by 50 members of the Salem church who lived among the farms of Cape Ann. Such stability, persistence, and unanimity among such a large group of the godly could not be overlooked. The official vote of the church was delayed until the next sacrament day, when more of the members would be present, but at that time a hand vote confirmed the consent of the Salem church. In September of 1667, Mr. Hale was ordained and the Cape Ann church was established. Other churches formed on the borders of Salem claimed small numbers of church members as well during these years. Three were dismissed to join the newly established Topsfield church in 1663, and six joined in the Wenham covenant of the same year.[37] The cycle of accommodation, dispersion and differentiation started with the initial land policy which reserved Cape Ann Side for the Old Planters and other areas for later arrivals who formed distinct subgroups had reached its inevitable conclusion.

These dismissals from the Salem church caused a dramatic dwindling of the covenanted church of Salem, which had never been as inclusive of the inhabitants as the churches of some inland towns.[38] The renewal of immigration from England after 1660 brought a stream of tradesmen and merchants to Salem, most of whom—unlike the majority of men in the original pre-1640 immigration—did not seek church membership. The reduced rate of church admissions after 1641, an increased death rate in Salem after 1665, and the creation of new churches from the original gathering, all served to decrease church membership of Salem men by half over the last 30 years of the charter period. This marked decrease, coupled with an increase in total population size, caused the percentage of church members within the population to drop even more precipitously—to 15.8% by 1683. The nearly uncontested acceptance of the Half-Way Covenant and other practices which decreased exclusivity under the encouragement of John Higginson did not prevent church membership from declining to levels not foreseen during the era of accommodation.

The leadership of Salem in the 1660s had good reason to fear for the future of the Puritan ideal, since few in the second generation seemed capable or desirous of meeting it, despite the easing of access to the church and to voting rights. Wealthy, godly, and politically powerful, the major leaders of the middle decades embodied the ideal of seventeenth century Puritan society, but their sons and the offspring of the first generation as a whole did not follow the pattern set by their fathers. Few of the men coming to maturity after 1650 acquired the seals of both covenants, and increasingly the particular signs of status were associated with identifiable economic and geographic subgroups of the population. In the 30 years after 1650, only 54 men joined the church, and only 55.6% of them also decided to take the oath of freemanship.

Adoption of Covenants	1630-1649	1650-1679
Both church member and freeman	138	30
Freeman only	28	32
Church member only	40	24

At the same time, the number of men made colony freemen without establishing full membership in the Salem church continued to rise. Although the General Court did not formally accept the motion of the Salem deputies in 1663 to extend freemanship to some who were not members of the particular churches of the colony, the practice was not unknown either before or after that date. After 1650 the "exceptions" to the colony law were more numerous than the group of men who became freemen in the prescribed manner by first becoming full members of the Salem church.

The men who joined the church without becoming freemen perceived both their self-interest and the nature of the community differently from those who were made freemen despite their lack of full standing in the church, and both groups were distinguishable from the small group who fit the ideal of the first generation. The differences among these three groups reflect the intensification of other divisions within the community. Before 1650, twenty-eight men were made freemen who had not joined the church. Eighteen of them acquired this status on arrival in Salem, probably in anticipation of full membership in the church which never occurred.[39] Only three men who grew up in Salem and two others who had lived in the town for more than two years at the time they took the oath were well known to the community; three others had been made colony freemen while residing in other towns, but never joined the Salem church after moving there.[40] Thus, before 1650 only five deliberate exceptions were made for residents of long-standing who had proven their worth in the community.

After 1650, only 2 new arrivals were granted freemanship, while 16 sons of earlier residents together with 9 first-generation residents of long standing were granted full political rights in the colony. Not only were these exceptions made deliberately to long term residents, but they were also reserved for particular residents. Two men were Salem Village farmers, but the remainder were seamen and merchants from the west end of the peninsula—the Town center. Among the 16 sons of earlier residents admitted as freemen were three Beverly planters and one resident of Marblehead, but the others were merchants and artisans from the town center with prominent names like Brown, Corwin, Gardner, Hathorne, Price, and Porter. Of the remaining five men who became freemen after 1650 without joining the church, two had received this status as earlier residents in another town, while the date of arrival for the last three is not known.

The earlier exceptions to the rule included 2 merchants, 4 seamen, 5 farmers, and 11 artisans of various sorts, only a few of whom ever became prominent in the town; but the men admitted as freemen after 1650 were either well known as public servants—George Corwin being the outstanding example—or were sons of prominent merchants in the town. Farmers and seamen, the groups concentrated in the area beyond the town bridge and in the eastern end of the peninsula respectively, were underrepresented among the men for whom the colonial legislation regarding the prerequisite for freemanship was suspended. Men from these precincts east and west of the town center had to follow the prescribed route— through the church—to be granted the status of freemen, while birth into a leading family provided an alternate path to full political rights for the sons of merchants in the center of town.

The men who joined the church without becoming freemen were quite a different lot. Before 1650, forty men failed to add freemanship to their list of Puritan credentials after joining the church, but 25 of these men either died or left the limits of Salem soon after inclusion in the church covenant. An additional five men joined the church after 1640 but lived in Beverly or among the farms of Salem Village, and failed to respond to the expectation that they would also become freemen of the colony. Only seven Salem residents of long standing who lived on the main peninsula joined the church before 1650 but never presented themselves to take the freeman's oath.[41] These seven men, together with the five farmers from beyond the bridge, were the men to whom the General Court addressed its order of 1647 that all church members should either take the freeman's oath or serve in offices anyway as if they had. In fact, one of the Beverly farmers and five of the seven residents of the town were elected at least once to office, and both John Gedney and William Lord among the residents of the peninsula were chosen as selectmen. Although these 12 Salem residents joined the church before 1650 without becoming freemen, half were nevertheless active in the political life of the town to some degree.

Again, between 1650 and 1679 few residents of the peninsula were admitted to the church who did not also become freemen. Although 2 dozen men were admitted to the covenant of the church who did not subsequently take the freeman's oath, 17 of them either left the town soon after admission or lived in the outlying precincts of Beverly and Marblehead;[42] only 4 lived on the main peninsula, and all resided in its eastern sector. While a growing number of Salem men became freemen after 1650 without joining the church, they were mostly merchants and artisans concentrated in the western end of the peninsula in the area around the meetinghouse; the few who joined the church but did not become freemen were farmers from the outlying districts or seamen from the eastern end of the peninsula. This pattern continued to intensify after 1680, when 4 new residents—all residing in the eastern sector of the town—and 15 sons of earlier residents were admitted to the church but failed to add the seal of freemanship; 12 of these sons lived in the Village, while only 2 were located in the western area of the peninsula. Thus, after 1650 freemanship became available to sons of the merchants and artisans who clustered in the heart of the town regardless of their standing in the church, while a growing number of the second generation who lived among the farms or in the eastern end of the town joined the church but ignored the injunction to become full members of Salem's political community.

While the number of men outside the church covenant who were nevertheless administered the freeman's oath increased slightly after 1650 and fewer men joined the church without adding the seal of the federal covenant, the most significant change marked by the midpoint of the seventeenth century was the precipitous decline in the number of men who became fully covenanted members of both church and state. In the 30 years after 1650, only 21.7% as many men became both church members and freemen as had been incorporated within the central institutions of the town in its first 2 decades. Four of those who joined the church and took the freeman's oath after 1650 were earlier residents, while 6 were more recent immigrants to the town, but 20 were sons of original settlers. While 11 of these 30 men lived in the western sector of the peninsula, there were 8 in the east end and 6 living among the farms; thus they were not as geographically distinct as a group as those who chose one or the other but not both of the major Puritan seals.

The meaning of the increasing differentiation of the signs of status among recognizable economic and geographic subgroups may be read from the record of service to the town by each of these groups.[43] Roughly three-quarters of the men who took the freeman's oath after 1650 held at

Office-Holding Among Men Made Freemen or
Church Members, 1650-89

	Free and Church Member	Free Only	Church Member Only
Percentage who served:			
in any office	63.4	73.5	40.5
as constables	22.0	14.7	23.8
as jurors	51.2	58.8	21.4
as selectmen	17.1	23.5	9.5

least one of the three town offices surveyed, while only two-fifths of the church members who failed to become freemen were called on to serve. Joining the church or becoming a freeman enhanced a man's chances of being called to town office, but the latter was clearly more important for the generation coming to maturity after 1650. Indeed, the residents who acquired full colonial voting rights without the "required" church membership were not only more likely to be elected than those who followed the stipulated path to freemanship, but were also more apt to be reelected:

	Free and Church Member	Free Only	Church Member Only
Average number of terms:			
Juror	3.0	4.0	3.1
Selectman	4.7	7.3	4.5
Constable	1.0	1.0	1.0

Not surprisingly, the freemen who were not within the church covenant had a different conception of the community from those carrying both of the Puritan seals, and these men held an increasing share in Salem's political life after the first generation. No agreement about the good of the whole could be reached after the separability of the covenants became a social fact among the generation entering into them after 1650, especially when clear differences of residence, occupation, and political participation covaried with the choice of taking the freeman's oath, or joining the church, or both.

Only the longevity of the major selectmen held off the inevitable results of the divisibility of the signs of status among their sons and the newer immigrants to Salem. Only 6 new immigrants after 1650 adopted the seals of both covenants before 1689, and they were joined by only 20 of the sons and grandsons of Salem's early residents for both communion in the church and meetings of the freemen. As the free saints of the first generation died, they were not replaced in equal numbers by younger men. The organic view of leadership propounded and established by Winthrop and others of his era was clearly doomed. Still, the major leaders of the middle decades of the colonial period continued to exert a strong influence on the town for another decade after the loss of hegemony in 1668:

Service as Selectman

	Major leaders		Their sons		Other new selectmen	
	No.	Ave. years in office	No.	Ave. years in office	No.	Ave. years in office
1668	2	16.0	1	1.0	4	1.5
1669	3	17.3	1	1.0	3	1.3
1670	2	19.5	2	1.5	3	2.3
1671	3	19.7	2	2.0	2	2.0
1672	5	20.2	1	3.0	1	3.0
1673	2	26.0	1	3.0	4	3.0
1674	4	20.8	1	4.0	2	2.0
1675	2	27.0	1	5.0	4	1.0
1676	2	23.0	3	3.7	2	5.0
1677	1	24.0	3	4.7	3	3.7
1678	0	0.0	0	0.0	7	1.6

Although the major leaders were a majority of the board of selectmen in only one year after 1668, three factors combined to make their influence dominant. First, they were far more experienced than the men elected to sit with them on the board of selectmen; only two of the fourteen new selectmen between 1668 and 1680 had been elected prior to 1668, while the major leaders brought with them the authority of age and decades of experience. Second, in 7 of the 10 years after 1668 the sons of the major leaders together with their fathers constituted a majority of the board. Although none of the sons elected by 1679 joined the church, all but John Porter Jr. were freemen; these sons were undoubtedly influenced by the major selectmen more directly than were the other new second-generation selectmen who had not grown up in households headed by a major leader of the first generation.

Finally, the continued election of the major leaders as the town's representatives in colonial affairs augmented their authority within the board of selectmen.

	Deputy		Assistant	
	Terms	Dates	Terms	Dates
Henry Bartholemew	19	1645-84		
Edmund Batter	17	1637-82		
William Hathorne	24	1635-61	18	1662-79
William Brown	6	1654-80	4	1680-83
George Corwin	7	1666-76		

Only Walter Price and John Porter among the major leaders were inactive after 1668; each served one term as deputy in 1665 and 1668 respectively, but neither became assistants. The other five major leaders completely dominated Salem's voice in colonial affairs until 1677, and three of them continued to serve with the five younger men elected as deputies after that date.[44] Although the hegemony of these older merchants were challenged on the board of selectmen after 1668 by the second generation of Putnams in Salem Village and by a new generation of merchants—notably the Gardners from east end, and John Ruck and Bartholemew Gedney who lived in the west end—they continued to represent the interests of the Salem freemen in colonial affairs for another decade, as their sons took on leadership roles within the civic institutions of the town.

By 1684 the last of the major leaders retired from colonial office. Their sons not only failed to inherit the undisputed claim to represent the town of Salem at this level, but also lost what little control they had been able to assert within the town at the same time their fathers left their posts as deputies and assistants:

Service as Selectman

| | Sons of Major Leaders | | Other New Selectmen | |
	No.	Ave. years in office	No.	Ave. years in office
1679	4	4.5	3	2.0
1680	5	4.4	2	4.5
1681	4	5.8	2	1.5
1682	5	6.0	2	5.0
1683	5	7.0	2	6.0
1684	3	4.7	4	4.8
1685	1	7.0	6	3.0
1686	1	5.0	6	3.2
1687	1	8.0	6	2.8
1688	1	9.0	6	3.6
1689	1	10.0	6	4.7

John Hathorne, son of Salem's most prominent citizen during the entire period, served his last year as selectman in 1684 and his last as deputy in 1686; John Porter Jr., John Corwin, and William Brown Jr. were all out of both offices by 1683. John Price continued to serve until his death in 1689, and Israel Porter was elected for the last time in 1686, but they were the remnants of Salem's leading families of the previous generation.

After the loss of the charter in 1684, a new group of merchants took over the leadership of Salem. While some were sons of merchants who had achieved sufficient wealth and prestige to be elected to the town's highest office, others were very recent arrivals whose wealth had not been earned in the Puritan town. These men brought new views of the good of the whole to the board of selectmen. Meanwhile, Jonathan Corwin, after serving one term as selectman in 1680 was defeated in the elections of 1684 and 1685 and was demoted to the constabulary in 1686.[45]

The major leaders of Salem in the charter period emerged in the 1640s at the apex of a status hierarchy grounded in land and reflected in the church. Even after 1668, these men continued to predominate on the boards of selectmen and retained control of Salem's voice in colonial affairs, but the community of which they were still the leading citizens was producing in these years a new group of leaders who would take over in the provincial period. Maintaining a sense of unity in Salem among economically specialized neighborhoods whose most prominent residents increasingly regarded church membership and freemanship as separable symbols of status rather than as seals of universal covenants required new strategies for managing the affairs of the town from those major leaders and their sons who continued to be elected as selectmen.

Chapter Ten

The Consequences of Dispersion and Differentiation, 1668-1684: The Church

The dispersion of Salem's residents and their concentration in economically specialized districts was built into Salem's earliest land policies, and was accelerated by later practices of the town. The town meeting and the selectmen in the middle decades acquiesced in the demands of outlying inhabitants for more control over their precincts by appointing indigenous constables for each area and permitting men who lived in each district to be called to public work only in their own neighborhoods. Although these practices intensified the separation of the various districts from the town center, the leaders of Salem valued primary interaction sufficiently to overlook the inevitable consequences for the unity of the town.

Faced with both a new tide of commercially-minded immigrants after 1660 who did not adopt the seals of the covenants on arrival in Salem, and the failure of the second generation to achieve the symbols of "good order" of the first, leaders of both church and town eased the standards for inclusion. Church membership was opened to the children of the saints, and both colony freemanship and the local vote were newly available to those who were not church members due to changes in policy during the 1660s. Instead of having the intended unifying effect, however, these changes merely increased the differentiation of identifiable geographic subgroups within the town. The separation of Beverly from Salem in 1667 and the election of the Putnams to the board of selectmen after 1665 as the voice of the Salem Village farmers were inevitable consequences of dispersion and differentiation within the population. The Quakers in the same period dealt the first blow to the unity of the church, and by 1667 the town reluctantly exempted them from the maintenance of the ministry.

The divisibility of status, regional specialization, and religious disunity were all in evidence by 1668. After depending on the merchant-selectmen to exert a unifying force for two decades, the town in that year attempted to reassert the original basis for the social and religious order created by the founders: voluntary support of both church and civic institutions and their leaders. The town meeting insisted, in the face of a decade-long record to the contrary, that the minister's maintenance could be raised by voluntary contribution; they asked the selectmen to be certain that the constables maintained their watch, and they decided to raise the town rates themselves instead of waiting for the selectmen to do so.[1] While these decisions were couched as orders to the selectmen, they were in fact a call to voluntarism for the town as a whole.

After a 1 year hiatus in 1668, the major leaders and their sons were again elected to the town's highest office, and dominated the board of selectmen for another 16 years. During this period, the intensity of the differentiation of neighborhoods increased, provoking new challenges for the leaders of the town. Simultaneously, they attempted to reestablish the peninsula as the focus for unity by approving three major public buildings—a new church, a town house and a jail—which had the unintended effect of increasing resistance to taxation among residents of precincts which felt increasingly estranged from the town center. In 1676 the tenuous balance between dispersion and unity was upset by the crushing taxes imposed by the General Court to support the costs of King Philip's War. By 1684, little remained of the spirit of voluntarism or the definition of unity the town had tried to reassert in 1668. While the increasing distinctions between the Salem precincts had earlier not resulted in conflict, after 1668 each neighborhood would present a direct challenge to the cohesion of the town.

Beverly was formally and peacably separated from Salem in 1667,[2] but the process of intensifying the identities of other areas continued. The residents of the North Neck requested a separate watch due to their fear of Indians in the area in 1668, and the selectmen agreed that "if the inhabitants desire a watch there the constable shall set the watch there by the inhabitants of the North Neck there."[3] The following year two new burial grounds—one in Glass House field beyond the bridge and the other near Ipswich River—were approved for the "convenience" of the residents of those districts.[4] In 1674 the Salem foot companies were divided, with John Corwin placed in command of the western troop as Joseph Gardner took over the militia in the east end of the town.[5] The following year the selectmen appointed two farmers from beyond the bridge as sergeants for the western company, and two other men residing on the peninsula were commissioned but allowed to choose which company they would serve.[6] Constables and surveyors had always served in the districts where they lived, but their tasks were not by definition communal exercises. The decisions made after 1668 meant that training days and funerals would no longer provide an opportunity to maintain frequent primary interactions between residents of the town center and those from outlying areas; instead, these would become occasions for the development of cohesion within subgroups—whose geographic boundaries coincided with different occupational concentrations—thereby diminishing the sense of the whole town as a social unit. Sabbath services and town meetings were the only remaining communal exercises inclusive of the entire town.

Given the new representation of Village interests by the Putnams after 1665 and the continuing differentiation of that and other neighborhoods, it is hardly surprising that in 1672 a group of Villagers renewed their attempts to form a separate church. The immediate catalyst was the recommendation by the selectmen in 1670 to build a new meetinghouse. Repairs had been made periodically and new seats authorized to accommodate the slowly but steadily growing population, but by 1670 the town meeting asked the selectmen to decide whether to repair the meetinghouse yet again or to build a new, larger one. The selectmen recommended the latter, and were authorized to oversee the building of it. The new structure was "not to exceed the sum of one thousand pounds price" to be raised by a rate calculated by the selectmen.[7] At the same meeting where the town approved a new church large enough for the entire town to gather in at a cost exceeding the total of all rates for the previous two years, they refused requests from residents of Beverly and Salem Village for enlargements to their commons.[8] The special interests of outlying groups were denied while the unity of the whole was promoted by the decision to build a new and larger church.

The vote of the town meeting went counter to the interests of the Salem Village farmers, who had only three years before asked for total separation from the Salem church. They wrote a petition to be delivered to the town meeting prior to the vote, hoping thereby to protect their interests:

> We whose names are here subscribed, taking into consideration the motion that is now on foot concerning the building of a new meetinghouse now at Salem, have with one consent agreed not to contribute to the same at all (not knowing how long it may be beneficial to us), unless you likewise of the Town will share with us when we shall build one for ourselves.[9]

Through a parliamentary maneuver, the moderator of the town meeting at which the petition was to have been presented avoided any mention of the dissent of the farmers, so they grudgingly paid the taxes for a new meetinghouse from which they fervently wished to be separated.[10] Frustrated in their attempts to achieve a measure of local control from either the Salem church or from the town meeting, the farmers turned to the General Court with their next request for permission to maintain their own minister, claiming that in response to their previous petitions "the Town have given us no answer, although we have used all the means we could."[11] While the Deputies consented to the farmers' request, the Assistants did not concur.[12]

Two years later in 1672 the farmers again approached the town meeting with their petition, and this time achieved a mixed success. They were allowed to maintain their own minister, "provided always, that they shall bear all other charges whatsoever among themselves, both with respect to their meetinghouse, and minister's house . . . and also bear their proportion of all other public charges in the town."[13] This vote was confirmed later that year by the General Court.[14] Henceforth the few church members of the Village would continue to travel to the Salem church for sacraments, since only a covenanted church with an ordained minister could offer them and the Village had not yet succeeded in achieving this total separation from the Salem church, but the majority of the Village residents would attend the regular Sabbath services in the Village and never again have reason to travel weekly to Salem Town. For some there would be economic roles which drew them regularly to the peninsula, and a few would serve in offices which required meetings in a central location; but the regular weekly contacts among the Villagers and the Townspeople would no longer occur. Just as the Beverly residents had petitioned for permission to maintain their own minister in 1659, after the Salem town meeting hired Higginson at nearly double his predecessor's salary and built him a home costing four times as much as the older parsonage, the Villagers reacted to the decision to build a new church. Both decisions were attempts to unify the town, which only resulted in further separation of its increasingly distinct parts.

Emboldened by their success in obtaining permission to maintain their own ministry, the Villagers petitioned for full separation from the Town, but were frustrated in their attempts to acquire township status for another 80 years.[15] Although the question was "agitated" for the remainder of the charter period the town meeting successfully delayed in providing an answer. Finally, when a vote was taken in 1689, the answer was negative.[16] Unwilling to let Salem Village go the way of Beverly, the town meeting exempted the Villagers only from the maintenance of the ministry of Salem and not from other public charges for highways, public works, and the poor. Yet the constables who collected the Village rates were from the Village, as were the men called on to perform public work in the precincts, as they had been for years. What little unity was preserved by the half-way measures of the town meeting rested on financial and political control of the Village by the Town, and not on the maintenance of interaction.

If another reason for the reluctance of the Townsmen to allow separate institutions to develop in the Village was a feeling that the Villagers were not ready for this move, their fears were soon confirmed. Once freed from some of their obligations to the Salem church, the Villagers began to quarrel among themselves. In 1679 one faction of 16 persons wanted to remove Mr. Bailey, their preacher of 6 years, while 49 persons signed petitions to retain him.[17] The Salem church, of which some of the petitioners and Mr. Bailey were members, was asked for advice. After noting that "there was much agitation on all sides," the church reported "that business being long and many of the brethren gone that we could not make a church act of advice in the case."[18] In the midst of appeals by some of the petitioners to the General Court, the Salem church finally issued its opinion: that due to the small number (and percentage) of church members in Salem Village, following the will of the majority of the inhabitants would be the only peaceful solution. Following the will of the majority was considered by the Salem church to be a temporary measure, however. As more Salem Village residents became church members, they alone would be expected to exercise control over church affairs in the Village.[19] Since leadership in the Village and in its church were not congruent, and the number of church members was small, democracy was used as a temporary expedient.

Despite the victory of the majority of the Village residents who wished to retain Mr. Bailey, he resigned his position, and the following year the "brethren at the Farms" sent another letter to the Salem church asking approval of their new preacher, George Burroughs. The old conflict was still alive, and again the Salem church—which contained both Porters and Putnams among its members—did not wish to act. However, "after some agitation the church agreed thus far that they did so far approve as to have nothing against it."[20]

While the differing interests of Village and Town were recognized and faced in the 1670s, the resolution of the status of the Village church did not come until 1689. By 1686 when Burroughs was replaced by Deodat Lawson as minister, there were 14 Village farmers who were members of the church; 3 years later that number had increased to 17 men and 10 women who signed the covenant which formally inaugurated the Salem Village church.[21] None of the Porters or any of their relatives by marriage appear among the members of the newly covenanted church; they chose to remain with the Salem church, and left the control of religious life in the Village to the Putnams, who constituted 11 of the 27 original signers of the Village covenant.

Throughout the various controversies between Village and Town, the farmers consistently cited distance from the Salem meetinghouse as their primary reason for wishing more control of their own affairs. The principles of church membership they drew up at their first church meeting in 1689 indicate that serious differences over polity may have been at the core of their disaffection with the Salem church as well. Under Higginson's leadership and in an effort to gather more saints to the church, the Salem church had agreed to admit new members after examination conducted privately by the minister; if none spoke in dissent, the applicant was then automatically admitted. The Villagers made it the business of their first official church meeting to reassert the necessity of public confession:

> That such as offered to join in church membership shall be admitted before, and in presence of, the whole congregation . . . unless we find it needful to be more private . . . That persons (that is of the male-kind) can hold forth . . . with their own tongues and mouths . . . But where natural impediments hinder, we would not lay too much stress upon [a verbal confession] but admit of a written confession and profession, taken from the person or persons by our Pastor.[22]

"Natural impediments" referred to the shyness or lack of articulation of women; even they, however, were to make a written statement which could be made public. Further, the Village church members specifically rejected the practice of admission by silent consent of members: "Persons shall not be admitted by a mere negative: that is to say, without some testimony for them from the Brethren."[23] The founders of the Village church were clearly trying to reestablish the purity of New England church polity of the first generation. Higginson, in trying to preserve the godly state, tried to open the church to more men who would thereby maintain the bond between sacred and secular leadership. The Villagers, having felt excluded from secular leadership for decades, opted instead for the purity of the church. This critical difference in outlook between Town and Village churchmen first appeared in writing in 1689, but undoubtedly underlay the struggles between the two sections of Salem which erupted during the 1670s.

The Villagers were not the only inhabitants who challenged the unity of the Salem church in these years. A consequence of the increasing social, if not legal separation between the various subgroups of the population was a precipitous decline in the spirit of voluntarism on which the covenant rested. In 1668 the town meeting had attempted to maintain a semblance of voluntary support for the church, by agreeing to raise Higginson's maintenance by "voluntary contribution into the deacons's box," but facing reality they added that "those persons who do not contribute or not contribute to their ability and estates shall be rated by the select-men in being."[24] The maintenance of the minister was to be raised by rate only where necessary, in an effort to preserve at least a vestige of communal unity based on voluntarism. The vacillation of the town continued until 1671, when Higginson agreed to accept his salary in a specified cordage of wood and cash raised by rate alone, "and the trouble to be taken off from him in the gathering of it from several persons."[25] After more than a decade in Salem, Higginson agreed that a regular income required the abandonment of both voluntary contributions and the somewhat more coercive method of house-to-house subscription. Having gone for periods of up to a year with no income in the previous decade while the town meeting discussed his welfare, Higginson had little choice but to acquiesce in this decision.[26]

Even after the town, with Higginson's reluctant concurrence, dropped all pretence of voluntarism after 1672 and ordered the minister's salary raised by rates to be gathered by the constables in the same manner as the town and colony rates, there were problems with the collection of the tax. The difference between the rates assigned to the constables and the amounts collected was made up from the sale and rent of various parcels of town land. Three times during the next decade committees were established to "search" for land which could be used to cover the town's debts to the minister.[27] When Reverend Nicholet arrived in 1672 to assist Higginson in the work of the ministry the town agreed that his maintenance would be raised "by a free voluntary contribution every Lord's day."[28] Nicholet generated more popular support from the townspeople than Higginson during his brief tenure in Salem, so he may have received sufficient money each Sunday to satisfy his needs. When another assistant for Higginson was hired in 1682, however, the terms of his calling specified that his maintenance would be raised by a rate assigned by the selectmen and gathered by the constables.[29] Despite the approval of Higginson's rate in the previous year, the town meeting "voted it is left to the selectmen to take care that Mr. John Higginson his maintenance shall be paid him this year the best way they can."[30] Even the formal approval of rates in the town meeting for the maintenance of the ministry was not enough to assure that the proper amount could be collected.

During these same years when the Salem church was facing resistance not only from the Villagers but also from others who did not wish to support the Salem ministry, yet another group of residents attempted a division of the church. Though dwindling in membership during the 1660s, the church had accommodated itself with remarkably little internal conflict to changes in polity which divided New England ministers and fractured other New England churches for decades after the synod of 1662.

Having survived the doctrinal debates of the period, the Salem church was soon plunged into bitter divisions on other grounds, which extended beyond the church and into the community. The church had eased requirements for membership for the children of church members, but what of those outside the covenant who desired the benefits of church membership? During the 1670s, they attempted to clear another path: the creation of a second church.

Their efforts centered around Mr. Charles Nicholet, who arrived from Virginia in 1672 at a time when John Higginson was asking for an assistant to help him discharge his duties as minister. Nicholet preached to the Salem congregation several times before he was "invited to continue for a year in a way of trial as a help in preaching the Gospel."[31] Before the end of the trial year, in February of 1673 the residents of Salem invited Mr. Nicholet to continue for another year.[32] Unlike the first invitation, which had been suggested by John Higginson, decided by a "vote of the Church and people together on the Lord's Day as had been done formerly,"[33] and confirmed by a town meeting,[34] this invitation was the result of a vote of the inhabitants at a general town meeting and was carried out without the approval of Mr. Higginson, who within the year had become disenchanted with his assistant.

Higginson, anticipating a renewal of the call to Nicholet for the following year, called a meeting of the church members in February of 1674 to inform them of his objections to such a move. He declared Nicholet's preaching "not desirable," and stated that "the truth and peace was much endangered by his continuance here so long." Finally, Higginson charged that he had received no assistance from Nicholet as had been the intention of the church's original invitation, but rather had experienced "much affliction and oppression which he lay under by his means."[35]

The extended debate which followed demonstrated the depth of the division within the church over Nicholet's tenure. The nature of the issues is not described in the records, but since we know Higginson to have been a strong critic of the growing mercantile spirit in Salem, we may assume that he found Nicholet's preaching "not desirable" for its support of commercial growth in particular and the covenant of works in general. Nicholet's Virginia connections also must have aroused Higginson's suspicions about the Anglican leanings of some of his Salem admirers, particularly those who had arrived in the new tide of immigration after 1660 and some of whom had accumulated wealth which rivalled that of the town's major leaders. When agreement within the congregation was acknowledged by those assembled to be clearly impossible, Higginson withdrew his request for a vote, which would only have consolidated the factions.

One month later the selectmen called a general town meeting "to know the mind of the town" concerning the renewal of Nicholet for another year; the meeting was held on March 26, 1674.[36] Seeing that the majority of the inhabitants sided with the minority of church members who wished to retain Nicholet, Higginson would only say that he "could not concur with them nor consent thereunto, and therefore should be only passive therein, he should not oppose."[37] The politics of consensus required that he withdraw from the debate. Nicholet thus began his third and stormiest year in Salem. In the early fall of 1674, Nicholet for no apparent reason began to preach a series of farewell sermons.[38] Whatever his intention, the result was a general town meeting vote in October to appoint Nicholet for life and to build a new meetinghouse at the eastern end of the peninsula.[39]

A series of annual defeats at the hands of the townspeople had been bearable for Higginson; the prospect of permanent "affliction and oppression" was not. Especially alarming was the approval of a new meetinghouse, when the "old" one, specifically built to accommodate the increased population of the entire town, had been standing only two years. Although no official request had been made for a division of the church, Higginson correctly surmised that the move for a new meetinghouse signalled "an attempt of diverse of the nonmembers to gather another church in this place."[40] Higginson had been willing to remain silent when the issue was the choice of his assistant, but the constraints of consensus were no match for his concern for the unity of the church. Since the tools of consensus were clearly no longer adequate to resolve the conflict within the church—or indeed within the town—Higginson appealed to the governor and the Council for assistance.

Help came in December, 1674, in the form of a recommendation from the Council that the Salem church hold a meeting with elders and "messengers" from other churches as mediators.[41] Accordingly, in February of 1675, a church meeting was held in which Mr. Higginson "produced some exceptions in relation to Mr. Nicholet's doctrine and practice," and Mr. Nicholet pledged to "be more watchful and careful" in the future. His pledge was "voted as accepted for satisfaction with respect unto all that was past."[42]

If Higginson was satisfied by Nicholet's public acknowledgment of past errors, his relief was not to last long. The selectmen's minutes of March 7, 1675, note that the new 100 foot square meetinghouse had been laid out on the common.[43] A petition to the General Court, signed by "the greatest number of the town, and many of the church," proposed the establishment of a second church in Salem; not surprisingly, Nicholet was to be the minister.[44]

Instead of granting the petitioners' request, the General Court sent a committee to Salem in June to investigate the case personally; the degree of concern which the divisiveness in Salem aroused in the General Court is evidenced by the appointment of both the governor and deputy governor to the committee. The committee condemned the "general voting of such inhabitants in town affairs who are not expressly qualified to vote by law," the procedure which had been used in 1673 and 1674 to reappoint Nicholet and finally to install him for life.[45] However, they decided that Nicholet should remain "so the work of public preaching for the future be carried on jointly by Mr. Higginson and Mr. Nicholet as before."[46] The church was not to be divided, but Nicholet was to be allowed to stay, this compromise to be sealed by a public day of humiliation. Apparently this consensus was not acceptable to Nicholet, however, for he left Salem the following spring, becoming the last Salem minister to resign his post rather than die in office for over a century.[47]

Nicholet's departure did not heal the division, just as his arrival did not create the faction of which he became the focal point. Four years later in 1680, 147 Salem men petitioned the Quarterly Court for the establishment of a second church in Salem. Twenty-four men subsequently delivered a petition opposing this move.[48] An analysis of these petitions suggests the nature of the split within the town and the church, a division which Nicholet may have catalyzed and used for his own ends, but certainly did not create. Of the 94 Salem men who were church members in 1680, only 30 became directly involved in the appeals to the Quarterly Court, while nearly half of the nonmembers who appear on the country rate census of 1680 signed, all but 8 of them in favor of a second church.[49] Thus, nonmembers appear to have been proportionately more involved in the controversy than the church members themselves. Had the church members been equally united, the issue might not have been raised, but 13 church members, joined by 134 nonmembers, petitioned for a second church, while 17 church members and 8 nonmembers (5 of whom were sons of church members) opposed this move. Church polity was clearly not the issue: none of the proponents of a second church had applied for or been refused church membership.

Rather, their differences with the church stemmed from the changed character of the town itself. In 1680 fewer than one-quarter of the inhabitants made their living from the land; the remainder were artisans, merchants and seamen whose economic interests, views concerning the social order, and style of living were frequently berated from the pulpit of the Salem church. Like the Villagers, who masked differences over polity with pleas for separation based on distance, these petitioners cited rapid population increases and the size of the meetinghouse of 1672 which "will not contain above two-thirds of us with any convenience the which is made a general plea for abstaining from the public worship of God whereby the Sabbath is greatly profaned" as their reasons for requesting a second church. They did not mention that once inside the church they did not like what they were hearing.

As early as 1663, Higginson had been alarmed by the growing mercantile spirit. He warned in an election sermon of that year:

> My fathers and brethren, this is never to be forgotten, that New England is originally a plantation of religion, not a plantation of trade.
>
> Let merchants and such as are increasing cent per cent remember this, let others that have come over since at several times understand this, that worldly gain was not the end and design of the people of New England, but religion. And if any man amongst us make religion as twelve and the world as thirteen, let such a one know he hath neither the spirit of a *true New England man* nor yet of a *sincere Christian*. [50]

The apprehension motivating Higginson's denunciation was amply justified. Two-thirds of the petitioners for a second church had "come over" since 1660, compared to 16.7% of the opponents;[51] 85% were merchants, seamen, and artisans. Seamen alone accounted for one-third of the signatures, twice as many as any other occupational group.[52]

Higginson's identification of the "true New England man" with the "sincere Christian" reflected a fundamental principle of Puritan utopianism: that the secular world and the spiritual realm were coterminous, that the economic and political rewards of the secular world were signs of spiritual rewards, and that leadership and wealth should be coincident with saintliness. Throughout the first generation, this bond was maintained by the practice of the policy of accommodation, but by the end of the second generation it was clear that the differentiation of the population and the separability of the seals of the covenants had dissolved the basis for unity. Whether or not the church was to be divided, the town was clearly composed of differentiated subgroups.

The specialization of neighborhoods within the town is reflected in the residence patterns of the signers of the two petitions. Only 29.9% of those proposing a new church were from the west end of the peninsula, compared to 62.5% of those against dividing the church, while 56.4% of the proponents lived in the more heavily populated east end, the district containing most of the wharves and all of the shipyards and fishing lots.[53] Only 15 signers of both petitions pursued agricultural occupations, and all but 3 of them lived beyond the bridge at the west end of the Town. In the area surrounding and west of the meetinghouse to the bridge lived most of the merchants and those craftsmen not related to the maritime trades; residences of seamen, fishermen, and those whose crafts supplied and maintained shipping were predominantly located in the eastern end of the peninsula.[54]

The seamen, tradesmen and merchants arriving after 1660 settled in the central and eastern parts of the town, and remarkably few of them became church members. Therefore, by 1683 the constables' districts west of the bridge had a substantially higher percentage of church members than the districts within the town. This trend was accelerated by the separation of Beverly from Salem in 1668 and the semi-independence of the Village after 1672, the two areas in which land had been granted and laid out as individual farms by the early selectmen. In contrast, the smaller allotments of land granted to the open field farmers who received house lots in the town and shares in the common fields nearer the peninsula meant that their sons had been compelled to supplement their incomes by learning trades, thus intensifying the concentration of tradesmen within the peninsula, men who identified with the commercial spirit of the new immigrants to Salem after 1660 at whom Higginson's railings were directed.

While neighborhood specialization had contributed to the dissolution of the unity of the early town, the decline in the rate of church membership and freemanship also played a role. Nearly all of the difference in the positions taken in the conflict over the church by residents of the western sector of the peninsula can be explained on the basis of their status as freemen and church members. Nine of the ten freemen who were also church members and resided in the area around the meeting-house were against permitting the construction of a second church in the eastern end of the town, while seven of the nine freemen living in the western area who had not joined the church were willing to permit the division. Only six other free church members agreed that there should be another church in the eastern end of the peninsula, and four of them lived there while two resided among the farms. Taken together, residence in one of the three clearly differentiated neighborhoods of Salem and the seals of the covenants described differences among Salem's inhabitants over one of its two central institutions. (See the table on p. 133.)

By 1670, the leadership of Salem's civic institutions reflected the changes in residential patterns and the decline in the adoption of the seals of the covenants. Before that date, one-third of the selectmen were farmers, but after 1670 only two additional yeomen were elected—Lt. Richard Leach and his son John—both of whom lived west of the town bridge. The remainder of the newly elected selectmen after 1670 were all residents of the peninsula, and were involved in business or trades. Given the decreasing proportion of church members in the population, the increase in numbers of wealthy men who did not join the church, and the change in the voting laws to include substantial citizens who were not church mem-

Neighborhood	Freeman Only	Church Member Only	Both
West End			
for 2nd church	7	2	1
against	2	2	9
East End			
for	1	6	4
against	0	2	1
Beyond bridge			
for	2	3	2
against	1	1	0

bers or freemen, the previously strong correlation between church membership and holding the office of selectman began to break down. Of those who served as selectmen before 1670, 89.1% were church members at the time of their first election to that office. After 1670, only 4 of 26 men (15.4%) had joined the church prior to their election as selectmen. Thus, the board of selectmen no longer mirrored status within the church.

This disjunction between leadership and church membership was a highly visible fact within the community. The selectmen, together with the minister and deacons, determined the assignment of pews in the meetinghouse. This, the only official joint responsibility of town and church officials throughout the charter period, was the point at which spiritual and secular definitions of the elite were supposed to merge and be made visible.[55] Sermons from the pulpit were thus not the only messages received by the congregation. Since church services were the only regular large-scale gatherings of Salem residents, seating arrangements within the meetinghouse were important weekly reminders of deference patterns within the community. By 1670 it was clear, however, that the secular and spiritual bond had been fractured in Salem. Increasing numbers of merchants and selectmen did not become church members, yet they used their political position to assure themselves of the seats designated for the elite of the community.[56] Thus, the seating patterns within the meetinghouse no longer reflected the status of the church and its members, but mirrored instead deference patterns outside. Given two increasingly divergent deference models—the one spelled out by Higginson, and the one that could be seen within the congregation—the vast majority of the inhabitants found the one based on human accomplishment more compelling than the view that all earthly rewards flowed from a state of grace, and a minority of the church members were left to defend the unity of church and town in 1680.

This divergence of previously inseparable designations—"election" by God, and being chosen as selectman—is reflected in the controversy over a second church. Of the 24 men on the list of those opposing the creation of a second church, 5 had served as selectmen by 1680; all had been first elected before 1670, and all were both freemen and church members. In contrast, of the 10 men with experience as selectmen who favored the establishment of another church, 8 were elected for the first time after 1670;[57] while all were freemen, only 2 of the 10—William Hathorne and his son John, who took up the mantle of his father's leadership in 1679—were church members.[58] Freemanship and town office were available to men on both sides of the conflict, but church membership was not.[59]

While the men opposed to the division of the church were not unlike the leaders of the movement for a second church in their access to secular leadership, the latter group attracted a large following which stood completely outside the town's central institutions.

Petitioners[60]	For Second Church	Against Second Church
Met property requirement and became freemen	12	11
Met property requirement but weren't freemen	17	2
Didn't meet property requirement but were freemen	8	7
Neither	98	1

Among the proponents were twice as many men who met the property requirements in effect for the local vote, while the numbers of freemen were nearly equally distributed on both sides. The largest number of proponents were those who had not taken the freemen's oath, yet qualified to vote in local elections on the basis of their economic standing. The support of all but one of the petitioners who stood outside full participation in the town meeting went to the leaders of the movement for a second church—men who in general were not church members but nevertheless were elected to the town's highest office after 1670.

The question of who was authorized to vote in decisions affecting the church thus became an urgent matter. If only church members participated in the decision, the issue would virtually split the congregation, with a bare majority of the petitioners against a division; this voting base had been the clear preference of the Salem church in their advice to the Village farmers during the conflict over Reverend Bailey the previous year. However, the General Court had declared that all who were eligible for the local franchise in secular matters could indeed vote in questions affecting the church, a criterion which would have resulted in a clear victory for the proponents of a second church in Salem. Finally, the general populace seemed overwhelmingly in favor of a new church in the eastern end of the peninsula, and their views could not easily be dismissed since the Salem church members had finally agreed during the Bailey conflict that following the will of the majority of the inhabitants of the Village would be the only peaceable solution given the small number and percentage of church members in the precinct. The principle of inclusion, always a motivating force in Salem's ecclesiastical history, now threatened the very unity that inclusion had originally been intended to buttress.

The history of service to the town by the petitioners further complicated the issue. By 1680, the church members opposed to the second church were not distinguishable from the leading proponents in terms of election to local office. Compared to the general population of Salem, those men who became involved in signing petitions both for and against a second church were more active in town government. Although a larger proportion of those against a new church served in each of the local offices surveyed, the group wishing to establish a second church contained four times as many men who had served as constables and jury members, and three times as many selectmen. Their rate of church membership, however, was below that of the general population (8.6% compared to 15.7%), and far less than the rate of church membership among those who wanted to maintain a single church in Salem (70.8%). Estranged from the Salem church, yet bearing the largest share of the responsibility for running the town, the proponents saw the establishment of a second church as their only means of obtaining status in a religious institution equivalent to their status in secular affairs.

Distinguished as a group by their late arrival in Salem, concentration in the east end of the town, low rate of admission to the church, and extensive participation in town politics, those who appealed to the Quarterly Court for the establishment of a second church were also younger than those who opposed them. The average age of those against the division of the church was 66, while that of the proponents was 46.[61] The latter petition was signed in roughly deferential order, the first 20 signers forming a distinct subgroup.[62] These "top twenty" probably met to write (and sign) the petition, which was then circulated for additional signatures. All 20 were freemen, 9 had been selectmen, 8 were church members, and all but 1 had served in at least one town office, yet their average age of 47 was not significantly higher than that of the group as a whole. The conflict over the church was also an intergenerational struggle. If this marked difference in ages between the two groups was an important factor in the decision not to build another meetinghouse, it also portended the dominance of the commercially-minded segment of the population. By 1689, 42% of those who had opposed the division had died, compared to 21.4% who favored it. By attrition of the older generation, if not by the surrender of their institutions and ideals, the values of the new merchants and tradesmen would prevail.

In the end, the major division between the group of men who opposed the establishment of a second church and those who promoted it, was not along occupational or residential lines, but rather separated those who were not alarmed by differentiation within the community from those whose view of the social order depended on unity. Like their opponents, the majority of the "top twenty" lived in the west end of town, including six of the nine merchants; but unlike their opponents, they attracted the support of the seamen and tradesmen along the harbor to the east. The remainder of their support (13.7%) came from 16 men who lived west of the bridge, 11 of whom were farmers. These men could not have agreed that the site of the new meetinghouse would be more "convenient" for them, since it would be half a mile further to the east. Rather, they saw a chance to endorse the principle which underlay the case they themselves had been pleading for 13 years: the separation of residents in the Village from the church at Salem to form a covenanted church among the farms. The residents of the eastern end of the peninsula could not appreciate the anti-commercial views of Higginson—views which were likely shared by the farmers—but on the other hand the farmers had in mind a pure form of the covenanted church which would have further narrowed the membership base of the peninsula which was already greatly diminished. The men who tried to hold both ends of their fragmented community together in one church for all of these subgroups had an impossible task.

The newcomers to Salem had not caused this division alone. Although support for a second church came largely from those who arrived in Salem after 1660, all but one of the leaders had arrived by 1642 or were sons of men who had arrived by then. Like the opponents of a second church, these men expected religious and secular success to covary, but they saw these elements as equally desirable parts of an individual life rather than as inseparable components of a social system. The late arrivals did not therefore "take over" the town, either through election to public office or by instigating a division in the church.[63] Instead, they formed a natural alliance with the earlier settlers and their sons who also chafed under the preaching from the Salem pulpit. The lives of the opponents also centered around trade. However, those who attempted to block the new church were united more by their common belief in the unity of town and church than by their economic interests. They insisted on the no longer practiced principle that a single political unit should be served by one church from whose membership all leadership of the town should be derived—a principle specified by colony law in the first years which had been abrogated by the town of Salem each time they permitted a precinct to maintain its own minister. Still, the opponents when faced with the railings of Higginson about the further differentiation within the town on economic grounds attempted to curb their profit motive within Puritan guidelines, and clung to their severely threatened concept of community.

In the end they won. Although the Quarterly Court approved the request for a second church on the endorsement of the selectmen—4 of whom had signed the petition—the East Church in Salem was not established for another 40 years.[64] No record of the conflict was made in either the town records or the church records in 1680, so the reasons for the decision not to act on the Court's approval cannot be known with certainty. Both sides had appealed to outside authorities to resolve a difference that ran deeply through the community. Perhaps by the time the Court acted, proponents and opponents alike realized as Higginson had five years before that to force the issue would result in conflict which the institutions of the town could no longer contain, and therefore simply withdrew the question. Despite the victory by default of the opponents of the second church, the price paid for unity was high. Higginson, in an effort to extend the boundaries of inclusion and thus blunt the drive for division began to baptize children of nonmembers in 1678,[65] but even this measure did not alter the position of the church within the community. While the population of Salem continued to increase after 1680, church membership continued to decline. By 1689, only 67 men were members of the Salem church, fewer than in 1637, while the population had tripled in that time. (See Appendix C, Table II.)

The division within the Salem church was not easily smoothed over. In January of 1680, the members elected two new deacons to assist "our brother Horne having been deacon of this church above this fifty years being now very ancient."[66] Hilliard Veren and John Hathorne were chosen, but Hathorne refused the post. He had been the clear leader of the faction trying to establish a second church, and was one of the few church members among them who was also a freeman, had served as selectman, and was preeminently wealthy. While he did not withdraw from church membership, he did not choose to serve as deacon. That same year, John Higginson Jr.—son of the minister and the leading opponent of the division of the church—refused election as selectman and paid the one pound fine. These two leading merchants, both sons of the leading lights of Salem's civil and ecclesiastical institutions in the previous decades, no longer stood at the pinnacle of the system in which one's calling, the quest for salvation, and civic duty were inseparable.

As a means for healing the conflict which had not only weakened the church but made apparent divided interests within the leadership of the town, Reverend Higginson suggested a renewal of the covenant—the method used after the Williams episode and the Quaker threat—but at first his motion was "left to consideration."[67] Finally, in March "the direction for renewing our church covenant after several agitations about it was agreed on by the church to be solemnly read (as consented) by the church the next fast day."[68] Two elements of the new covenant were familiar: the original statement of 1629, and a statement of humiliation for past sins and failure to walk together as "the Lord's Covenant People."[69] Several articles of church polity were also restated, but there was a new emphasis as well: the reform of individual behavior. In addition to promising to act "without formality and hypocrisy, and more fully and faithfully than heretofore, to discharge all covenant duties one toward another in a way of church communion," the members pledged to be more careful about the catechizing of their children. Finally they agreed:

> We do further engage (the Lord helping of us) to endeavor to keep ourselves pure from the sins of the times, and what lies in us to help forward the reformation of the same in places where we live, denying all ungodly and worldly lusts, living soberly, righteously, and godly in this present world, making conscience to walk so as to give no offense nor to give occasion to others to sin or to speak evil of our holy profession.[70]

It could no longer be assumed that the church would function as the guide for the reform of the town, but individual members could—by avoiding the "lusts" of the secular world—have some minimal effect "where we live." While none of the earlier covenants had hinted at a better order beyond death, by 1680 the members saw a clear distinction between "this present world" and a better order. Higginson himself could recall that order from the past, when as a boy of 14 he had joined in the covenant of 1629. While his language may have been nostalgic, it clearly marked the greatly reduced place of the church in Salem. Church and town were no longer a single whole, within which individuals ranged in a unitary hierarchy. The saints could no longer claim authority as secular leaders by virtue of their church membership, so they turned instead to the reform of individual behavior and looked to a better order elsewhere than in Salem. The church had become an enclave for the few who clung to a "holy profession" in a highly differentiated town.

Chapter Eleven

The Consequences of Dispersion and Differentiation, 1668-1684: The Town

The major leaders of Salem after 1647—the merchant-selectmen and the commercial farmer, John Porter—provided the focus for unity in the town during years in which religious cohesion was weakened by Quakers and the sense of a single community was destroyed by continued dispersion and differentiation of the population into occupationally coherent precincts. By 1668, the resulting decline in voluntarism among the populace caused them to turn away from their major leaders even as they called for a new resurgence of cooperation with authority in their orders to the selectmen of that year. While the older leaders continued to be elected sporadically through the next decade, in only two years after 1667 did they constitute a majority of the board. Unable to agree on common symbols of authority vested visibly in particular persons, the electorate created a higher degree of turnover in the office of selectman than had existed since the 1640s. As the sons of the major leaders were elected to office after 1668, together with their fathers they served more than half of the available terms in office for the decade, but the solidarity of earlier boards was missing. The growing divisions within the town rather than the decrepitude of the six merchants and John Porter caused their loss of hegemony. Only Walter Price died in office, while the others lived from 4 to 18 years after their last terms in office.

Dates	% of Terms Served by Leaders	% of Terms Served by Their Sons	Total
1636-46	16.25%	0.0%	16.25%
1647-68	71.7	0.0	71.7
1669-83	24.8	37.1	61.9
1684-89	0.0	19.5	19.5

The immediate cause of the defeat of the sons of former major leaders after 1683 was the emergence of a new breed of merchants, compounded by the conflict over the colonial charter. But other events in the preceding years presaged their loss of leadership. The major leaders of the middle decades together with their sons constituted a majority of the board of selectmen in all but two of the years between 1668 and 1683, years in which they faced major new challenges to their concept of community. The crushing expenses of King Philip's War, the new tide of non-Puritan immigrants, and controversies within the church all combined to alter the structure of the community and the function of its leaders.

All of these changes occurred against a background of continued specialization of Salem's precincts, which had its own effect on the patterns of leadership. The unity represented by the merchant-selectmen depended on universally agreed upon standards for hierarchy, made visible in land and over time in service to the community. As long as land, church membership, and leaderhip were seen as three facets of the same status model, the merchants could serve as a unified and recognizable elite. However, at the same time they emerged as leaders of the town in the late 1640s, the acquisition of land became based on individual achievement. The tie between land and leadership was broken, and the landscape was no longer formed by a single hierarchical model or reflective of it. Eventually this disjunction would require a new explanation for service to the town, a new way for the voters to recognize their leaders; they found it in the representation of special neighborhood interests. Roger Conant was the first of these regional representatives; within a decade the Cape Ann farmers had won the right to maintain their own ministry, and in 1667 they were incorporated as the new town of Beverly. The election of Thomas Putnam as selectman in 1665 was the result of a similar new coherence of neighborhood feeling in the Village, among farmers who had acquired their farms by purchase for the most part. Most of the largest landowners in the precinct were not church members and did not participate in the civic life of the town; they were not only distinct occupationally from the merchants and artisans of the peninsula, but were also attuned to a different model of success, one which depended on individual achievement rather than ascribed status.

During the turbulent years after 1668 when the old guard struggled to maintain a single church for the residents of the peninsula, they also faced challenges from the farmers to unity of Salem's civic life. The first confrontation came in the year before the signal town meeting of 1668, and may have helped to provoke it. The Village farmers circulated two petitions in an attempt to gain more control over their own precinct. The first, a petition for separation from the Salem church, was signed by only six church members and was duly rejected, but the second petition which was addressed not to the town but to the General Court shows the deepening sense of estrangement between the commercial town and its one remaining agricultural precinct. Thirty-one farmers subscribed to this petition asking for release from the Salem town watch, claiming "the remoteness of our habitations from the town . . . the distance of our houses, one from another . . . the weakness of many of our families . . . the opportunity and advantage that Indians and other ill-affected persons have by knowledge-before that such and such families are such nights left destitute of help to two or three miles about."[1] While the General Court granted the farmers' request, several of the signers continued to be harassed by fines several years thereafter by the selectmen for failure to attend the watch.[2]

After more than a decade of seeking more autonomy—always unsuccessfully—through their representatives to the board of selectmen, the Village farmers turned again to the General Court in 1677 in another attempt at increased independence from Town-based institutions, this time from the Salem militia. The General Court responded:

> In answer to the petition of Salem Villagers for a foot company, it is ordered, that all those of the said Village that live in the west side of Ipswich road may be freed from Capt. Corwin's company, and shall be exercised at home by Lieutenant Richard Leech, who is hereby appointed their lieutenant, leaving it to the militia of Salem to bound the two companies of Salem.[3]

Even the General Court realized that when the farmers crossed the Ipswich Road and then the town bridge on their way to drill with the Salem militia on the Town common, they were no longer "at home."

Although the Town and the Village had ceased to constitute a community of interest, the Town refused to separate the farmers from its tax base for another 82 years. Had the Village itself been more unified, a condition it never achieved due to its initial pattern of settlement as dispersed farms and the fact that the merchants of the town continued to maintain large farms there, the voices of its representatives might have been harder to ignore. The entry of the Putnams to the board of selectmen after 1665 could have portended the same fate for the Village that had already occurred in Beverly—the creation of a separate church followed closely by township status—but the history of the Villagers was to be quite different for at least two reasons. First, while Conant had been a true peer of the dominant selectmen of the peninsula in age, background, and experience, by 1667 the major leaders who dominated the board had served an average of 16.8 years each in office. They could overwhelm the farmers not only with their votes, but also with their experience. A second reason for the disadvantageous position of the Salem Village selectmen was the clear rivalry between the major families of the Village, the Porters and the Putnams, which was mirrored among their neighbors.[4] The Village itself was deeply divided. In the same year that Thomas Putnam was elected as selectman for the first of the many years that a Putnam would represent the interests of the Village, John Porter's son followed his father's example and bought a house on the peninsula to be closer to his mercantile connections.[5]

The major impact of the new representatives of sectional interests was thus to demonstrate publicly a new source of disunity within the town of Salem. The merchant-selectmen and their ally John Porter no longer served as effective symbols of a general communal mission for the Putnams and their neighbors whose lands were four to seven miles from the Town center. The presence of the farmers in the leadership group of the town represented a loss of consensus, but was no real threat to the dominant peninsular interests as long as the Village itself was divided. The majority of the board of selectmen continued to be merchants from the Town center, who were able to outvote or ignore the Village representatives throughout the remainder of the charter period. Still, the Putnams could inject a discordant note into the meetings of the selectmen, which they did on numerous occasions.

Meanwhile, the intensification of other neighborhoods continued. The harbor area was a magnet for the new immigrants after 1660 who were seamen and followed mercantile trades, while other occupational groups also settled in ways which confirmed the distinctions among neighborhoods. By 1684, the few farmers who remained on the peninsula felt sufficiently estranged from their own neighborhoods to petition for the right to manage the North Field without any interference from the town leaders. Throughout the period, the selectmen had been careful to appoint surveyors of fences and highways from the areas in which the work was to be done, but by 1684 the proprietors of one of the two large common fields asked for and received the authority to select their own surveyors of fences. The selectmen retained the power to approve their choices, but the North Field yeomen had won the right to conduct a crucial piece of annual business among themselves.[6] Thus even within the peninsula there were clear divisions by the end of the charter period.

Within this context of increasing differentiation of neighborhoods and recognition of distinct and sometimes conflicting interests, there were a number of financial drains on the town after 1668 which served to exacerbate existing divisions and create new ones. There had been no major public works in the period of the hegemony of the merchants, but after 1668 the town approved the building of the first jail in 1669, a new meetinghouse in 1670, and a town house in 1672. While the jail was built with money received from the sale of land confiscated from Quakers,[7] the church and the town house added greatly to the rate of taxation of the inhabitants. Prior to 1669, the town rates had exceeded £100 (exclusive of the maintenance of the ministry) only four times: in 1654 the inhabitants paid that amount for the fort alone; in 1657 the construction of a new minister's house costing £50 raised the total tax to £123, and in 1659 a new house was built for John Higginson costing £200; repairs to the meetinghouse the following year brought the total town tax to £137.[8] All of these rates except the last one were spread among the constables for Village, Town, and Cape Ann. By 1669, the Beverly residents had been exempted from Salem taxes, and the total needed rose to £118 from an average of £60 for the earlier years of the decade.[9] Expenses for the previous year had also exceeded the amounts turned over the selectmen by the constables, so William Hathorne, George Corwin and Henry Bartholemew were instructed "to call together all persons indebted to the town as well former constables as all others upon any consideration whatsoever."[10] In December of 1669 the town meeting approved a rate of £65, but the selectmen the next month had accumulated bills for twice that amount and moved "for the raising further of the town rate."[11] In previous years a single annual allotment half as large had been sufficient to cover the usual expenses—payment of the wolf bounty, care of the poor, repair of highways, costs of the militia, and wood for the elders—but by 1669 the needs of the town had increased, the tax base had been narrowed, and the residents seemed less willing to pay.

The most troublesome task confronting the new, more representative board of selectmen in 1668 was thus the collection of taxes. They ordered the constables to take a census of "estates ratable" in their "respective wards" for the assignment of a rate, "and those that refuse, to return their names, and to be paid for their pains by the town."[12] Constables had occasionally been paid for their work in the past, but only in extraordinary circumstances; Thomas Putnam, constable for the Farms in 1655, was given 20s. "for his pains" in collecting the tax for the fort, but other constables were not given equal consideration.[13] Recognizing the difficulty of the constables' job in 1668, the selectmen for the first time offered a general financial incentive to all of them for the proper execution of the task.[14] The town meeting simultaneously adopted new methods for collection of past-due amounts owed to the minister, by ordering a specially appointed committee to "make issue on persons that did not formerly give or are since come into the town to give their voluntary contribution."[15] The measures used by the new selectmen were similar to those employed by the major leaders of the previous twenty years, but the problem they faced had intensified: the decline of voluntarism based on universal agreement about the good of the whole.

The next crisis came in 1673, by which time the town rate had returned to its usual lower level, but a tax of £470 was assessed in addition to cover the first half of the cost of raising the new meetinghouse agreed to in 1670. Notations scattered through the earlier records indicate that occasional abatements were made by the selectmen for special reasons, but this new tax for the meetinghouse strained a whole group of the residents of Salem. They did not pay, and appeared at the town meeting of March, 1674, to request "the abatement of some part of their meetinghouse rate."[16] The town meeting had also approved the construction of a new town house in 1672 using the materials from the old meetinghouse, but the inability of the taxpayers to sustain additional costs delayed the completion of that project until 1679.[17] Resistance to paying higher taxes for centrally located public works was also undoubtedly part of the reason for the delays and delinquency of many of the residents.

In 1675, after failing to gather the full rates for the meetinghouse despite threats of arrest to the constables,[18] the taxpayers of Salem were assessed seven "great rates" by the colony for the expenses of fighting King Philip's War; the total levied on the town of Salem was £764, far more than the town had already failed to gather for its own church.[19] By 1676, the colony tax had risen to sixteen "great rates" totalling £1510; again in 1677 the colony taxes were extraordinary—nine rates, or a total of £1245— after which they returned to a level which was higher than in pre-war years but a substantial relief from the crushing taxation of 1675 to 1677.[20]

The phenomenal increase in taxation during these years had important consequences for the roles of the officers of the town. The constabulary, which had always had the lowest proportion of church members, freemen, early arrivals, and large landowners among its ranks, became very difficult to fill. Refusals of the office were rare before the 1670s. In 1655, Benjamin Felton "being spoken to by the selectmen to gather his part of the Castle [Hill] rate: his answer is he will not gather it," so the selectmen chose two of their own number to "agree with Henry Skerry or any other for the gathering of part of the town rate."[21] No fine was imposed on Felton for refusal, and there was no mention of special financial incentives for his replacement. Only once before 1670 had constables been fined for nonperformance of their duty—in 1659 when two of the three had difficulty collecting the minister's maintenance due to the resistance of Quakers[22]—but when this crisis passed so did the penalty. Eleazer Hathorne and William Brown Jr., both sons of major selectmen, were "freed from being constables for this year" by the town meeting in 1665, and were not penalized for their refusal to serve. However, there was some concern about finding qualified men, and the town agreed that they should not be reduced to choosing anyone "until they have been two years an inhabitant."[23] To ease the burden of the office in an effort to make it more attractive, the constables were "discharged from whipping any this year and the town is to provide on for that service" in 1667.[24] New financial incentives were also provided. In 1668 the constables were to be paid if they encountered any difficulty in collecting their rates and had to "return" the names of resisters, but they were not compensated for the ordinary task of gathering the rates.[25] By 1672, however, it had become routine to abate the constables' own rates in exchange for their service.[26] Even this incentive was not sufficient for all who were asked to serve; in 1675, John Turner was elected as constable but "made an agreement" with John Clifford to take his place which the town "accepted."[27] The following year, at the height of the heaviest taxation by the colony, four constables refused election before three could be found who would accept the post; the town meeting established a £5 fine for those who refused, an amount five times higher than the fee for refusal of the selectman's post established in 1670. Even this amount was regarded as insufficient deterrence, as the Salem deputies successfully petitioned the General Court to allow the town to exceed the colony-wide limit and impose a fine of £10 for refusal to serve as constable,[28] yet in 1681 Thomas Maule paid this amount in preference to carrying out his assigned duties as constable.[29] Simultaneously, to entice three men to accept the job in 1676, the town meeting paid them each £5, again five times more than any previous constable had been allotted for his trouble.[30]

Despite the lower rates after 1677, the difficulty of finding men who would accept the post continued. In 1686, "Nathaniel Silsby refusing to serve as constable for this year and in regard he expressed his willingness to serve another year it is voted that he be discharged for this year from that choice."[31] His replacement also refused the post, however, so the town meeting agreed that they would "accept of John Chaplin to serve as constable in the room of Isaac Foot if Foot do hire him and will be engaged to the town for the rates credited to Chaplin."[32] Foot could refuse, but only at his expense, to collect the rates assigned to him; he could not, however, avoid the responsibility for the full collection.

The constable's job had become increasingly onerous, not because it was more time-consuming due to population growth, but because more inhabitants refused to pay. In 1678 the number of constables was doubled, further reducing the burden on any one man.[33] Still, the liability for the taxes due was a serious concern given the increasing number of inhabitants who could not or would not pay. Constable Nicholas Manning still owed £70 of the minister's rate to William Brown—the selectman who had finally covered that expense—in 1676, four years after Manning had served as constable.[34] By 1681 he had managed to pay back most of what he owed, but he was still short £2 7s. 10d. of the town and country rates he was to have collected nearly a decade earlier. Accordingly, a piece of his land was "distressed" and given over to the town to clear up his debt.[35] As would be expected, the rate of delinquency was high during the period of King Philip's War, and the constables of those years carried major debts to the town.[36] However, the rate of delinquency did not decrease after 1677, indicating that the problem was only partly due to the rate of taxation; there was also an increasing reluctance or inability to pay. By 1679, various bills were charged directly to the constables, so their failure to collect the full rate meant that they were not only debtors to the town but also to various providers of services who were owed money by the town.[37] It was one thing to be indebted to the community, and quite another to face neighbors who had become creditors. Various methods were used to assure eventual payment. In 1679, Eleazer Giles still owed £95 5s. of his 1676 rates, and bound himself and his heirs to full repayment in a contract with the town.[38] The alternative after that date was a lawsuit initiated by the selectmen on behalf of the town, a power granted to the selectmen by the town meeting in every year after 1679. The instructions of the town were clear: "The selectmen shall have . . . power to call the constables unto account and to sue and fully prosecute at law all such as are in the town's debt."[39] Four of the six constables for 1683 were sued in 1684, and the selectmen ordered two of their own number to "take out execution against those constables sued at the last Salem Court for what they stand indebted to the town at this time."[40] Faced with the loss of their own property, three of the constables somehow paid the remainder of the rates assigned to them; but Philip English, constable for the harbor ward, did not and had a portion of his land seized. The following year, he had accumulated enough money to buy it back, but his experience could not have served as an incentive for others in his neighborhood to enter into the town's service.[41] The constables for the next two years did no better: by November of 1685, only £46 of the minister's maintenance of over £300 had been paid. Alarmed by this debt, which not even the wealthiest of the selectmen could personally cover until the rates were collected, they called four of the constables from 1684 and all but one of the six from 1685 to account in 1686.

These nine delinquent constables met again with the selectmen in July to settle accounts, but by October none of them had fully paid and all were "arrested to the next county court at Salem."[42] Accepting the constable's post had become almost a guarantee of eventual prosecution.

The difficulty in collecting the rates assigned had two sources: the inability of an increasing number of residents to pay their rates, and the unwillingness of others to yield to taxation. The few abatements of taxes granted by the selectmen in the middle decades had been for extraordinary reasons—the loss of a ship, or a physical disability—but the frequency of abatements after 1670 demonstrates that a new class had emerged in Salem: those who simply could not afford to pay, year after year.[43] These abatements accounted for some of the difference between the rates originally assigned to the constables and the amounts eventually received, but the selectmen carefully deducted each abatement from the constables' debts. The remainder, far more than the total value of the abatements, was owed by inhabitants who simply avoided payment. Voluntary support of the ministry had been a problem ever since the arrival of the Quakers in the 1650s, but the unwillingness to support the basic services provided by the town was a new phenomenon.

Other declensions in the voluntary spirit of the population exacerbated the problems of taxation which consumed much of the time of the selectmen after 1670 and the energies of the constables. Men called to repair highways were reimbursed for the time they lost from their respective callings as early as 1653, but all were expected to share in the work; thus whatever drain these services caused on the town's accounts was universally reimbursed to the taxpayers in exchange for their service. The bills granted by the selectmen by 1677 indicate that some of the work previously done collectively was by that date contracted out to particular men, and at higher rates than had been paid previously.[44] In addition, others were paid for work which had previously been done gratis as part of the natural obligations of residence in a Puritan town. For example. Thomas Oliver was paid "twenty shillings for going about the town to inquire after inmates" in 1671, and in 1676 Constable Obadiah Rich was abated £1 1s. 9d. of his own rates "for going to the Council about getting disbursements allowed."[45] Similar examples abound in the itemized audits of the constables' accounts included in the minutes of the selectmen after 1670. The only service routinely paid for by rate before that date was the school; in 1668 Edward Norris was granted £5 from the regular town rate, and received in addition fees paid directly by parents.[46] The town meeting continued to vacillate over the voluntary support of the ministry, for the church, unlike the school, was intended as a universal institution for the community, and the covenant theology on which it was based required free-will financial support. All other services in the town prior to 1670 followed the model of the church—universal, voluntary participation— but after that date an increasing number were paid for as the schoolteacher had been, by rate.

Finally, the increase in the number of poor people in Salem required larger rates for the remainder of the population. The care of the poor had been handled by the town meeting and the selectmen during the middle years of the century in highly personalized ways. Some were given food by the rest of the householders; in 1643 John Moore received one-half peck of corn from every family in the town and more "from such as are better able to bestow more according as God shall enable them," and in 1658 William Chichester's widow was given one-half bushel of corn per week by the selectmen.[47] In 1645 two men received cows from the town in an effort to make them self-sufficient, while other families were helped by placing their children out in other homes.[48] Still other men were helped by giving them the "odd jobs" of the town—cleaning the meetinghouse, ringing the meetinghouse bell for meetings and funerals, and beating the town drum.[49] In 1653, Richard Stackhouse was allowed to keep the ferry "for the relief of his family."[50] In 1656, the town had to pay the cowkeep from the town rate, but this was a temporary expedient as it was hoped that the fees from the next year would cover the "pay" given to this poor man.[51] Clearly the preferred way to deal with the few people in Salem in these years who could not support themselves was to provide food and jobs, not to give monetary support from a town rate. However, after 1670 the number of poor had exceeded the capacity of the town to deal with them in highly personalized ways. Where the ferry had once been used as a source of support for Richard Stackhouse, it was by 1678 used as a source of direct income for the town which was spent for whatever needs were most pressing—the salary of the schoolteacher in some years, and the care of the poor in others.[52]

The town had responded previously to cases of individual need in direct and simple ways, but after 1670 the town records reveal that the poor had become a nameless group who were given assistance in the form of money. At first, the poor were granted aid directly from the town rate,[53] and after King Philip's War this source was supplemented by contributions made to the elders of the church and distributed by the selectmen.[54] In 1682 a £65 rate for the poor was approved by the town meeting—a larger amount than the average total town tax in the 1660s.[55] By 1683, even these two regular sources were not sufficient, and the town meeting "voted that the selectmen are desired to supply the urgent necessity of several poor amongst us and to be repaid by the town, until the town take further care."[56] Finally, in 1685 the town meeting decided that some measures had to be taken to relieve the drain caused by the poor on the town's finances:

> Voted that the town do appoint and empower Bartholemew Gedney, Esq., Capt. William Brown, Samuel Gardner Sr., Jonathan Corwin, John Hathorne, and Thomas Gardner . . . to be a committee for the settlement of an employment for the poor in

spinning, etc., and if there be occasion may make use of about fifty pounds of money of the town's stock for the buying of a stock of wool for the end aforesaid and that they do their utmost to secure the said money so as that it may be returned to the town in due time.[57]

The poor had become an amorphous group, to be set to a single occupation instead of being helped to self-sufficiency on their own terms, in an effort to relieve the burden they placed on the town. While an almshouse was not officially established until 1698, the impersonality of the measures taken in 1685 describe a new mentality, quite different from the one in effect in 1645 when the "elders and townsmen" judged John Bachelder to be "the poorest man or at least he that most was in want," and gave him a cow.[58] By the end of the charter period, wealthy men like Ebenezer Gardner and William Brown were designating portions of their wills for the "poor honest people of Salem," who had become a group set apart from the general population.[59]

In 1688 the selectmen reported to the town meeting that a rate of £174 would be required to meet the "charge of necessity for the maintenance of the poor, repair of bridges, highways, repairing of meetinghouse, town house, school house, cage and stocks."[60] The amount had tripled since the 1660s, and several of the expenditures were new. Public buildings unknown in the town before 1670 now required repair, and the people who had not been able to "accommodate" themselves in the town through their own achievements needed alms. The leaders of Salem had intensified the dispersion of the population, built new public structures to reinforce the centrality of the peninsula, and admitted inhabitants who could not be accommodated; now they would have to find new ways to pay for the consequences of these policies.

As early as 1662 the town had been alarmed by the increase in the numbers of men in Salem who were not householders. In that year they encroached on the common to enable two residents to build houses, and in 1663 Henry West received a similar parcel: a "plot to build a house of two rods in length and twenty foot in breadth at one end and eighteen foot the other end."[61] Similarly small house lots were laid out by both the town meeting and the selectmen in that year and the next,[62] after which the town meeting stopped the granting of further land by either group. By 1671, the pressure for house lots had again intensified, and a few more were laid out on the common; John Launder was one of the new residents allowed to build a house there on a tiny plot, "paying for it as other men did for theirs."[63] In 1672, the town meeting agreed that "it is left to the selectmen to sell house lots in the swampy land in the common . . . to such persons as shall need them, provided they build houses on them, in two years time, after granted to them, but if not then to return to the town again."[64] These sales accomplished two purposes: the settlement of inhabitants as "sober men and householders," and some relief from the burdens of taxation.[65]

Having discovered a new source of income in the house lots on the common, the town turned to the arable acreage surrounding the peninsula. In 1673 they ordered a survey of "common land the town hath amongst the farms," and the surveyors found 11 parcels of varying sizes lying between previous grants, between individually owned land and the town bounds, and even within earlier grants.[66] Some of this land was sold, and the revenue added to the town's account; in 1678 the selectmen used a portion to "satisfy Mr. Higginson according to the town's agreement."[67] Like the Beverly farmers a generation earlier, the Villagers objected strenuously to the sale of lands they had grown accustomed to using as commons, and carried their claims to the Quarterly Court.[68] The use of the income to support a minister from whose church they wished to be separated was another direct affront. They won the principle of retaining as much common as was needed to support their own minister, for later in 1678 the selectmen claimed that they could not help to resolve a border dispute between Beverly and Wenham by giving them a tract of land since it had already been reserved to the Villagers for that purpose.[69] Still, the policy of using the town's land to generate income had been established.

The remainder of the acreage was leased, thereby adding a new source of regular income other than taxation; in 1677, this revenue was used to pay the schoolmaster.[70] In 1677 and 1679, and again in 1682, the town authorized further "searches" for land which could be leased; even the islands in the harbor were rented for income.[71] After 1678, the selectmen's minutes became increasingly complicated as they calculated rents into the amounts required for the support of various services in the town. By 1688, the income was nearly sufficient to cover the expenses of caring for the poor that year—an amount which 20 years earlier would have supported all of the needs of the town.[72] While earlier selectmen had been stewards of the landscape, making certain that every inhabitant was settled according to his needs and merit, the selectmen after 1673 were managers of income property, with the town's balance sheet determining the choices made. Suits of constables, distribution of general funds for the poor, and monitoring rents and leases were all new duties of the selectmen after 1670, and all were carried out on an increasingly impersonal basis. While most of the rates approved before that date were for reimbursement to the selectmen for services already rendered, the costs of running the town had increased beyond the personal capacity of the selectmen to cover them. The financial crises of the 1670s created a new role for the selectmen—strict management of the funds needed to support the services needed in an increasingly complex town.

The only new source of income generated in this period had the effect of furthering the distinctions between the various areas of the town as well. Each house lot sold on the common increased the concentration of residents in the eastern end of the peninsula. By 1684 there was no more room for shipyards or wharves on the main peninsula, so permission was granted to build them at Winter Island.[73] Even that area, previously reserved for fishermen, was crowded; in 1685 the selectmen had to arbitrate a dispute over space for "the pitching of flakes, setting of presses, houses, etc., by which means they obstruct each other in their fishing concerns there."[74] Simultaneously, the Village residents became a more distinct group as they maintained their own minister, were relieved of the Town watch, and gained the right to manage what remained of their commons. The merchant-selectmen and their sons who continued to dominate the board of selectmen until 1684 became "overseers" of a town which had grown well beyond the limits of accommodation.[75]

There were still signs, however, that the ideal was to extend these limits to include as many as possible in the central institutions of the town. In 1678, Higginson again expanded the coverage of baptism, this time to children of parents who were not themselves church members, in an attempt to enlarge the boundaries of the church to make them more nearly coterminous with the town.[76] In that same year, the General Court passed a measure which was also intended to include more men in civil institutions. During 1673 and 1674, only 14 men appeared before the town meeting to take the oath of fidelity which was one of the requirements not only for voting but also for serving as a jury member, constable, or selectman if one were not a freeman of the colony.[77] Thomas Flint was allowed to refuse his election as constable in 1673 "not being capable by law," but this excuse was eliminated in 1678 when all males over the age 16 were required by colonial law to come before the constables of their respective wards to take the oath.[78] Even the decision to sell house lots on the common, while it was motivated partially by financial duress, was an attempt to reestablish Salem as a town of settled householders. In fact, none of these measures worked: church membership continued to decline, the number of men who were not householders rose, and the oath of fidelity was not universally taken. In 1678, two hundred seventy-nine men were recorded as having taken the oath, but by 1686 the selectmen could turn in to the Quarterly Court a list of only 102 men who had become eligible for jury duty by taking the oath.[79]

While the ideal of inclusion was still promoted by lowering of the standards for entrance to the church covenant and by the direct order of

the General Court for participation in civil affairs, the town reacted to
the obvious failure of the earlier policy of inclusion by becoming more
concerned about its limits. Admissions to the town carried new restrictions, and there was an increase in the frequency of warnings out of
Salem. In 1671, Samuel Stevens was "received to be an inhabitant so long
as he behaves himself well in the town"; by 1678 a new category of
residency was created for John Champlin, who was "permitted to dwell
in the town during the town's pleasure."[80] While earlier arrivals had been
admitted on the condition that they took "effectual course" to bring their
wives, or with the stipulation that they purchase house lots, these men
were granted conditional and temporary residency.[81] Early arrivals to
Salem were granted land in the hope that they would become full members of the church; after 1670, men were admitted with conditions concerning their behavior, and in the hope that they would stay off the poor
rolls.

As the conditions of admission became more detailed, the frequency
of warnings out increased. After 1657 there was a 20s. fine for harboring
a stranger in the town in an effort to keep Quakers out of the community.[82] Still, only four "strangers" were warned out before 1669, while
two residents gave security to the town for two temporary, skilled laborers.[83] The arrival of the notorious Quaker Thomas Maule in 1669 led two
Salem residents to be fined 20s. each for keeping him at their houses, and
the next year the town officially reminded all residents of the policy. In
addition, Thomas Oliver was hired to "go from house to house about the
town once a month to inquire what strangers do come or have privily
thrust themselves into the town."[84] The selectmen feared not only troub-
lemakers like Maule, but also those newcomers who could add to the
ranks of the poor who were already straining the town's treasury. During
the next decade, seven men were expelled from the town, while those
residents who had "entertained" them were fined.[85] Two strangers were
allowed to remain after settled residents had given security to "the town
from any damage or charge that may arise thereupon."[86] Although the
influx of refugees to Salem during King Philip's War made maintaining
the town's social boundaries more difficult during these years, the actions
of the selectmen both before and after the war made clear their intentions
to close the town to schismatics and those of questionable behavior or
financial status. Even after 1680, the selectmen continued to enforce the
regulation against strangers. Leonard Bockwith was given ten days to
leave the town in 1680, and a warning was issued "that no inhabitant of
the town do afterwards entertain him upon the utmost penalty."[87] Three
years later the selectmen discovered that "there is one John Chase come
into the bounds of this town" who was to be told by the constable "that

the selectmen are not willing he should reside in this town."[88] A "pie baker" was also summarily expelled the next year.[89] After 1684, however, the colony took over the task of admitting new residents, so the decisions of the selectmen became secondary and less personal, and expulsions ceased.[90]

While the efforts to maintain the boundaries of the town appear to have to been successful to 1684, the same cannot be said for the attempts either within the church or within the civil institutions of Salem to reestablish the cohesion of the population through greater participation. The constables were not the only officials to be penalized for refusal to serve; in 1670 a £1 fine was established for turning down election as a selectman, and in 1675 the town meeting established a 5s. fine for not responding to warrants for work from the highway surveyors.[91] Even those whose civic responsibilities were purely customary had to be reminded of their duties; when five licenses for inns and taverns were renewed in 1681, the selectmen admonished "every one of them, both tavern and innholder, suitably to provide for the accommodation of the courts and jurors likewise all other matters of a public concern proper for them."[92] The largest fine for refusal of any post prior to 1670 had been the 3s. penalty for failure to work on the fort in 1655—a one-time, extraordinary task—yet two decades later the town agreed to assess any man who failed to answer a warrant for work in his own neighborhood on the highways a higher penalty of 5s.[93] Even the cohesion within neighborhoods was insufficient to guarantee cooperation in public work. Refusal of election to town office occurred only once before 1668, but the size of the fines established after that date and the occasional entries indicating that at least some men considered their freedom from obligations to the town worth the price, show that voluntary service was in decline not only among the generality of the population but occasionally among the leaders themselves.

There is also evidence that attendance at town meetings continued to decline after the fine for lack of participation was established in 1654.[94] Three years later when Thomas Goldthwaite asked the town meeting to remit his fine for cutting trees on the common, his request was "referred until there be a fuller town meeting."[95] The following year, the elections for deputies were held at the town meeting indicating that only freemen had appeared, in contrast to earlier years when separate meetings of the freemen had to be warned for this purpose.[96] Nevertheless, it appears that attendance among the freemen was good in this period. In 1659, William Hathorne received 116 votes in the election for selectmen, indicating that at least that number were present. Since the population of adult males in Salem at that time was approximately 350, Hathorne was elected by nearly one-third of the men of the town, probably most of the total eligible to vote even after the changes in the franchise requirements made in 1658. The new colony law stipulated that in addition to the freemen of the town, any man who was 24 years old and a "settled householder" of good and honest character, had an estate valued at £20 in a single country rate, and took the oath of fidelity, could serve as a jury member and vote in local elections—though not for deputies—as if he were a freeman. Only the right to select Salem's colonial representatives was denied those men who could meet these criteria but did not become freemen.[97] The property requirement replaced the stipulation in the voting laws of 1647 that the freemen of each town could decide which men among those over 21 years of age who had taken the oath of fidelity would be admitted to the "liberties" of the town.

Since attendance was not taken at town meetings and no tax lists survive from this period which would permit an estimate of the men who could have met this set of criteria, the votes for Hathorne in 1659 merely establish a minimum number for the group of enfranchised men in Salem at that time—a proportion which stood somewhere between the 42% of the adult male population who were eligible to vote in 1647 due to their status as freemen, and the substantially lower percentage of freemen (28%) in the Salem population by 1666.[98] Others were specifically guaranteed the right to speak at the town meetings, further obfuscating the question of the degree of actual participation in town politics at mid-century.[99]

Since tax lists are available in addition to records of freemanship for the next generation, however, the decline in the proportion of inhabitants who could exercise voting rights in the town can be demonstrated. Sixty-three freemen appear on the tax list of 1683, the first available for the colonial period, comprising 11.5% of the taxpayers that year. An additional 36 men met the minimum property requirement for the franchise. Even if all of them met the other qualifications of the law of 1658—being a settled inhabitant and householder of good and honest conversation, taking the oath of fidelity, and being at least 24 years old—the 99 men who were either freemen or fulfilled the franchise requirements would still constitute only 18% of the taxpaying population that year.[100] The General Court order of 1678 requiring all adult males to take the oath of fidelity may have helped to fill juries and the constabulary, but it did not add substantially to the number of residents who could vote at town meetings on issues of taxation, services, public works, and leadership.

In fact, the number who could vote was smaller than 99 for 2 reasons. First, men were taxed after the age of 21, while the franchise requirements set a minimum age of 24; second, the property requirement was raised from £20 of ratable estate to £80 in 1670 for new applicants for the franchise.[101] Men who had voted under the old standards could continue to do so, but new residents and sons reaching maturity after 1670 had to satisfy the requirement of that date. Thus, while a minimum of one-third of the residents actually voted for William Hathorne in 1659, at most one-sixth were even eligible to vote by 1683.

At least 54 men did exercise their voting rights in 1683, since William Hathorne's son John received that number of votes as the most popular selectman chosen that year. The largest number of votes for any single man sets the minimum attendance of voting residents at the town meetings

	Highest Vote	Lowest Vote[102]	No. of Candidates	County Rate[103] Census
1680[104]	60	39	n.k.	307
1681	55	29	n.k.	310
1683	54	35	18	310
1684	33	25	10	300
1685	32	14	13	300

after 1680, a number which steadily declined. By 1683, Hathorne was supported in his election by fewer than 10% of the men taxed in the town that year, or just over half the eligible voters according to the most generous estimate.[105]

Two different explanations may be proposed for the decreasing numbers of men voting for the leading selectmen, but either one produces the inescapable conclusion that even the men who drew the most deference from the voters by 1680 were elected to the town's highest office by a small fraction of the populace. The method of voting in Salem seems to have varied in these years. In 1681, the voters were instructed to "vote the lists all together, and if any man's name be twice in the lists or there be more votes than seven that or those lists shall be rejected."[106] The instructions leave little doubt that all nominations were made before elections began, and that candidates were considered together by each voter, who then cast a secret ballot to contain no more than seven names and no duplications. This practice is at variance from what we know about other towns, and from other practices in Salem during these years. In 1683, the number of votes recorded for "nominations" was identical to the ballots for "election"—suggesting that as each nomination was made, the eligible voters were asked to cast their votes for or against the nominee.[107] This was probably the method used earlier, since the high rate of retention of incumbents during the middle decades of the seventeenth century suggests both that they were nominated first, and that few voted against them. Such elections were "simply plebescites on the sole candidate up for consideration, and so almost everything depended on who was nominated first and then upon whether others who had other candidates could be prevented from voting against any but their own."[108] Still another method appears, however, in 1685, when the votes recorded for nominations are at variance with a separate list of votes recorded for election; in that year, there were clearly two separate processes, with full votes taken at the nomination stage.[109] If there were many more voters present than the highest votes noted above for the 1680s would indicate—whatever the voting method—then winning an election meant less than full approbation from the electorate, some of whom held out for "their own." Alternatively, we may assume a high degree of consensus among the voters who were present between 1680 and 1685, and conclude that the most successful candidate assumed office with the full support of the eligible voters, who constituted only 10% of those on the country rate census by the middle of the decade, while the least successful nominee among those actually elected garnered the votes of only 5% of that same group. Since the country rate census for 1683 is substantially lower than the actual tax list extant for that year which contains 550 names, the selectmen in these years were in fact chosen by an even smaller percentage of the adult male population. The 54 votes cast for John Hathorne in 1683 account for fewer than 10% of the men taxed that year, and the decrease in the highest votes in the next two years signalled a further decline in consensus or actual participation, or both. While the 7 men elected in 1683 accumulated a total of 297 votes of support for their nominations from their fellow townsmen, the selectmen of 1685 mustered only 119 votes among them, and in both years over a third of the affirmative votes for nominees were cast for losing candidates.[110] This record stands in marked contrast to the election of 1659, in which there were only 8 candidates, and they received 442 affirmative votes in all.[111]

As town politics passed beyond the limits of accommodation, not only were fewer men included in the process of decision-making, but there was also a new confusion of the hierarchy of leadership. The larger number of nominees in the 1680s in itself suggests a breakdown in consensus among the Salem voters concerning the criteria for leadership. While 5 sons of the earlier merchant leaders who swept the election of 1659 were among the nominees in 1683, and all of them were elected, there were 13 other men nominated as well. Among them were merchants recently arrived in Salem, Salem Village farmers, three members of the mercantile Gardner family from the east end of the town, and assorted others.

The distribution of eligible voters among the various precincts of the town suggests one reason for the lingering success of candidates with last names of Corwin, Brown, Price, Hathorne and Porter in 1683, despite the plethora of candidates. A survey of the tax list of that year shows that

41.4% of those who met voting requirements lived in the same neighborhood as these men: the west end of the peninsula. Only 13.3% of the
taxpayers in the east end of town were eligible to vote, compared to
22.8% of their neighbors to the west.[112]

Percentage of Eligible Voters by Neighborhood

	1683	1689
West End	41.4%	38.6%
East End	29.3	28.9
Salem Village	29.3	32.5
	100.0%	100.0%

While the concentration of voters was higher in the west end, the population was larger in the eastern sector, with the result that this neighborhood contained 29.3% of the voting population.

If the east end was the most populous of the three major neighborhoods
of the town, Salem Village was the fastest growing. Between 1683 and
1689, there was a 29.6% increase in taxable population in the two constables' wards west of the town bridge; the two wards which comprised
the west end of the town increased in taxable population by only 2.2% in
the same six-year period, while the east decreased slightly (6.4%).

Distribution of Population by District

	1683	1689
West End	32.7%	31.5%
East End	39.6	34.9
Salem Village	27.7	33.6
	100.0%	100.0%

Simultaneously there was a decrease in the percentage of the eligible
voters who resided in the west end, to the advantage of the Salem Village
districts.

While the diminished proportion of the Salem electorate residing in the
west end is reflected in the increased residential diversity of the selectmen
after 1684, the most important story told by these figures is the decrease
in the absolute numbers of potential voters in each of the three districts
between 1683 and 1689, and a decrease in the total eligible from 99 to 83
men. Whatever advantage candidates from the west end had enjoyed previously was dissipated after 1683 as both population and eligible voters
were more evenly spread throughout the three major districts of the town
by 1689. In the same period, however, while the total taxable population
increased from 536 to 590, the eligible voters decreased by 16.2%. In

contrast to the previous generation in which a much larger electorate had routinely returned the same small group of recognized leaders to office year after year, the voters of the 1680s were faced annually with a large array of candidates totalling approximately one-sixth of their own ranks.

Among this larger group of candidates, the sons of former major leaders were unable to establish their primacy after the suspension of the charter in 1684. John Corwin, William Brown Jr., John Hathorne, and Israel Porter were all defeated in the elections of 1684 and 1685 after serving from 4 to 12 terms in near succession prior to that date. Only John Price among the sons of outstanding earlier selectmen retained his position throughout the decade until his death in 1689. The willingness of an earlier generation to trust a small and clearly defined group of centrally located merchants to define the good of the whole gave way in the final decade of the charter period to the promotion of candidates representing diverse occupational and residential groups within the boundaries of the town. Ironically, when the electoral base was broad in the middle decades, there was a small, stable group of well-defined leaders. With the dramatic narrowing of the voting segment of the population came a new pattern of diffuse and "representative" leadership.[113] Indeed, after 1668 the board of selectmen more nearly resembled the diversity of the board in its first decade, with the crucial difference that now this diversity was firmly planted in distinct neighborhoods.

The "good order" envisioned in 1629 had rested on three basic assumptions—that all would be included according to their needs and abilities, that the lesser sort would recognize and voluntarily submit to authority, and that anyone who was basically "honest" and practiced general godly behavior could participate in filling in the particular definition "good order" received in the organization of the new town. The instruments of cohesion were not elaborated, since it could be anticipated that those who chose to "walk together" in coming to Salem would develop a new definition of unity in the new environment. By the middle decades, inclusion in the civil workings of the town had become problematic; the proportion of men who could fully participate in town meetings declined from nearly half to just over a quarter during the period of the hegemony of the merchants, but at least during this period the voters could recognize their leaders—the merchant-selectmen of the middle decades who embodied all of the symbols of status in their church membership, land-owning, and freemanship. Continued dispersion and differentiation of the population, which was positively encouraged by the town and its leaders during these years, led however to the dissociation of the symbols of authority on which the major leaders' power had rested. By the final decades of the colonial period, it was clear that the "recognition" of "natural" leaders was no longer simple; the major selectmen of the peninsula could no longer provide a focus for the unity of the town.

With both of the first assumptions which underlay the hopes for "good order" in the first generation seriously in question by the end of the second generation, the town—like the church—turned to the third of its instruments for achieving cohesion within the community: godly behavior of individuals. The attempts to buttress the principle of inclusion by changes in the voting laws and to stem the resulting decline in voluntarism by establishing fines for non-participation of all sorts did not work. In what appears in retrospect to have been a series of desperate acts, the town leaders after 1670 began to "manage" the behavior of the residents just as they had learned to manage the land, the poor, and the finances of the town in an increasingly impersonal manner.

The heightened concern for the behavior of residents took a variety of forms. There had been numerous orders before 1670 regarding cutting of trees from the common, mending of fences, and maintaining fire ladders, but all of these instructions were intended to protect property.[114] Similarly, the constable's watch, which was in effect as early as 1655 during the summer months since there was an order that year to repair the town house "for the school and watch," was intended to protect the town from external dangers.[115] Throughout the 1660s, the constables warned four men each night from May to September to maintain a perambulation to watch for fire and Indians.[116] When residents of the North Neck became concerned in 1668 about "Indians residing thereabouts," they were authorized to maintain a watch for themselves as the Cape Ann farmers had done since 1664.[117] The only other general orders issued before 1670 regarding the behavior of inhabitants were the town meeting directives of 1644 concerning attendance of Sabbath services and of 1654 requiring freemen to attend town meetings.[118] The selectmen were also empowered by 1657 to regulate seating within the meetinghouse to reflect "good order" within the congregation. All of these orders were directed to the population in general, and do not show any larger concern about deviance.

After 1670, the selectmen began to issue orders which demonstrate their concern about the incidence of ungodly behavior. In 1672, they ordered that twelve persons named in their minutes were not to "frequent the ordinaries, nor spend their time and estates in tippling." The next year, one of the offenders was excused from the list, but five more were added.[119] If they could not assure that every man would become a householder, at least the selectmen could try to assure that the town consisted of sober men. Despite these efforts, by 1681 Reverend Higginson despaired of indigenous controls, and asked the General Court to restrict the total number of inns and taverns to be licensed in Salem.[120]

More serious was the concern about the "children and youth that are not brought up in some honest calling and taught to read as the law directs." Earlier, the selectmen had "placed out" children of indigent residents as a form of poor relief, but by 1673 the measure was used as a rebuke to negligent parents. While the selectmen named five men whose children would be immediately removed from their households, they warned that "we also intend to take the like course with all such children and youth as we shall find in the like condition."[121] The family was the "first society" from which the authority of church and state were derived according to Puritan social thought.[122] The failure of family discipline was thus a threat to the entire social order. If parents could not be trusted to teach their children properly, the selectmen would intervene directly.

The earlier order concerning absence from and inattention during Sabbath services also required reiteration and strengthening. Where two men had been assigned to walk about the town during the services to look for those who were absent without cause in 1644, by 1676 measures were also needed to assure that those who attended remained until the conclusion of the service:

> It is ordered by the selectmen that the three constables do attend at the three great doors of the meetinghouse every Lord's Day, at the end of sermon, both forenoon and afternoon, and to keep the doors fast and suffer none to go out before the whole exercise be ended, unless it be such as they conceive have necessary occasion, and to take notice of any such as shall presume to go forth as abovesaid and present their names as the law directs.[123]

Having exhausted the resources of the constables in this task, the selectmen hired Reuben Guppy and William Lord to watch the boys on the stairs "and if any are unruly to present their names as the law directs."[124] Reuben Guppy was given the further task "to keep the dogs out of the meeting house," which must have been a considerable job since he was "allowed his whole rates for the year ensuing" for its performance.[125]

By the following year, the absence of residents from the church had become a greater concern than the behavior of those who did attend, so the selectmen borrowed the constables from their duty at the doors to check this more serious abuse:

> Whereas there hath been several complaints of several persons that do profane the Sabbath by unseasonable walking abroad, even at the time of public exercise etc., the selectmen have agreed each of them, to take their turns with the constables to walk abroad on the Lord's Day, both forenoon and afternoon, morning and evening, to redress such miscarriages as they shall at any time meet withall.[126]

The constables still had to be back at the meetinghouse "before the public exercise be ended" to close the doors, and had "warrants given them to prosecute this order."[127]

If the selectmen were to assure the sobriety, child-rearing methods, and church attendance of the populace in addition to their burgeoning workload in monitoring the constables' accounts and caring for the poor, they would need more assistance than the constables could provide. Accordingly, in 1675 the General Court established a new appointive office— inspector of families—to assist the constables in detecting abuses in the proper upbringing of children. The selectmen appointed 25 men to the task, and instructed them "to attend the next County Court . . . to receive their orders."[128] Again the next year 21 men were assigned this duty, and the exact limits of the neighborhoods for which they were responsible were specified; in each case, the "inspectors" resided among those families they were to watch.[129] In 1679 these appointees were renamed "tithingmen," but their duties remained the same,[130] and in 1680 their number was standardized at three per tax ward.[131] Having acquired these new agents of godliness, the selectmen assigned them additional duties: the "prevention of the profanation of the Sabbath by boys playing in and about the meetinghouse and disorderly running down the stairs before the blessing is pronounced." Apparently the selectmen could not depend on either the constables or the tithingmen to maintain order, despite their increased numbers, and so asked five additional men "to inspect the same and to return the names of such as are profane and disorderly to authority that they may be punished according to their crimes" in 1681.[132] The selectmen by appointing tithingmen to maintain order in the meetinghouse and to be aware of the quality of instruction given to children in their homes had not only created a new layer of administration in Salem, but had also changed the meaning of watchfulness. When the church members of 1636 had agreed to "teach our children and servants, the knowledge of God and his will, that they may serve him also," the end had been the unity of church and town;[133] after 1679, with tithingmen responsible for overseeing only the families in their immediate neighborhoods, the aim had been reduced to godly behavior alone. Weeding out unruliness and profanity were the new sights of the selectmen, since the cohesion of church and town was no longer at stake.

Changes in the instructions given to the constables concerning their watch underscore the fact that Salem's greatest perceived danger after 1670 lay not in Indians or fire but in the behavior of its own residents. In 1677 the selectmen reminded all inhabitants to "get a suitable ladder" for use in case of fire, and in 1679 the selectmen approved expenditures for "so many hooks and instruments as may be necessary in case of fire," while the constables were empowered to fine anyone who had not followed the order about ladders "ten shillings for every week's neglect"; but there were more detailed instructions concerning behavior than there were about measures taken to protect property.[134] The danger posed by Indians had also been revived by King Philip's War, so a joint meeting of the selectmen and the militia officers in 1679 resulted in an order "that there shall not any Indian lodge within the town one night but shall depart out of the town by sun setting, and shall not return again into the town until sun rising," with imprisonment the penalty.[135] Still, the orders repeated to the constables regarding the watch after 1679 emphasized neither fire nor Indians but the deviance of the residents themselves:

> You are hereby required in his majesty's name, to warn thirteen men every night to watch and to be exact to see the full number appears and attends; the one half at least to be sober, honest men and householders, one of which you shall commit the charge and care of the watch unto, and warn them to be very careful to examine any night walkers, strangers or others who are abroad at unseasonable hours, and to secure any suspicious person that cannot give a good account of their business.[136]

The constables' watch had stood at four men for the peninsula since 1661, but the selectmen of 1679 increased it more than three-fold; they also extended its duration, by requiring six men to continue through the winter months.[137] While the newly enlarged group of watchmen patrolled the peninsula each night, the constables were instructed to initiate a "strict inquisition throughout their whole divisions" to discover if any inhabitants were harboring "inmates," or strangers.[138] The proliferation of watchmen had not resulted in the abatement of anxiety about illegal residents; indeed, as the need for internal controls increased, so did the stridency of the warnings out of the town.

By 1684, the instructions to the watchmen became even more specific: in addition to following all of the orders of 1679, they were to enforce a ten o'clock curfew, and hold any violators "secure . . . until the morning and carry them before the next magistrate." The same fate awaited "any that carry themselves any ways debauchedly or shall be in drink."[139] These watchmen were not merely to observe those on the streets, either: they were told that "if there be any disorder in any house you are to inquire into it and, if there be occasion, to inform authority thereof." Finally they were "to require people to have a care of their lights"—the only reference to fire in the long list of instructions. Having told the watchmen what to do, the selectmen proceeded to tell them how to do it in language which suggests that the earlier performance of the watchmen had been less than desired: "You are to order the watch to have four men constantly walking abroad, two to the eastward and two to the westward, and so to relieve one another."[140] The six watchmen on winter duty were, in effect, told to keep constant surveillance on the residents of the peninsula, both those in the streets and those whose activities inside their homes might be discernable to one passing by.

All of these orders were delivered not directly to the men of the watch themselves, but to the constables who were to oversee their work. The use of layers of administration to check the performance of appointees was increasingly in evidence after 1670. While the selectmen as a whole supervised the tithingmen, who in turn "inspected" the families in their wards, by 1681 the board recognized the difficulty of carrying out their role in the Village and authorized John Putnam to supervise the tithing-men in that district.[141] The surveillance of the residents required primary contacts between the surveyors and the objects of their scrutiny, but so also did it mandate the close connection of surveyor and those responsible for overseeing the work. In focussing on the need to enforce godly be-havior, the selectmen were once again reinforcing neighborhood solidarity.

Most of the new concerns of the selectmen after 1670—drunkenness, church attendance, the care of children, strangers, and the general good behavior of the inhabitants—were delegated to the constables or to newly created appointed roles after 1679. The selectmen had effectively removed themselves from direct, personal contact with the people for whom their orders were intended. Instead, they spent their time as they had with those delegated the responsibility for taxes, the poor, and searches for land: overseeing those to whom the primary assignments had been given. By 1684, even the constables' watch required the attention of the select-men, who decided to "walk the rounds, each one twice in a week."[142] Even this degree of supervision was insufficient, as they were joined by the "commission officers that live in the town" to "take their turns . . . to see that the watch do their duty and that there be no disorder in the town" in 1685.[143] Despite the doubling of the number of constables in 1678 and the increase in the size of the watch in 1679, these officials could not collect the full taxes or maintain "order" in Salem.

The removal of the town's leaders from primary interactions with the townspeople permeated all aspects of their role after 1670. While earlier residents had personally appeared before the selectmen to request land from the town, in the final decades of the colonial period surveyors were appointed to find what land remained and the acreage was sold or rented; the medium of exchange was no longer a personal judgment, but money. After 1677, the deacons collected money for the poor, an amount which was supplemented by rates and disbursed not to individuals who had come to the attention of the selectmen in an ad hoc manner, but to groups of people who were recognized as a new and undesirable class. The con-stables were charged with the responsibility for paying for services in their own neighborhoods, with the selectmen assuming the role of over-seeing the accounts; no longer would they personally pay the men called to work on bridges and highways in their own neighborhoods. After 1687, the minister's maintenance was also paid by a third party, as the deacons took over this task. Even the new effort to control behavior among the residents required the use of intermediaries. Most of the interactions between the elected leaders of the town and the inhabitants were indirect after 1670, just as the selectmen themselves represented groups which were no longer in direct and regular contact with each other due to the differentiation of neighborhoods which had gained the right to provide many of their own services.

There was a similar distance created between the selectmen and the town meeting, which can be seen in the changes in methods of raising town rates. Even after the orders of 1668 from the town meeting to the selectmen that "you shall raise no money nor town rate without the vote of the town," and further that "you shall in no way engage the town so as to bring them into debt except in case of necessity of the poor,"[144] the major leaders who continued to be elected after that date pursued their earlier practices. In 1670, they called a town meeting "for to make a town rate and for all persons to acquaint the town what their several disburse-ments have been for the town that orders may be taken for payment."[145] The selectmen had continued to use their own judgment about the needs of the town, and had personally financed the consequences of their de-cisions. It took the financial crises of the 1670s—the building of the church and other public works, and the expenses of King Philip's War—to bring the practices of the selectmen into line with the orders of 1668. Only after the needs of the town had exceeded the personal capacity of the selectmen to finance its operation and wait for reimbursement did the town meeting regain the power to set its own priorities, by which time there was little agreement regarding the good of the whole. All still con-curred that the ministry had to be supported, and by 1682 the town meet-ing had delegated the raising of that rate to the selectmen; while the town meeting was willing to let the selectmen oversee the gathering of the minister's rate, which was a set amount agreed to in advance, they re-tained the power to set the other town rates.[146] Only once did they vote "that there be a town rate made by the selectmen," and its size was specified in advance "to the value of one hundred and twenty pounds in pay."[147] The role of the selectmen was merely to distribute the rates approved by the town meeting to the constables, and to assure payment by the constables by lawsuit if necessary.

After the suspension of the charter under the Andros regime, yet an-other wedge was driven between the town and the shrinking proportion of the inhabitants who were qualified to participate in decision-making. In 1688, the selectmen appealed directly to "two justices of the peace, one of them of the quorum of approbation of the same according to law" for approval of town rates. The list of needs was not exceptional—"the maintenance of the poor, repair of bridges, highways, repairing of meetinghouse, church, town house, school house, cage and stocks"—but the request for coverage of these usual expenses now required outside authority.[148] Later the same year the selectmen again appealed "unto John Hathorne, Esquire, and some other justice of the peace these several sums of money which is needful for the town's use in order to get a rate made."[149] The selectmen were forced again to set the priorities for the town as they had during the middle decades, but they had to seek authority to carry out their decisions beyond the town's own institutions.

The new dependence on authorities outside the town which confirmed the distance between Salem's residents and its leaders was new in the area of taxation, but was already a firmly established practice in other matters of concern to the town. The tithingmen had made their reports concerning the education of children and had presented profaners of the Sabbath not to the selectmen but to the Quarterly Court since 1676.[150] After 1679, the selectmen themselves sued delinquent constables in this forum. The new sharing of authority between colony and town affected even the admission of new residents after 1684, reducing the selectmen's role to the acceptance of a decision made elsewhere. Even after Andros had imposed the requirement that town rates be approved by justices of the peace, the selectmen of Salem sought additional "interference" in the affairs of Salem. In 1688 when the constables' watch was not properly maintained despite the best efforts of the selectmen to assure that the watch did its duty, the Quarterly Court intruded at this level of local government at the request of the selectmen for "assistance" and ordered the number of men in the watch increased.[151]

The suspension of the charter merely exacerbated an already well-developed pattern in Salem: the search for order at higher levels of government, well beyond Salem's indigenous institutions. The authority vested in the local forms of government was no longer sufficient to contain conflict within the boundaries of the town. Higginson had appealed to outside authorities in 1674 to resolve the controversy within the church, and then after the crisis had passed wrote a new church covenant in 1680 which hinted at a better "order" in another world. By the end of the charter period, the order of the town itself also depended on forces beyond its control.

Chapter Twelve

The Glorious Revolution: Salem in 1689

Salem's civil and ecclesiastical institutions, as well as its land policies, all derived from the legal base of the charter of 1629. The unique church polity as well as the forms of local government which emerged in the bay colony reflected the corporate base from which they had developed, a base which was threatened by the restoration of Charles II to the throne in 1661. Reports from the colony ever since Francis Bright—the Anglican minister sent by the company with Higginson and Skelton in 1629, who had returned to England in that year unhappy with the institution of the covenanted church—had established the clear impression that the leaders of the colony "intended to suspend their absolute obedience to the king's authority."[1] With the establishment of each new form of social organization developed in the wilderness, the colony ran the risk of convincing the mother country that any differences from traditional English practices were "repugnant" to the laws of England.

Charles II confirmed the charter in 1662, but conditioned his approval on the repeal of all laws "contrary and derogatory to our authority and government." Specifically, all persons of "good and honest conversation" had to be admitted to the full sacraments of the church, and the suffrage was to be extended to those who were not members of the church.[2] In fact, by that date the colony had itself extended the vote in a limited way to nonmembers of the church, and the ministers had realized that the declension of the second generation would require relaxation of the standards for membership. The failure of the Puritan ideal had led the leaders of the colony to take the first steps to bring their practices closer to the laws of England; but it was quite another matter to have the full suspension of the New England covenants mandated from "outside." A combination of distance, events in England, and the success of conciliatory measures taken by the Governor and General Court—among them a brilliant move to send masts for the King's Navy as a gift just after the disastrous fire in London in gratitude "for the many and continued

expressions of his tender care and fatherly respect to this his colony"—
kept the issue from resolution which would surely have been contrary to
the wishes of the majority of the leaders of the colony.[3] The orders of
1662 were effectively ignored, and the leaders of Salem proceeded to
buttress their covenants in the best way they could.

During the next generation, both the intensification of commerce on
the peninsula and the immigration of new residents who were less than
sympathetic to the Puritan institutions of the town altered the views of
at least some of the residents concerning the charter by the time the issue
emerged again in 1685 upon the accession of James II to the throne of
England. The two deputies sent to the General Court in 1684, both of
whom were merchant-selectmen who had served on the board of selectmen for years, advised the abandonment of the charter. They were a
minority in the General Court, but they had a following in Salem. When
the freemen of Salem met in 1686 to consider the issue, they instructed
their deputies not to resist the withdrawal of the charter should that occur
at the next session of the General Court, but to "peaceably withdraw
yourselves, as representing us no longer."[4] While other towns forcefully
opposed the removal of the charter, Salem's freemen were sufficiently
divided that conciliation required withdrawal from the debate.[5]

With the arrival of Andros in December of 1686, the fears of the colony
since 1629 were realized: the charter was revoked, and Andros proceeded
to replace the Quarterly Courts with justices of the peace and courts of
common pleas and to amalgamate Massachusetts Bay with the other New
England colonies according to royal order.[6] He appointed the two Salem
deputies who had earlier urged the withdrawal of the charter—William
Brown and Bartholemew Gedney—to his council,[7] and decreed that local
taxes could henceforth be raised by the selectmen in consultation with a
"commissioner" elected by the town meeting instead of by the town
meeting itself. There were few men in Salem eligible to vote in the town
meeting anyway—less than one-sixth of the population—but the issues
raised by the revocation of the charter served to reveal new divisions
within the leadership of the town. By 1689, both Brown and Gedney had
joined the party which overthrew Andros when news reached Boston of
the death of James II, but they were joined by John Hathorne whose
father had been a staunch resister of imperial claims in the past.[8] After
the restoration of the charter form of government in 1689, the freemen of
Salem elected Jonathan Corwin and John Price as their representatives,
instead of returning Hathorne, Gedney and Brown who had been their
choices in most previous years; Price had served once before, in 1679,
but Corwin was new to the General Court.[9] In addition to crises in the
town over the church, taxation, and behavior which had required the use

of outside intervention in the previous decade, the major leaders of Salem were now divided among themselves over yet another issue which was not internal to the town.

If the leadership of the town was divided, the taxpayers were not. In June of 1688 the selectmen together with the commissioner decided that the town needed a rate of £174 and asked two of their number to "move the case to the justices desiring . . . the allowance thereof."[10] Two months later the constables were asked to warn the inhabitants "to bring in an account of their estates" for the levy of a colony tax as well.[11] Since the town tax had not been collected, the selectmen calculated an "overplus" of £27 in money and £55 in country pay into the colony rates.[12] The needs of the town were pressing: the meetinghouse was crowded and needed several new galleries and some repairs estimated at £126; in addition, the town required £50 for the care of the poor to supplement the deacons' collection, £40 for the highways, and £11½ for "ye bellman for ringing the bell, for bulls and the herd, for repairing the school house and watch, and candles."[13] Somehow, in addition, the ministry would have to be supported. In November the selectmen discussed elaborate plans for the renovations of the meetinghouse and contracted the work to John Marston and Jeremiah Neale for £116.[14] Still, the rates had not been collected, and by November the total needs had increased to £226.[15]

There the matter rested throughout 1689. No town rates were collected, and the issue was not raised by the selectmen or by the town meeting. Some rents were received,[16] and one constable was sued for nonpayment from a previous year,[17] but the payment of highway workers and several others with outstanding accounts quickly depleted the town's stock. Only one poor woman was aided directly from the fund for that purpose, after which the selectmen were asked to give John Bly 10s. each and put the debt to themselves "on the town's account."[18] By February of 1690 the situation must have been serious, but the town meeting refused to change their stance. When it was "put to vote whether the former rates raised in November 1688 for the relief of the poor, repairing the meetinghouse, mending of highways, etc. committed to the constables should stand," the secretary recorded that it was "voted in the negative."[19] Someone moved for a new, and presumably reduced, rate instead, but that too was voted down. At the normal March meeting for the choice of selectmen and other town officers, the issue was raised, but it was "voted that the matter with respect to town rate is referred unto the next town meeting."[20] The town had put off the requests of the Villagers for separation from the Town in just this way for years, but now the tactic was directed against the central institutions and services of the town itself. Finally, in April the town meeting reconvened and approved a rate of £150—far smaller than the amount originally requested—and the rates were committed to the constables by the selectmen the following month.[21] While there was a movement from some "persons that complain that their rates are too high" at the September town meeting, they nevertheless approved a second rate of £150 in December.[22] The charter had been restored under a royally appointed governor, the membership of the board of selectmen had changed, and a new group of deputies was elected to represent Salem in the General Court; the taxpayers then returned to their earlier level of resistance to local rates. They grumbled, but they approved the rates.

Earlier crises in Salem had resulted in increased solidarity within the board of selectmen. The rapid rate of dispersion in the town's first decade of formal government led by 1647 to the election of centrally located, godly, wealthy merchants, who dominated the board for decades. As a result of the Quaker disruption in the late 1650s, their hegemony was intensified. Even after 1668, with Beverly separated from the town and the remainder of the inhabitants facing up to the decline in voluntarism among themselves in their orders to the board of that year, the townspeople continued until 1683 to reelect the major leaders of the middle decades and their sons. The issues which confronted the town after 1668, however, had the effect of dividing the merchants themselves.

Each of the major decisions made by the town's leaders in the last decades of the charter period resulted in clashes within the elite. During the decade-long controversy over a second church, the rising merchant John Higginson Jr. and his more experienced colleagues Bartholemew Gedney, Edmund Batter and Nathaniel Putnam tried to maintain the old church as the single institution of the peninsula, while the Hathornes, Corwins, Browns, Prices and several merchants new to the town led the movement for division. When anxiety over the charter erupted soon after the struggle over the church had subsided, the leaders were again divided. This time William Brown sided with Bartholemew Gedney, and both were rejected by the voters after the restoration of the charter in favor of Jonathan Corwin and John Price. Similarly, John Higginson and John Hathorne, who had led the opposing groups in the struggle over the church, and had turned down elections as selectman and deacon respectively in 1680, were nevertheless united in their desire to see the charter restored. Meanwhile, the meaning of leadership had been transformed by the changed nature of the population itself, exacerbated by the financial drains of King Philip's War; whoever was chosen by the ever dwindling electorate to serve in the town's highest office was confronted by management problems—over taxes and behavior primarily—which depersonalized the role of the selectmen.

The confusion of ideals among the second generation merchants and the suspension of the charter in 1684 opened the office to a new group of merchants. The sons of the earlier merchants could not build the record of service achieved by their fathers which had been based on the covariation in symbols of status, a shared view of the good of the whole, and personal assumption of the financial burdens of the town—all complemented by primary relationships with the inhabitants in the course of their stewardship of the town's accounts. The qualities required after 1680 were quite different: the management of money according to highly impersonal criteria, the coercion of taxpaying and "good behavior" through third parties, and appealing successfully to the county courts and the colony officers for additional authority when necessary. Only 4 of the 10 selectmen elected for the first time between 1680 and 1689 were church members, and Israel Porter joined after he had served 4 terms in office.[23] The status of prominent fathers, long term residents all, did not automatically guarantee their sons a similar role. Three men were first elected in 1685 and 1686 who had not grown up in Salem or arrived in the pre-1640 immigrations, defeating men with last names of Higginson, Putnam, Gardner, Batter, Brown, Corwin and Porter—with only John Price among the sons of former leaders consistently achieving reelection. The history of service to the town by the leading families of the middle decades and membership in the church did not sway the voters after the earlier symbols of status had been dissociated from both wealth and leadership. The sons of earlier leaders who were reelected, all but Price sporadically through the period, shared the responsibilities of the selectman's office with new merchants like William Hirst and Timothy Lindall, and the successful builder Daniel Andrew, all of whom arrived in Salem after 1660. Wealth had become the only shared characteristic of the men who were elected to the town's highest office.

Into this matrix of merchants, who shared nothing but their private economic pursuits, the Putnams of the Village reinserted themselves in 1689. Released from the town watch in 1670 and the maintenance of the town ministry in 1672, the Villagers had continued to pay full town rates for all services and public works except the ministry, for which they were assessed one-half the normal amount.[24] Their subsequent petitions for full separation of Village church and government had gone unanswered.[25] Lt. Thomas Putnam, who had initiated the Putnam presence on the board of selectmen in 1665, died in 1686; but his brother Nathaniel who had followed him in office in 1666 through 1668 was still alive, and still chafing under the dominance of the Town. So was his brother John, who had been elected for six terms between 1668 and 1681. With the exception of John Putnam's term in 1681, the Putnams had been absent from the board of selectmen for over a decade, but they took advantage of the general unrest over taxation and the charter, and the divisions among the merchants of the peninsula, and succeeded in reelecting both Nathaniel and John in 1689.[26] Their resistance to the leadership of the Town had been quiescent during the years of King Philip's War, but certainly contributed to the difficulty the constables experienced both during and after that period in collecting taxes in the Village. Their renewed political participation in the form of the elections of John and Nathaniel Putnam to the board in 1689 precipitated another crisis in leadership. Both Israel Porter and his brother-in-law Daniel Andrew who had also been elected refused to serve with the Putnam brothers; they were joined in their refusal by Jonathan Corwin and Timothy Lindall. Only Edward Flint, a yeoman of middling income— and one of the few of that occupation who continued to live on the peninsula—consented to serve the term to which he had been elected.[27] The gulf between Porters and Putnams was deep by 1689, so the refusal of Andrews and Porter can be explained in those terms; the reasons of Lindall and Corwin, both merchants of the peninsula, are less clear, but their feelings were not shared by at least four other merchants of the Town who were elected in their stead: John Higginson, John Price, and Samuel and Thomas Gardner. Again, the merchants appear to have been divided on one of the basic issues of the town in the last decades of the colonial period, the status of the Village, and again the breach did not correspond to divisions over other major issues among the merchants, since Higginson and Lindall had opposed the second church while Price and Corwin had promoted it and the Gardners had stayed out of the conflict despite the fact that they were the only ones from the East End of the Town where the new meetinghouse was to be located.

Having engineered their reelection in 1689, the Putnams lost no time in resuming their earlier campaign for autonomy for the Village. While the church members of the Village successfully petitioned for the right to form their own fully covenanted church that year and adopted a covenant which demonstrated the deep differences over polity which had underlaid their struggles with the Salem church since 1667,[28] the Putnam brothers attempted to get the question of full township status on the agenda of the town meeting. Finally, one month before their terms expired, a town meeting was called to discuss the town rates, which had not been collected for nearly two years; after both voting down the rates of 1688 and refusing to set new ones, the town meeting "voted that the request of our neighbors of the Village is referred unto the next general town meeting then to be agitated."[29] The question "whether our neighbors of the Village should be a township of themselves" was indeed raised at the following meeting, but it was "voted in the negative."[30] The farmers of the

Village would continue to be disappointed in their quest for greater autonomy from the commercial town until 1752, when the provincial government finally acquiesced in the nearly 100 year old request. Elections for selectmen were also on the agenda of the meeting in which the Villagers' request was denied. Now alerted to the intentions of the farmers, the electorate of 1690 retained John Putnam, but his brother Nathaniel was not reelected. Village representation on the board was reduced to a minority of one.

In its early years, the town of Salem had actively encouraged the separation of distinct groups from the peninsula; when the attempt to settle Wenham failed in 1638, the selectmen tried again in 1642, and the establishment of Beverly as late as 1667 fit the consistent pattern of accommodating the wishes of outlying precincts in a peaceful manner. By the time the Village had achieved sufficient coherence to mount a serious effort to achieve a similar resolution, however, the town of Salem had changed dramatically from the town when inclusion and accommodation had been the rule. Not only was the Village the town's only remaining agricultural precinct—an important consideration for an increasingly commercial town which could not hope any longer to provide for its own food needs—but its petitions also were delivered when the town was preoccupied with the possibility of division with the church, increasing resistance to taxation, and finally charter problems. The continuing ties many of the merchant-leaders had to the Village through their own land holdings there probably strengthened the resistance of this group of Townsmen to the requests for more autonomy from the Villagers. By 1689, the financial status of the town was sufficient reason to turn down the farmers' petition. Between 1683 and 1689, the population of the two constables' wards west of the town bridge had increased by nearly a third, while the peninsula wards actually decreased slightly.[31] While the town was finally willing to separate the Village church from its own— partly from exasperation over the conflicts within the Village which the Salem church had been unable to resolve—and therefore release the farmers from the costs of refurbishing the Salem meetinghouse in 1690, they could not afford to do more. The timing of the Villagers' request to coincide with the controversy over the town rate was unfortunate, and certainly did not help their cause.

If earlier decisions about the precincts had been based on principles of accommodation, by 1689 most decisions in the town of Salem were based on money, which had become the medium of exchange for all of the town's civic interactions. Land, originally a tool for inclusion and consensus, had become a commodity of the marketplace as early as 1650, but after 1670 the voluntary services of the residents were also transformed by placing them on a monetary basis. It was not inconsistent, therefore, that at the same town meeting in which the farmers' request for township status was denied two new merchants were elected to the board of selectmen.

These new additions to the town's leadership typify the transformation of the criteria for leadership in Salem in the last years of the charter period. The elections of Daniel Andrews, Timothy Lindall, and William Hirst in 1685 and 1686 had already demonstrated that newcomers to the town could be elected to the town's highest office; while Lindall joined the church and became a freeman, neither of the other two men did, but all had developed strong ties to Salem's mercantile community.[32] The new selectmen elected immediately after the Glorious Revolution—Stephen Sewall and Benjamin Gerrish—were also latecomers to Salem, in 1681 and 1676 respectively. Both were merchants with economic and political connections which extended well beyond the boundaries of the town.[33] Gerrish had been appointed by the General Court to enforce the Navigations Acts in 1682, was subsequently appointed clerk of the county court by Governor Dudley, and was reappointed collector of the port by Andros in 1689. On his arrival in Salem, he married into one of the leading merchant families, and proceeded to buy commercial and rental property on the peninsula.[34] By 1689, he paid one of the highest taxes in the town of Salem. Stephen Sewall was born in England, moved to Newbury with his family in 1661, and settled in Salem in 1681. Like Gerrish, he received a number of commissions during the period of the suspension of the charter, and was clerk of the inferior court of common pleas and general sessions of the peace established by Andros. Indeed, in 1689 when Andros visited Salem to question those who opposed his commission as governor, Sewall was his escort.[35] He too began immediately on his arrival in Salem to purchase property on the peninsula for commercial purposes, and by 1689 paid one of the highest taxes in the town. Neither of them was hurt by his connection with Andros, as they were elected to Salem's highest office immediately after his removal. Both their wealth and their wider colonial contacts were sufficient reasons for the Salem electorate to choose these men to manage the affairs of the town. Wealth had become not a sign of godliness, but an assurance of the capacity to administer a complex commercial community.[36]

The Glorious Revolution in Salem caused a tax revolt, new divisions among the older leaders of the town, a renewal of the "agitation" from the leaders of the Village, and the emergence of a new group of merchants within the leadership of the town. None of these elements was totally new, but by 1689 they coalesced to redefine the community as a series of

distinct and often conflicting districts with a leadership group whose common interests did not extend beyond the advancement of commerce.

Just as the criteria for leadership changed, so also did the town bear
little resemblance to the nucleated, covenanted community of the first
generation.[37] The decline in church membership and freemanship, apparent after 1650, had continued in the last decades of the colonial period
despite a flurry of admissions to the church during the anxious years of
King Philip's War and Higginson's consistent efforts to open the church.
While the proportion of church members in Salem had never exceeded
half of the heads of households, by 1683 it had fallen to 15.8%, and by
1689 a mere 12.2% of those who paid colony rates had joined the church.
There were even fewer freemen; 48 taxpayers in 1689, or 8.7% of the
total, had adopted the seal of the federal covenant. Only seven men from
the first generation who had acquired access to both the sacraments of
the church and full political participation remained as heads of households; the attrition of the only generation in Salem which had held the
seals of the covenants to be inseparable was nearly complete by 1689.
After the separation of the Village church, which removed another 17 men
from the Salem church rolls, there were only 50 men left in the church
whose unity Higginson had fought so doggedly to preserve.

Despite the attrition of the first generation and the removal of the Villagers from Constable Putnam's ward to form their own church, there
still remained some correlation between church membership and wealth
as the provincial period of Salem's history began.

**Percentage of Taxpayers in Each Bracket who were
Church Members or Freemen**

1689 Tax, in Pence	Church Members	Freemen	All
6-48	13.6%	9.1%	3.2%
50-60	6.3	4.6	50.0
62-84	12.9	7.1	18.2
86-120	28.9	21.1	19.0
132 and over	27.3	27.3	9.6
All Taxpayers:	12.2%	8.7%	100.0%

The same, although weaker, correlation held for freemanship. Virtually
all of the major landowners of 1650, and all of the minimal majority of
1640, had joined the church—and those in the latter group had been
freemen and town leaders as well—but by 1689 only 9 of the 33 wealthiest
men in Salem could take communion with the church, and before the end
of the year 2 of them had withdrawn to form the Village church.[38] The
covariation of wealth, church membership and leadership which had been
nearly inviolate during the hegemony of the merchants in the middle

decades of the century could not be sustained by the seven men who remained in Salem after 1689. While 4 of them were elected to the board of selectmen after that date,[39] they were joined by 15 others during the first decade of the provincial period who were not members of the church. The men who represented the model of the first generation had become a saving remnant. (See Appendix C, Table III.)

The consequences of dispersion and differentiation, seen as positive elements of the policy of accommodation by the early town leaders, can also be seen in the occupational distribution of the town's residents in the tax lists of 1689. Over 100 occupational titles were used by the colonists of Salem, which may be broadly grouped as agricultural, artisan, merchant, mariner, and "other";[40] despite differences among these groups in rates of immigration and removal during the colonial period, there was no significant difference in their representation in the population in 1637 and 1689:

Occupation	1637	1689	All Immigrants, 1626-1689
Agricultural	22.6%	23.7%	23.4%
Artisans	47.0	45.5	37.3
Merchants	6.1	7.7	8.2
Mariners	20.0	20.5	25.6
Other	4.3	2.6	5.5
	100.0%	100.0%	100.0%

From these figures it is also clear that the artisans had the highest retention rate, while mariners were most likely to move from Salem. However, continued immigration and natural increase balanced removals and deaths within the ranks of each of the major occupational groups during the charter period.

While the representation of various occupational groups remained remarkably stable, their dispersion into different neighborhoods was built into Salem's earliest land policies. By 1689, this pattern of settlement had resulted in the creation of clear distinctions in occupational distribution among the six wards of the town. The fishermen, mariners and seamen continued to be set apart from the rest of the population, as they had been since Marblehead and Winter Island were reserved for them in the 1630s, but now they concentrated in addition in the southeastern quadrant of the peninsula itself. The few seamen who lived in the west end of the peninsula had all arrived in Salem after 1670, demonstrating the crowded conditions in the eastern harbor ward by that time. On the whole, men who earned their living from the sea were as clearly demarcated from the rest of the population as they ever had been, but they now lived closer to those from whom they were nevertheless differentiated.[41]

	Agriculture	Artisans	Merchants	Mariners
East End				
Becket	4.2%	7.2%	14.3%	54.7%
Curtice	1.4	18.9	23.8	26.4
West End				
Derby	5.5	19.8	19.0	5.7
Pickering	5.6	27.1	38.1	7.5
Beyond Bridge				
Trask	33.3	13.5	0.0	3.8
Putnam	50.0	13.5	4.8	1.9
	100.0%	100.0%	100.0%	100.0%

The presence of increasing numbers of seamen on the peninsula was a matter of concern to the very merchants whose increasing prosperity depended on this segment of the Salem community; in 1689, Bartholemew Gedney, John Hathorne, and both William Brown Jr. and his brother Benjamin, went to a meeting of the selectmen to urge that the watch, enlarged by the Quarterly Court the previous year to eight men on the request of the selectmen, be again increased. While the routine of the earlier watches was to be maintained elsewhere within the peninsula, they decided that two men among the augmented watch were "constantly to walk on the Neck."[42] The separation of those who made their living from the sea was furthered by the daily pattern of life within the peninsula; while the seamen, mariners and fishermen would have reason to leave their immediate residential neighborhood to do business with the artisans who were concentrated to the north and west of them and to attend services in the meetinghouse, others would have little reason to frequent the neighborhood inhabited by the seamen.

The farmers, yeomen, and husbandmen were as clearly set apart in their own neighborhoods beyond the town bridge in the Village, on Ryal Side, and at Brooksby. Only a dozen farmers remained on the peninsula, most of them in the two western wards; a few fields remained in the areas between the meetinghouse and the bridge, and three men continued to farm on the North Neck where the Old Planters had originally sown their crops in 1626, but they were greatly outnumbered by their artisan and merchant neighbors. In the two wards west of the town bridge, the situation was reversed: the farmers outnumbered men of all other occupations combined by nearly two to one.

The merchants of course found their natural neighborhood in the peninsula; only one man who lived west of the bridge called himself a merchant, and he was taxed at the lower end of the scale in 1689. Within the wards of the peninsula, however, the merchants were distributed according to patterns of arrival in Salem. Only the Gardners among the merchants in Becket's ward—the one in which seamen outnumbered all other occupations combined by better than two to one—had arrived in Salem prior to 1674, while those who were clustered around the meetinghouse in the western wards included some more recent arrivals but also the sons of earlier residents.

The artisans were the most numerous occupational group in Salem throughout the colonial period, totalling 43.3% of those whose manner of earning a living is known in 1689. Within this broad category, however, the beginnings of clear neighborhood distinctions can be seen. Three-quarters of the artisans in the wards west of the bridge were engaged in trades which required a large investment of capital and resulted in the production of heavy goods—sawyers, masons, millers, and blacksmiths—while the "light" artisans, including such trades as glovemaking, tailoring, and pewter casting, were concentrated in the wards north of Essex Street, most of them in the western end of the peninsula. Those whose trades were closely associated with the sea—ship carpenters, coopers, and sailmakers—together with men in the building trades (glaziers, house carpenters, and turners) contributed to the concentration of artisans in the western ward on the harbor which by 1689 contained the largest number of artisans of all kinds. Thus the only ward within the peninsula in which few artisans appeared was the harbor area where most of the seamen lived. The beginnings of a district of retail shops had appeared in the area north of the main street of town, while the men whose trades supported commerce bought or built houses closer to the harbor. By 1689 the needs of the merchants had transformed the appearance of the town; they had built their wharves and warehouses along the South River, attracting to these neighborhoods the men who made their living from the sea and sea-related trades.[43] While the merchants themselves were still primarily concentrated in the area around the meetinghouse, the nucleated village of 1636 had long since ceased to be a reality.

If the various occupational groups in Salem were distinguished by their choice of residence by the end of the colonial period, they were also differentiated by wealth. The tax lists are not a reliable indicator of absolute economic standing, since the assets of merchants could not be viewed and rated in the same way that the acreage of a farmer or the tools of an artisan could be evaluated. The result was a highly regressive system of taxation in which the wealth of the merchants was certainly underrated, as can be seen from a comparison of the distribution of rates in 1689 with the distribution of wealth revealed by wills probated between 1660 and 1681:[44]

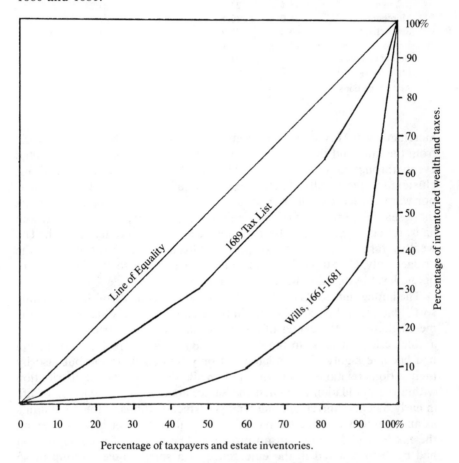

Percentage of taxpayers and estate inventories.

Since the wealth of the merchants was increasing compared to that of other segments of the population, the inequality revealed by the wills had probably increased among those who were taxed in 1689.[45] With this caveat, the tax lists can be used as a general indicator of the relative economic welfare of the inhabitants in that year.

Each occupational group had a distinct pattern of distribution across the range of tax brackets. The seamen and sea artisans had the highest proportion of taxpayers in the lowest ranges, while the merchants were by far the most likely to be rated at the highest level. Mobility was still a salient fact of life for both groups, however, as a number of ship carpenters by 1689 had risen to positions of wealth while one-quarter of the

Occupation	6-50	52-72	75-120	132-600 (pence)
Agricultural	24.3	32.4	33.8	9.5 = 100.0%
Seamen	48.4	23.4	23.5	4.7
Merchants	25.0	12.5	20.8	41.7
Sea Artisans	46.2	26.9	15.4	11.5
Heavy Artisans	22.9	37.1	37.1	2.9
Building Trades	31.4	31.4	28.6	8.6
Light Artisans	21.7	60.9	13.0	4.3
All Occupations	31.7	34.0	25.6	9.6 = 100.0%

merchants were taxed at the bottom of the range. Men who made a living from the land and those involved in the building trades were distributed evenly throughout the tax scale, while both "heavy" and "light" artisans clustered in the middle. The concentration of seamen in the eastern harbor ward caused that district to have the lowest average tax; but among these seamen lived some of the wealthiest merchants, nearly all of whom had arrived in Salem in the final decades of the colonial period. The wealthy farmers with one exception all lived in the wards west of the bridge; only Constable Pickering himself had risen to the highest economic level by farming within the peninsula.

The immigrants to Salem in the 1630s had been mostly of the "middling sort," had built their first houses in the area immediately surrounding the meetinghouse in the center of the peninsula, and had started to farm the arable acreage nearest to the peninsula. By 1689, the residents of Salem had become highly differentiated not only by neighborhood but also by their various relationships to the land. While the occupational distribution within the population remained the same, another of the features of life in early Salem—universal landowning—which had bound the inhabitants as an organic whole had been dramatically altered. Over half the men on the tax lists of 1689 owned no property. The failure of accommodation had by 1650 resulted in the emergence of a small landless group of 45 men, but by 1689 there were 76 men who owned no property in Constable Becket's ward alone. Only in Pickering's ward, which encompassed the land around the west harbor south of the main street as far as the town bridge, did the proportion of men who owned no property and had no hope of inheriting any also exceed one-quarter of the residents. (See Appendix B, Map 5.) Thus, the largest proportion of inhabitants in the tenant class of the town resided in its harbor wards; men who rented or leased property from others in these two wards alone accounted for over half (52.4%) of the landless within the limits of Salem in 1689. All but one of the farmers and all of the merchants in these wards owned property, but the seamen and artisans who lived along the harbor were not tied by

Landownership Among Taxpayers of 1689

	No Land, and None in Family	No Land, but Land in Family	Owned Land	Total
East End				
Becket	53.4%	11.0%	35.6%	100.0%
Curtice	28.6	27.4	44.0	
West End				
Derby	25.3	29.1	45.6	
Pickering	33.3	11.8	54.9	
Beyond Bridge				
Trask	25.6	23.2	51.2	
Putnam	25.0	27.9	47.1	
All Wards:	33.6%	21.4%	45.0%	100.0%

landowning to the commercial town for which they provided vital services.

The density of the population in the harbor wards by 1689 made it more difficult for newcomers to find their own accommodation in the town.

	Born in Salem	Arrived by 1650	By 1683	After 1683
No land, but land in family	79.4%	66.7%	3.5%	6.4%
No land, and none in family	20.6	33.3	96.5	93.6
	100.0%	100.0%	100.0%	100.0%

Most of those who had some reason to expect to inherit land had grown up in Salem or had arrived by 1650, while 83.8% of those without similar expectations had immigrated to Salem after the midpoint of the century. Within the farming areas beyond the bridge, three-quarters of the taxpayers in 1689 had some tie to the land, either their own or their fathers', but among the residents of Becket's ward the ratio was reversed. Distinguished by their low rate of church membership throughout the colonial period—12.1% compared to 22.5% of those of known occupation—their low level of taxpaying, and their clear consignment to the eastern wards of the peninsula, the seamen of Salem were a class apart from the general population. Among the farms, mobility was limited for one-quarter of the residents by the lack of land, while another quarter was dependent on their fathers—and in some cases grandfathers—for access to an agricultural livelihood. When the division of lands did occur, it would mean a reduction in the relative economic standing of those who remained during the next generation and the beginnings of migration to the interior of the colony where land was still available for others.[47]

Those who did own land in 1689, only 45% of the taxpayers, had accumulated their holdings in ways which further intensified the distinctions among neighborhoods and occupational groups. The merchants, always the largest landowning group in Salem, continued to invest in this stable commodity. While some in the later decades of the colonial period may have been motivated in their acquisition of arable acreage by the models provided by successful London merchants of the time, who bought large estates in hopes of moving into the ranks of the "gentlemen" from their status as tradesmen, all were attracted by the stability of wealth represented by land—wealth which could be passed from father to son, unlike the business of the merchants itself which was based on their own personal reputations and contacts in England, and on ships which occasionally sank.[48] Land was thus the basis of a stable income. Tenants could easily be found among the landless one-quarter of the men who lived among the farms; so also could they be found among the artisans and seamen of the peninsula, so the merchants bought and built houses as income property as well.

The merchants of course stood out among the purchasers of land in Salem, but clear distinctions emerge even between lesser occupational groups. Only 2 of the light artisans bought houses south of Essex Street, while the seamen who purchased residential property did just the opposite: only 6 of the 26 mariners who eventually became homeowners lived north of that natural dividing line which ran the length of the peninsula from the bridge to the neck. Among the artisans, 41% supplemented these purchases with some arable acreage, while only 7% of the seamen added farmland to their holdings. Many of the artisans thus continued to practice the kind of subsistence farming which had typified their existence in the early decades, while the mariners were clearly a part of a purely commercial enterprise. The artisans had several advantages over the seamen as purchasers of land: more of them were sons of Salem residents, they accumulated the necessary capital for their purchases at an earlier age, and they continued to buy property later in the period than the seamen, who were victims of an increasingly tight market.[49] Half of the artisans living in Salem in 1689 had acquired a house by the age of 25, but only a quarter of the seamen had sufficient capital by that time. Even at the lower levels of the economic hierarchy, men of different occupational groups led lives that bore little resemblance to each other.

The patterns of immigration to Salem after the Restoration show that

Salem was increasingly attractive to merchants and those whose occupations supported mercantile development—seamen and artisans with direct connections to trade—and less so to farmers and other kinds of artisans.

Percentage of Each Occupational Group Arriving in Three Generations

Occupation	Arrived 1624-1640	1641-60	1661-89	Total
Agriculture	45.0%	29.5%	25.6%	100.0%
Seamen	30.9	20.0	49.1	
Merchants	36.1	22.2	41.7	
Artisans	50.0	18.8	31.2	
All Occupations	44.3%	21.0%	34.7%	100.0%

The merchants among the latecomers quickly bought property in Salem, but the seamen did not, which may have contributed to their higher level of transience. Only one half of the taxpayers in the eastern harbor ward in 1683 were still on the rolls in 1689, a far lower percentage than for any other ward. Despite the more rapid growth in the farm wards, they had the highest rate of persistence during the last decade of the colonial period. The decrease in taxpayers in the east end of the peninsula, far from indicating a decline either in the number of seamen or the importance of mercantile development, showed that these neighborhoods were too crowded in 1683 to accommodate all who were there, some of whom moved to the less densely populated west end by 1689.[50]

Mobility and Persistence[51]

Ward	# of Taxpayers in 1683	# of Taxpayers in 1689	% on Both Lists
East End			
English/Becket	140	125	50.0%
Phelps/Curtice	99	90	73.7
West End			
Lambert/Derby	73	83	64.4
Hirst/Pickering	84	94	64.3
Beyond Bridge			
Hayward/Trask	67	89	74.6
Pope/Putnam	83	109	78.3%

The high turnover in the eastern wards meant that the socialization of new residents, given the fragmentation of the town's central institutions, would be substantially different from the experience of immigrants during the period of accommodation and inclusion. The increase in population in the farm wards shows the difficulties faced by second-generation residents of these wards as well by the end of the colonial period. One half of these taxpayers owned no land in 1689, due primarily to the number of children of the second generation who were coming to maturity—and to landlessness—in a precinct that had reached its limits to growth.

Despite the pressure for land in the farm wards, they accounted for an increasing share of the taxes paid in Salem, a further reason for the reluctance of the Town to separate the Village from its tax rolls. The colony taxes assessed in 1689 were 2½ rates—five times the rate charged in 1683; by adjusting the rates to an equivalent base, the changing relative economic position of the various wards can be seen.[52]

Ward	1683 Rate x 5			1689 Rates		% Change	% Pop. Change
	Lbs.	Shs.	Pence	Lbs.	Shs.		
East End							
English/Becket	32	10		25	00	−23.1	−10.7
Phelps/Curtice	27	10		25	00	− 9.1	− 9.1
West End							
Lambert/Derby	31	5		21	00	−32.8	+13.7
Hirst/Pickering	27	5		26	00	− 4.6	+11.9
Beyond Bridge							
Hayward/Trask	20	16	8[d]	22	00	+ 5.6	+32.8
Pope/Putnam	25	00		31	00	+24.0	+31.3

The average tax per person went down in every ward but Curtice's in the six years of royal governorship at the end of the colonial period. Still, the farmers were paying an increasing share of Salem's taxes, which was a major reason for the resistance the Putnams experienced as they led the drive for more autonomy for the Village. In the peninsula wards, the average tax declined, but the reduction was not equally shared. While some made a marginal living, the merchants continued to increase their share of Salem's wealth.

The inhabitants of Salem by 1689 formed clearly differentiated subgroups characterized by visible distinctions in neighborhood, occupation, mobility, and participation in the town's central institutions. Each of these distinctions must have been equally discernable to the residents of the peninsula in 1689, all of whom were removed from regular interaction with the farmers beyond the bridge by that date as well. Some elements of the earlier pattern of settlement still remained as a vestige of an organic community within the peninsula. Sixty-three men continued to meet as proprietors of the South Field, a group consisting primarily of artisans and merchants who lived in the west end of the town—its traditional center.[53] Nearly all were sons of the earliest immigrants to whom these openfield plots had been allocated in the initial division of land. Only 10 men bought into the South Field group after 1640, so the number of native sons among the proprietors was double their proportion of the population as a whole in 1689. These men who gathered annually to make decisions about crops, dates for grazing of animals in the fall, and other traditional business of open field life were a small and familiar group, bound by several generations of mutual experience. The common field proprietors and the members of the church were the only groups still practicing consensual politics by the end of the charter period. There was no basis for a wider practice of mutual pursuit of common ends within the town itself, since the earlier symbols of authority had been disassociated from leadership, and the limits of inclusion in the land system and the town's central institutions on which the voluntarism of an earlier age had rested had long since been exceeded.

The meaning of the land itself had changed. Where once it had marked each man's place in a Puritan hierarchy, land use patterns now labelled roles in a commercial town. The remaining open field farmers felt the need to manage their own affairs instead of leaving it to the selectmen to appoint their surveyors; the North Field group, which had won the right to select their own in 1684 subject to the approval of the selectmen, did not bother to turn in the names of their choices in 1689.[54] Among the farmers beyond the bridge, land holdings were still a reliable indicator of status and prestige, but only 30% of the assets of the merchants were made visible in the landscape by the end of the charter period due to the increase of shipping and other commercial ventures.[55]

The meaning of wealth had also been altered, both for those who had none and for those who were at the pinnacle of economic success. In the early nucleated village, each resident could expect to make some contribution to the good of the whole. All were maintained above the level of subsistence, and those who fell below that line were given assistance in forms which helped to bring them back to economic health—a few more acres of land, or a cow. By 1689 these measures could no longer be sustained for a new class among whom poverty was not a temporary condition. The town meeting expected to hear each year that rates for the poor were needed—in amounts that exceeded the total town tax of the 1660s.

At the other end of the scale, 35 men paid more than 10s. in the colonial assessment of 1689, representing just under 6% of the taxpayers. These were the men to whom the town would naturally look for leadership:

Ward	Agriculture	Merchant	Artisan	Seaman
East End				
Becket		4	1	1
Curtice		3		2
West End				
Derby		4	1	
Pickering	1	5	1	
Beyond Bridge				
Trask	2		1	
Putnam	7			
	10	16	4	3

With the exception of Constable Pickering, all of the wealthy farmers lived in the wards west of the town bridge, seven of them in the Village. The merchants were not only spread throughout the districts of the Town, but those who had arrived in Salem since 1660 paid higher taxes than the men who had grown up in the town. Of the five men who paid over a pound, all were merchants, and three had immigrated since 1674. These newcomers, whose "guiding principles were not social stability, order, and the discipline of the senses, but mobility, growth, and the enjoyment of life,"[56] had stood completely outside the political life of the town before the suspension of the charter in 1684. Salem, unlike Boston, was spared the conflict over the establishment of an Anglican church during the Andros administration,[57] but these new merchants still provided a new model of economic success for the sons of Salem's early merchant-leaders. While anti-commercial sermons still issued from the pulpit of the Salem church, they saw a new group of merchants recently arrived in Salem whose wealth exceeded their own and whose views of the social order differed markedly from those of their fathers. Already divided over the church and the status of the Village, the sons of the earlier leaders were also divided over the challenge to "good order" presented by the most successful of the new immigrants. Some, like William Brown and Bartholemew Gedney, joined with the new merchants in urging the withdrawal of the charter, which they saw as a means of furthering their business interests, while others held fast to the view that the overthrow of Andros was essential to restore the tie between church and state which was the basis of the social covenant.

Just as the Putnams had taken advantage of these divisions within what had been for decades a stable leadership group, so also did some of the new merchants rise to political roles commensurate with their economic prominence in the town after 1684.[58] William Hirst and Timothy Lindall, both among the top taxpayers in 1689, were the first to be elected in 1685, but for the next few years the board was still composed primarily of men with names more familiar in the town—Gardner, Higginson, Price and Gedney. A merchant like Philip English, who first appeared in Salem in 1665 and by 1689 was among the top five taxpayers, could be elected as constable by 1683, but not as selectman.[59]

By 1689 it was clear that the wealthiest men in Salem were not a homogeneous group. Some were farmers promoting the autonomy of their own precinct, others were members of the second and third generation whose interests diverged over the issues of the 1670s and 1680s, and still others were an entirely new kind of merchant whose economic success had not yet provided them access to the major leadership positions of the town. This last group turned instead to the cultivation of wider colonial contacts which not only furthered their business interests, but also led to commissions by the royal governor with political implications for the town.[60] The Glorious Revolution caused the realignment of leadership and wealth in Salem, as the way was cleared for these men to assume their place in the town's civic institutions as well. With their proven talents as shrewd managers, and given their connections to higher political authorities increasingly needed to buttress the powers of the local selectmen as they attempted to collect taxes and regulate behavior, these merchants could provide the kind of management needed in the highly differentiated town. Whatever definition unity received at the hands of the new merchants and the farmers and older merchants with whom they served would be based strictly on shared economic goals. The correlation of wealth and political power was reaffirmed, but money had become an urban symbol instead of a visible sign of the seals of the covenants, and political involvement was motivated by the desire for economic growth rather than by the concern of the few for the good of the many.

The meetinghouse itself, center of the early town, had a new meaning by 1689. Church seating, once as reliable as land in indicating the position of each inhabitant within the community, demonstrated instead the disjunction between economic and religious standards of success. The selectmen of 1689, after choosing the fence surveyors for the year as they had done for decades, ordered that their names be "set on the meetinghouse," which was still a prominent landmark.[61] But the meetinghouse was no longer in the middle of the population center, which had moved east toward the harbor, and the church it contained was no longer central to the functioning of the town. Gathered weekly within its bolted doors, the inhabitants heard jeremiads reminding them that they were not what God had intended his transplants to New England to become, and that "good order" was no longer to be found in Salem.

At the end of his third decade in the Salem pulpit and on the eve of the restoration of the charter in 1690, Reverend John Higginson could look back over 60 years of Salem's history and reflect on the changes in the little community whose church he had struggled to maintain as a pillar of unity. As a boy of 15, he had joined in the original church covenant of 1629, and knew something of the town in which that fledgling church took shape. As an old man of 76, he was a practiced preacher of jeremiads against what that community had become.

The original definition of community in Salem which emerged from the Massachusetts Bay Company's instructions, the church covenant, and the pattern of land distribution, included several key elements. This was to be a nucleated town in which every inhabitant held some stake in the land. While a diversity of economic pursuits was evident from these earliest years, each householder's allotment of land marked his place in a single hierarchy. Inclusiveness was the goal of the early policies of accommodation, but it was expected that those at the top of this hierarchy would be church members and would take on the burdens of leadership for the new community, and these expectations were met. This single ranking, made visible in the landscape, not only prescribed deference patterns for all members of the community but also inextricably linked wealth with godliness and leadership. The standards for inclusion were generous: accommodation into the town was open to all who were "peaceable men, and of honest life and conversation, and desirous to live amongst us and conform themselves to good order and government," while entrance to the smaller community of the church required only the additional agreement to "walk together" in the ways of God—ways which were not specified.[62] Separation of different occupational subgroups of the population was a natural consequence of this willingness to accommodate heterogeneity, as open field farmers needed house lots in the town and strips in nearby fields while the open field farmers could take up larger farms further from the town center, and the fishermen could be expected to pursue their livelihoods on a rocky peninsula not suitable for farming. This degree of dispersion and specialization was not seen as a threat to the unity of the town, since a single hierarchy bound all of its parts into a clearly articulated whole which was firmly centered on the peninsula and its church. As the Old Planters moved to their capacious farms on Cape Ann Side, they were issued instructions to keep up their bridges and roads in order to maintain their connection with the town center, but their removal from the peninsula was not, at least initially, seen as a threat to the unity of the town.

The little community thus had both an ideological basis for unity, and a strong faith in the power of a single hierarchy reflected in the landscape.

In retrospect, this faith seems misplaced. The consolidation of the interests of the Beverly planters by the end of the first generation was only a harbinger of future coalitions which would emerge in other areas, even within neighborhoods of the peninsula itself by the end of the charter period. The ideological unity of the town was further weakened by the incursions of Quakers in the years just before Higginson returned to Salem as its new minister in 1660.

The town Higginson found as a man of 46 was considerably different from the one he had left as a youth. The continuing dispersion and differentiation of the population in the intervening years had resulted in the emergence of a small group of centrally located merchants as the early undisputed leaders of the town. As symbols of the original conception of the community they were virtually ideal: wealthy, godly, and holding land in all sectors of the town, they were the natural group to turn to for leadership to reinforce the ideological unity of the community. The numbers of landless men, together with the rising number of self-made men whose wealth was not translated into leadership, strained the original assumptions about the nature of the community, but the merchants' land still stood as an effective symbol of the earlier model.

As Higginson adapted church policy in a vain attempt to restore the church to its former function as an all-inclusive, unifying institution of the community, the selectmen went about the business of the town in ways which reinforced their primary contacts with its inhabitants. In the end, neither effort to hold the community together could succeed. The centrifugal forces set in motion in the original dispersion and differentiation of the population resulted in clear neighborhood distinctions inimical to the concept of a unitary community. Outlying districts wanted their own representatives in positions of power in the town and won the right to manage many of their own affairs within their precincts; the seals of the covenants—freemanship and church membership—were more appealing to some subgroups than to others, with the result that status within each area depended on one or another but not both, thereby destroying the old ideals of a single hierarchy.

The strains within the old order were fully apparent by the 1670s, and were exacerbated by King Philip's War, the renewal of immigration from England, and the retirement of the major leaders of the middle decades from office. Expensive public works commissioned by these leaders had only resulted in heightened resistance from various neighborhoods to these obvious attempts to reassert the centrality of the peninsula as a unifying principle for the town.

While Higginson preached his jeremiads and succeeded in preventing divisions of the church, the generation of leaders who took up the task of managing the town's affairs only succeeded in altering the function of leadership. New layers of administration were added within each precinct, and the primary ties of the selectmen with the community as a whole virtually ceased. Salem had become a collection of neighborhoods with functional economic interrelationships, held together by a formal political apparatus, whose leaders recognized the primacy of the precincts by assigning all duties involving face-to-face contacts to secondary officials who lived in the neighborhoods they served. The town was still nominally centered on the peninsula, but outlying districts had their own meeting-houses, burial grounds, militia companies, and public servants in the form of constables, fence surveyors, tithingmen, and a host of others. This reinforcement of neighborhood distinctiveness added to the already obvious differences between various areas, especially the separability of the seals of the covenants for various subgroups, and the clear occupational specializations within particular geographic areas. Even within the peninsula, the life of a mariner was quite different from that of an artisan, and both were easily distinguishable from farmers or merchants. Rates of mobility, patterns of landowning, ages at which landowning became possible, average degrees of wealth, and decisions to become freemen or church members, all varied within occupational subgroups identified with particular areas; if these differences show up clearly in charts made by twentieth-century historians, they must have been powerful social facts on a daily basis for the inhabitants of Salem in the late seventeenth century. With the organic unity of the town envisioned in 1629 transformed into purely formal bonds by the end of the charter period, the leaders of both church and town gave up any hope of basing their community on the covariation of land, leadership and godliness, and instead turned back to the one remaining instrument of cohesion which remained from the original social theory: the reform and control of individual behavior. The proliferation of orders about the constables' watch (and the dramatic increase in numbers of men assigned to this duty), the creation of a new host of tithingmen to watch over families, and the language of the final church covenant of the charter period which emphasizes the reform of individual behavior and hints at a better order in another world, all evidence a frenetic attempt to pin the community's hopes for unity not on the town or even on its neighborhoods, but on the smallest of social units—families and individuals. The original social theory of Salem, which assumed broadly acceptable standards of behavior among the general populace and emphasized the symbols of hierarchy as a unifying device was reduced to an insistence on strict adherence to Puritan standards of behavior. No alternative social theory was available, which might have made sense of the pluralism which was manifest within the town by the end of the charter period.

The absence of new principles of coherence was evident in the conflicts over the church as well. Those who opposed the creation of a second church on the peninsula acted according to the old style of leadership: they were "the few," acting on behalf of what they hoped were "the many." They made no attempts to collect additional signatures from sympathizers, and argued that the old values of congruence between church and town should be maintained at all cost, values which they believed required them to act on behalf of the whole from their positions of preeminence. The proponents of a second church, on the other hand, wrote a document which was circulated among their supporters in an effort to sway the General Court to their point of view through sheer force of numbers. Nevertheless, the proponents held the same view of the ideal community as the old guard; the two groups differed only in the definition of the proper boundaries within which wealth, godliness and leadership would coalesce. The opponents were nostalgic for the time when the entire town could meet this criterion; the proponents wanted to subdivide the church in order to restore the unity of neighborhoods according to exactly the same standard. Neither group had available to it any new theory which might have rationalized the pluralism which actually existed in Salem. Thus, the controversy subsided; formal unity was maintained through coercion, and both town and church turned their attention to individual behavior as the only ground remaining for social coherence.

The Glorious Revolution cleared the way for a new breed of merchants to join the already fragmented leadership group of Salem, thereby realigning wealth with power in the board of selectmen. Restoring the church to its former position of preeminence in the community was not the major goal of these men, however, most of whom were not members themselves. Instead, they used their influence to promote the economic growth of the town, and of their precincts in particular. Good order would have to derive from their efforts to confine the behavior of individuals within acceptable standards, since there was no longer any larger ideological format shared by all precincts which could generate universal support for a single definition of community. The outbreak of witchcraft in the Village, the most dramatic efflorescence of social dissonance in colonial New England, just a few short months after the restoration of the charter in 1690 could thus not have occurred in a more likely setting. Aberrations in individual behavior had become the central concern in a town which for years had struggled to cope with increasing social divisions among its parts, divisions for which none of the groups could provide a satisfactory explanation in the terms of the old Puritan social theory derived from the practice of accommodation. The meaning of landownership, membership in the church, wealth, and the exercise of political power had been transformed; it would be the task of the next generation to provide a new definition of "good order."

Notes

Chapter One

1. Philip J. Greven, Jr., *Four Generations: Population, Land and Family in Colonial Andover, Massachusetts* (Ithaca: Cornell University Press, 1970); Sumner Chilton Powell, *Puritan Village: The Formation of a New England Town* (Middletown: Wesleyan University Press, 1964); John Demos, *A Little Commonwealth: Family Life in Plymouth Colony* (New York: Oxford University Press, 1970); Kenneth A. Lockridge, *A New England Town: The First Hundred Years* (New York: W.W. Norton & Co., 1970). A recent study of Salem confirms the pattern: Richard P. Gildrie, *Salem Massachusetts, 1626-1683: A Covenant Community* (Charlottesville: University Press of Virginia, 1975).

2. For examples of such boundary disputes with Beverly, Wenham and Salem Village, see *Records of the Governor and Company of the Massachusetts Bay in New England, 1628-1686*, Nathaniel B. Shurtleff ed. (5 volumes; Boston: William White, 1853-1854), vol. V, pp. 186, 208. Hereafter cited as *Mass. Bay Recs.*

3. Mr. Alford's 200-acre grant in 1636 was given "where it is allotted to him provided that in case he depart to leave it desiring no advantage by it." ("Town Records of Salem, Massachusetts, 1634-1659," *Essex Institute Historical Collections*, vol. IX [1868], p. 22. Hereafter cited as T.R. vol. I.)

4. *Ibid.*, p. 24.

5. 147 buyers were non-residents, constituting 9.3% of all sales.

6. T.R. vol. 1, p. 8.

7. *Salem Town Records, 1659-1680* (Salem: Essex Institute, 1913), pp. 7, 221. Hereafter cited as T.R. vol. II.

8. *Ibid.*, p. 61.

9. *Ibid.*

10. T.R. vol. I, pp. 201-2.

11. *Ibid.*, p. 209.

12. T.R. vol. II, p. 50; cases of two joiners hired by James Brown and Bartholemew Gedney.

13. *Ibid.*, p. 112.

14. *Ibid.*

15. Based on 778 household heads whose arrival dates are known. (50.9%) An additional 29.1% of the historical population were sons of immigrants. The arrival dates for the remainder (20%) are not known, but their retention rate of 94% fits the post-1650 arrival group.

16. Lockridge describes this process for Dedham, whose first residents had "taken up temporary residence in several of the earliest settlements along the shores of the Bay." *New England Town*, p. 3.

17. Adjusted for deaths (not counted).

18. Marblehead 8 (all in 1680s); Beverly 2; Lynn and Ipswich 1. Beverly was set off from Salem in 1667; Marblehead did not have its own church until 1684, but enjoyed a measure of independence before that time.

19. Bernard Bailyn, *New England Merchants in the Seventeenth Century* (Cambridge: Harvard University Press, 1955), pp. 135-38, 180. Bailyn overestimates this phenomenon for Salem based on his data for Boston. However, the rate of extralocal marriage after the Glorious Revolution rises dramatically in Salem: 1690-1710 = 22%, or 89 of 405 marriages. *Vital Records of Salem, Massachusetts, to the End of the Year 1849* (Salem: Essex Institute, 1916).

20. Bailyn, *New England Merchants,* p. 122.

21. Conrad M. Arensberg and Solon T. Kimball, *Culture and Community* (Gloucester, Mass.: Peter Smith, 1972), pp. 69-70; Arensberg defines "community" as bounded by space, time, and limits of kin systems. Also note that the large size of families helped to create very extensive in-law networks.

22. Despite the separation of new towns within the original boundaries, the population of Salem continued to increase throughout the charter period. By 1689, there were 590 men on the tax rolls—hence the maximum figure. However, some of these taxpayers were sons still living in their fathers' households, and therefore would not meet the criteria for the "historical population" of this study, which consisted of heads of households. The figure of 590 therefore sets a maximum limit for the historical population's greatest size of any point during the charter period.

23. John Higham. "Hanging Together: Divergent Unities in American History," *Journal of American History,* vol. LXI (June, 1974), p. 11.

24. Richard C. Beeman, "The New Social History and the Search for 'Community' in Colonial America," *American Quarterly,* vol. XXIX (Fall, 1977), pp. 432-33.

25. Robert Redfield, *The Little Community* (Chicago: The University of Chicago Press, 1960); see especially pp. 113-31. The similarity (or at least analogy) between Redfield's diachrony which proceeds from the horizontal to the vertical dimension and Higham's survey of American history which proceeds from the ideological ("a bedrock of order, purpose, and cohesion," *Ibid.*, p. 11) to the technical (with its emphasis on "impersonal, utilitarian, and functionally interlocking" relations which feature "interdependence," *Ibid.*, p. 19) should be noted.

26. Gildrie, p. 1, *et passim.*

Chapter Two

1. Two of the primary federal theorists in New England were John Cotton and Thomas Hooker; their role in the development of the social covenant is described in Perry Miller, *The New England Mind: The Seventeenth Century* (New York: The Macmillan Company, 1939). See especially pp. 398-431.

2. Darrett Rutman, *Husbandmen of Plymouth* (Boston: Beacon Press, 1967), pp. 4-7; Powell, *Puritan Village,* p. 74.

3. Sidney Perley, *History of Salem, Massachusetts* (Salem: Sidney Perley, 1924), vol. I, p. 83.

4. *Ibid.*

5. *Ibid.,* pp. 65-67.

6. *Ibid.,* pp. 94.

7. Edmund S. Morgan, ed., *The Founding of Massachusetts: Historians and the Sources* (New York: The Bobbs-Merrill Company, Inc., 1964), p. 454.

8. J.B. Felt, *Annals of Salem* (Salem: W. & S.B. Ives, 1845), vol. I, p. 149.

9. Morgan, *Founding,* p. 454.

10. *Ibid.*

11. John White, *The Planters Plea* (London: 1630), reprinted in *Proceedings of the Massachusetts Historical Society,* 3d. ser., 62 (Boston: 1929), pp. 378-79. Salem is the Hebrew word for peace.

12. Miller, *New England Mind,* p. 415; Edmund Morgan, *The Puritan Family; Religion and Domestic Relations in Seventeenth-Century New England* (New York: Harper and Row, Publishers, Inc., 1966), pp. 161-68.

13. Joan Thirsk, "The Family," *Past and Present,* vol. XXVI (April, 1964), pp. 116-22. See also Joan Thirsk, ed., *The Agrarian History of England and Wales, 1500-1640* (Cambridge: Cambridge University Press, 1967), vol. IV, pp. 9-12, 23-24, 48-49, 455-56.

14. Morgan, *Founding*, p. 454.

15. *Mass. Bay Recs.* vol. I, p. 43.

16. Morgan, *Founding*, p. 468.

17. Perley, vol. I, p. 310; *Mass. Bay Recs,* vol. I, pp. 43-44.

18. Morgan, *Founding*, pp. 474-75.

19. *Ibid.,* p. 468.

20. Perley, vol. I, p. 255.

21. T.R. vol. I, p. 8.

22. Perley, vol. I, p. 255.

23. T.R. vol. I, pp. 34-35; J.B. Felt, vol. I, pp. 184-87. See Appendix B, Map 2.

24. Wood, *New England's Prospect* (London: Printed by T. Cotes for I. Bellamie, 1634; Boston: Printed for the Society, 1865).

25. T.R. vol. I, p. 28. See Appendix B, Map 2.

26. Perley, vol. I, p. 175; 9/8/1636.

27. T.R. vol. I, pp. 8-15.

28. *Ibid.,* p. 10.

29. *Ibid.,* p. 28.

30. *Ibid.,* p. 35. See Appendix B, Map 2.

31. *Ibid.,* p. 44.

32. *Ibid.,* pp. 19-27.

33. Perley, vol. I, p. 391.

34. *Ibid.*

35. *Ibid.,* p. 311. The others received their large grants according to another qualification: "Each person who came over at his own expense and was an adventurer in the common stock had forthwith allotted to him fifty acres of land for each individual in his family." If a man did not contribute to the common stock but paid his own way, he received 50 acres plus "as much more as the governor and council deemed necessary according

to his expenses and standing." 50 acres were granted for the transport of each servant as well. See *Mass. Bay Recs.* vol. I, p. 43. (May 19, 1629); vol. I, pp. 363-65 (May 21, 1629); also J.B. Felt, vol.I, pp. 117 and 149.

36. J.B. Felt, vol. II, p. 211.

37. T.R. vol. I, p. 27. See Appendix B, Map 2.

38. *Ibid.,* pp. 33, 36, 41, 55, 63, 66, 67, 76, 80, 83, 84, 88, 92.

39. *Ibid.,* pp. 27-28.

40. *Ibid.,* pp. 101-4.

41. *Ibid.,* p. 61.

42. The frequent interlineations and corrections in Ralph Fogg's list of the previous year show that this task was also a challenge in 1636.

43. For the categorization used to describe the dozens of occupational titles used by Salem residents in the charter period, see Appendix A.

Chapter Three

1. T.R. vol. I, p. 41.

2. *Ibid.,* pp. 44, 47.

3. *Ibid.,* p. 47.

4. Perley vol. I, p. 428.

5. *Ibid.,* p. 129.

6. Morgan, *Founding,* p. 454.

7. T.R. vol. I, pp. 27-28.

8. *Ibid.,* p. 28.

9. *Ibid.,* p. 47.

10. *Ibid.*

11. Of the 34 residents on Fogg's list of 1636 who do not reappear on the 1637 Conant list, 24 had received a grant from the town. 10 of the inhabitants who left during the year released grants of 50 acres or more. Altogether, those who left for other towns (and a few who returned to England) restored 1150 acres to the town's available supply of land, 12.3% of the total confirmed as grants on Fogg's list the year before.

12. T.R. vol. I, p. 54.

13. *Ibid.*

14. *Mass. Bay Recs.* vol. II, p. 109. See Appendix B, Map 2.

15. *Ibid.,* pp. 77, 98.

16. *Ibid.* See Appendix B, Map 2.

17. Perley vol. II, pp. 149-50.

18. Edward Johnson, *Wonder-Working Providence of Sion's Saviour* (1654), reprinted, Edward Gallagher ed. (Delmar, New York: Scholars' Facsimiles and Reprints, Inc., 1974), p. 189.

19. E.g. Watertown, Sudbury and Dedham. Powell, *Puritan Village,* pp. 92-146. Lockridge, *A New England Town,* pp. 93-103.

20. Of those known: Samuel Sharp, elder; Hugh Peter and Edward Norris, ministers; Francis Johnson and John Hathorne, merchants; Robert Moulton, shipbuilder; Edmund Batter, maltster; Captain Richard Davenport, gentleman.

21. Andover, Sudbury and Dedham had elites ranging from 6 to 10 people, but Dedham had only 46 household heads in 1637. Greven, *Four Generations,* pp. 46, 58. Powell, *Puritan Village,* p. 189. Lockridge, *A New England Town,* pp. 9-10, 70-72.

22. J. B. Felt, vol. II, p. 410. Felt "calculated" 950 people in 1639. My own population survey shows that 371 household heads had arrived by 1640, but 40 are also known to have left Salem and 30 others to have died in Salem by that time.

23. Town officers for the purposes of this computation include deputies, selectmen, constables and jury members.

24. Richard Gildrie describes the practice of rewarding church membership and service in town offices with land grants as an "established pattern" in the period from 1636 to 1650; he cites Price as an example, but does not mention Cromwell. In fact, the policy of accommodation was in sufficient conflict with this practice to produce a mixed land-granting record prior to 1650, *after* which Gildrie's statement becomes entirely correct, but little land was granted after this date. Gildrie, p. 73.

25. Richard Davenport received 80 acres in 1636 and 125 more by 1640; Daniel Ray's original grant of 160 acres was augmented by 70 acres in 1637. In addition, three men who had been in the minimal majority of 1636 received new grants: John Humphries added 300 acres to his previous 200, Hugh Peter added 200 to his previous 300, and Thomas Scruggs got 10 acres in addition to his previous 300. The other six new men in the minimal majority of 1640 all received their first and only grants after 1636: Emanuel Downing, 500 acres; Francis Felmingham, John Hathorne, Alan Kenniston, William Pester and Thomas Scudder, all 200 acres.

26. J.B. Felt estimates that the total population actually dropped from 1200 to 1068 between 1644 and 1654. (Felt, vol. II, p. 410) My own calculation based on known dates of arrival and departure shows a near steady state population between 1640 and 1660, holding at approximately 300 families. There were 45 landless men living in Salem in 1650.

27. T.R. vol. I, p. 170.

28. *Ibid.*, p. 169.

29. *Ibid.*, p. 170.

30. E.g., *Ibid.*, pp. 172ff.

31. E.g., *Ibid.*, pp. 170-71.

32. *Ibid.*, p. 164.

33. *Ibid.*

34. *Ibid.*, p. 173.

35. *Ibid.*, p. 221.

36. *Ibid.*, p. 174.

37. *Ibid.*, p. 176.

Chapter Four

1. Morgan, *Founding,* pp. 453-54.

2. *Ibid.*, p. 454.

3. Thomas Morton, *New English Canaan* (Amsterdam, 1637; facsimile edition, Amsterdam, 1969), pp. 158-59. Morton was hostile to the new colony and to Endicott's methods; his account, while biting, is probably accurate.

4. *Mass. Bay Recs.*, vol. II, p. 366.

5. *Ibid.*, pp. 117-18; the history of this development is chronicled by Robert Emmet Wall, Jr., *Massachusetts Bay: The Crucial Decade* (New Haven: Yale University Press, 1972), pp. 6-10.

6. T.R. vol. II, p. 37; T.R. vol. III, pp. 162-63.

7. Wall, *Crucial Decade,* pp. 6-10.

8. *Mass. Bay Recs.*, vol. I, p. 125.

9. Perley, vol. I, p. 198. Two other East Anglian deputies were elected in 1635, but the General Court refused to seat them due to their support of Roger Williams. *Mass. Bay Recs.*, vol. I, p. 156.

10. He served at only one additional session, in May of 1639.

11. Perley, vol. I, p. 284.

12. *Mass. Bay Recs.*, vol. I, p. 156.

13. The scope of this problem is laid out by R.H. Rawney, *The Agrarian Problem in the Sixteenth Century* (London: Longmans, Green, and Co., 1912).

14. T.R. vol. I, p. 7. William P. Upham, author of the forward to the published town records, speculates: "Previous to the time [1636] Salem seems to have had a sort of separate or independent government, retaining in some respects the character of a General Court, which properly belonged to it prior to the arrival of Winthrop. Its limits were not accurately defined, or even known. As late as May 2, 1636, the records speak of certain orders as passed 'at a general court or town meeting of Salem. . . .' It is possible that the whole subject of the jurisdiction of the Salem government was referred to the Lords, and that our earliest records, from 1628 to 1634, under the administration of Endicott and his council, were carried to England, and may yet be discovered there."

15. *Ibid.*, p. 8.

16. *Ibid.*

17. *Mass. Bay Recs.*, vol. I, p. 161.

18. *Ibid.*, p. 172.

19. *Ibid.* See also volume II, pp. 4, 6-9, 163, 180 for early instructions of the General Court to selectmen concerning laying out of highways, care of children, etc.

20. Winthrop, *Journal*, 1630-1649, 2 volumes, James Kendall Hosmer ed. (New York: C. Scribner's Sons, 1908), vol. I, p. 179.

21. T.R. vol. I, pp. 210, 224; T.R. vol. III, p. 197. The town decided to elect only five selectmen in 1657, in an unsuccessful move to eliminate Joseph Boyce, who was a Quaker. In 1659 the town again tried this ploy, and this time successfully, as Boyce was the sixth-ranking nominee. In 1688, the board was reduced to six due to the rising number of refusals of the post.

22. Andover, Sudbury and Dedham had elites ranging from 6 to 10 people, but Dedham had half the population of Salem in 1637.

23. Perley, vol. I, p. 447; *Mass. Bay Recs.*, vol. I, p. 211.

24. This degree of turnover in office was not atypical among New England towns in the period prior to 1647. 30% of Salem's selectmen to 1647 served five terms or more, the same proportion as in Watertown. Other towns surveyed include Boston, 43%; Cambridge, 15%; Charlestown, 29%; Dedham, 38%; Gloucester, 20%; and Salisbury, 25%. Wall, *Crucial Decade,* p. 25.

25. Elections for 1640 and 1641 are not noted in the town records; the names of six men in 1640 and four in 1641 are noted in the margins of the selectmen's minutes. If others were elected, they did not attend these meetings, and so are unknown.

26. Nathaniel Morton eulogized Endicott's early work in Salem, and noted: "There he continued, until the jurisdiction of the Massachusetts saw reason to desire his removal to Boston, for the more convenient administration of justice, as Governor of the said jurisdiction, to which he was frequently elected for many years together with little intermission."*New England's Memorial,* p. 177.

27. T.R. vol. I, p. 88.

28. *Ibid.,* p. 100.

29. *Ibid.,* p. 99.

30. *Ibid.,* p. 106.

31. *Ibid.,* p. 121.

32. *Ibid.,* pp. 121-23.

33. *Ibid.,* pp. 123-24.

34. *Ibid.,* pp. 124-25.

35. *Ibid.,* p. 138.

36. *Ibid.,* pp. 137, 141.

37. *Ibid.,* p. 140.

38. *Ibid.,* p. 131. (1644)

39. *Ibid.,* p. 140.

40. *Ibid.*

41. *Ibid.,* p. 144.

42. *Ibid.,* p. 145.

43. Paul Boyer and Stephen Nissenbaum, *Salem Possessed: The Social Origins of Witch-craft* (Cambridge: Harvard University Press, 1974), pp. 117-23.

44. See Lockridge, *New England Town*, pp. 42-46, for an analysis of a similarly small group (10 men) who dominated Dedham's local government—60% of all available selectman's posts between 1639 and 1687.

45. Number of purchases made after 1650: William Brown, 26; George Corwin, 21; Walter Price, 15; John Porter, 20. Porter also bought a farm of 500 acres before 1650, and held the most acreage of the entire group.

46. T.R. vol. I, pp. 147-48.

47. *Ibid.*, p. 147.

48. *Ibid.*, p. 151.

49. *Ibid.*, p. 215.

50. *Ibid.*, p. 203; T.R. vol. II, p. 2.

51. *Ibid.*, pp. 175 (1654; 3 grants), 179 (1654), 202 (1657), 220 (1658), 223 (1659; 2 grants).

52. *Ibid.*, p. 182.

53. *Ibid.*, p. 183.

54. *Mass. Bay Recs.*, vol. IV, p. 376. May 28, 1659.

55. T.R. vol. I, p. 222.

56. T.R. vol. II, p. 2.

57. T.R. vol. I, p. 125.

58. *Ibid.*, p. 179.

59. Perley, vol. I, p. 244.

60. Kai Erikson counted 51 in Essex County between 1657 and 1667. *Wayward Puritans: A Study in the Sociology of Deviance* (New York: John Wiley & Sons, Inc., 1966), p. 176. Gildrie describes Salem as "the core of Quaker agitation in the Bay Colony," p. 130.

61. For Hathorne's views, see Gildrie, pp. 133-37.

62. Perley, vol. II, p. 245.

63. T.R. vol. I, p. 231. The 5 merchants and their votes were Hathorne 116, Batter 70, Brown 61, Price 48, and Corwin 46. 2 men identified with the Quakers, Joseph Boyce and Thomas Gardner, received 35 and 32 votes each, while John Porter received 34 votes.

64. Perley, vol. II, pp. 247-50.

65. T.R. vol. II, p. 2.

Chapter Five

1. Gildrie, pp. 4-5.

2. Perley, vol. I, p. 79.

3. William Bradford, *Of Plymouth Plantation,* Introduction and Notes by Samuel Eliot Morison (New York: Knopf, 1966), pp. 205, 233-37. Nathaniel Morton tells a more lurid tale of Lyford's expulsion, replete with attempts to divide the Plymouth church and to damage further the reputation of the colony among its enemies in England by secretly dispatching vilifying letters. *New England's Memorial* . . . (Cambridge: Printed by S.G. and M.J. for John Usher of Boston, 1669); edited and reprinted by Howard J. Hall (New York: Scholars' Facsimiles and Reprints, 1937), pp. 53-61.

4. William Hubbard, *A General History of New England from the Discovery to 1680* (2nd edition; Boston: C.C. Little and J. Brown, 1878), p. 108.

5. Richard D. Pierce, ed., *Records of the First Church in Salem, 1629-1736,* Introduction by Robert E. Moody (Salem: Essex Institute, 1974), xxii.

6. Morgan, *Founding,* p. 453.

7. *Ibid.*

8. Nathaniel Morton in retrospect called both Higginson and Skelton "Non-conformists, who having suffered much in their native land upon that account, they came over with a professed intention of practicing Reformation." *New England's Memorial,* p. 74.

9. Morgan, *Founding,* p. 457.

10. Bradford, 223. Reprinted by Nathaniel Morton in *New England's Memorial,* pp. 73-74.

11. William Bradford, "Governor Bradford's Letter-Book," *Collections of the Massachusetts Historical Society,* ser. I, vol. 3 (Boston: 1794; reprinted by Munroe and Francis, no. 4 Cornhill, Boston, 1810), pp. 67-68.

12. Salem Church Records, 1629-1736 (typewritten copy of the manuscript; Salem, Massachusetts: Essex Institute), p. 3. Hereafter cited as *Church Records.*

13. Nathaniel Morton, *New England's Memorial*, pp. 75-76.

14. *Ibid.*, p. 76.

15. Morgan, *Founding*, 462.

16. Cotton Mather, *Magnalia Christi Americana: Or, the Ecclesiastical History of New-England, from Its First Planting in the Year 1620, unto the Year of our Lord, 1698* (London: 1702), book I, Ch. IV, p. 19. Also noted by Nathaniel Morton, pp. 77-78.

17. Gildrie, p. 21.

18. Hubbard, 181-82.

19. David D. Hall, "John Cotton's Letter to Samuel Skelton," *William and Mary Quarterly*, 3d ser., 22 (1965), pp. 482-85. See also Gildrie, p. 22.

20. John Winthrop, *Journal, 1630-1649*, ed. James K. Hosmer (2 volumes; New York: 1908), vol. I, pp. 52-53.

21. Williams' dismissal from the Plymouth church was a matter of extended debate. Plymouth leaders already knew of Williams' "singular opinions," but decided that "there being then many able men in the Bay, they would better deal with him than [they] themselves could." (Nathaniel Morton, p. 78.) Thus Plymouth's problem became Salem's.

22. For example, the Boston church sent a "public admonition" entitled "Errors in Doctrine" (Nathaniel Morton, pp. 81-82).

23. *Mass. Bay Recs.* vol. I, p. 156.

24. *Ibid.*, p. 158. See also Nathaniel Morton, pp. 79-80.

25. *Ibid.*, p. 161.

26. *Mass. Bay Recs.*, vol. I, p. 156.

27. Perley, vol. I, pp. 268-69.

28. *Mass. Bay Recs.*, vol. I, p. 147 (May 6, 1635); p. 165 (March 3, 1636).

29. *Church Records*, p. 3.

30. *Ibid.*, pp. 4-5.

31. *Ibid.*, p. 4.

32. There were 141 men on Ralph Fogg's list of land grants in 1636, and 203 on Conant's meadow division list of 1637; the new covenant was adopted in December of 1636.

33. From the years 1638-1641, 115 new arrivals are known; if all who arrived in 1637 are included on Conant's list of that year, the total (not accounting for deaths and removals) male population in 1641 could have been a maximum of 318. Thus, the 147 men within the church covenant in 1641 would be 46.2% of the adult male population. Note that Wall says there were only 246 men in Salem in 1647 (p. 39)—possibly due to the formation of new towns within the original limits.

34. *Mass. Bay Recs.*, vol. I, p. 332.

35. Edmund Morgan, *Visible Saints: The History of a Puritan Idea* (Ithaca: Cornell University Press, 1965), pp. 80-112.

36. Gildrie, p. 85. 158 of 238 land-owning families had at least one church member (66.4%); however, there were 45 landless heads of households in 1650, so Gildrie's figure is too high, and should be instead approximately 55.8%.

37. Powell, *Puritan Village,* p. 144; Lockridge, *New England Town,* p. 31.

38. *Mass. Bay Recs.*, vol. I, pp. 211-12. These men were Thomas Scruggs, William Alford, Mr. Comyns, Robert Moulton, and George King. Meanwhile, 59 men were disarmed in Boston, and 12 in Newbury, Roxbury, Ipswich and Charlestown. Nathaniel Morton noted that the "great troubles in the country" were "especially at Boston." (*New England's Memorial,* p. 106.)

39. *Ibid.,* p. 247.

40. Gildrie, pp. 49-50; Morgan, *Roger Williams: The Church and the State* (New York: Harcourt, Brace & World, 1967), p. 140.

41. Gildrie, pp. 77-83. See also Nathaniel Morton, *New England's Memorial,* pp. 108-11.

42. T.R. vol. I, p. 131.

43. *Ibid.*

44. *Ibid.,* p. 140.

Chapter Six

1. The number does not include adult sons of men with land who had none of their own.

2. T.R. vol. I, pp. 151-52.

3. T.R. vol. II, p. 108. His rates were abated again in 1683 (T.R. vol. III, p. 86).

4. *Ibid.,* pp. 110, 124.

5. *Ibid.,* p. 125.

6. *Ibid.,* p. 210.

7. *Ibid.,* pp. 211, 213; T.R. vol. III, pp. 121, 143.

8. T.R. vol. II, pp. 28-29.

9. *Ibid.,* pp. 37-38.

10. *Ibid.,* pp. 188, 263, 289, 290.

11. T.R. vol. III, p. 94.

12. *Ibid.,* pp. 153, 183.

13. T.R. vol. II, pp. 323-26. Altogether she received £2 1s. in five allotments.

14. Perley, vol. II, pp. 193, 405.

15. T.R. vol. II, pp. 242, 270. These inspectors went to each house to inquire about the instruction of children and domestic relations; they reported their findings to the Quarterly Court. (Morgan, *Puritan Family,* pp. 148-49.

16. T.R. vol. III, p. 38.

17. *Ibid.,* p. 150.

18. Deed no. 70150. Numbers have been assigned to all deeds from 1638 to 1689, 1458 in all, in the order in which they appear in the Essex County Registry of Deeds.

19. T.R. vol. III, p. 259.

20. Thirty-nine percent are residential sales: farms, houses, house lots; the remainder are upland, meadow, marsh, and miscellaneous town lots.

21. These figures do not include men who were born in Salem or arrived as minors, nor the few men whose dates of arrival are unknown; these groups make up the remainder of the historical population of 1529 household heads.

22. Between 1644 and 1650, 1755 acres were conveyed by grant while 2126 acres were deeded away.

23. The Hathornes, John and William, and Daniel Ray (a Salem Village farmer).

24. The overall wealth of the merchants was still higher than that of the farmers, since the merchants' wealth was expressed not only in land, but also in other forms of capital. For all of the county, 30% of the merchants' wealth was in land, compared to 80% of the farmers' assets. Manfred Jonas, "Wills of Early Settlers of Essex County, Massachusetts," *Essex Institute Historical Collections,* vol. XCVI (1960), pp. 229, 231.

25. *Mass. Bay Recs.*, vol. II, p. 266. Salem agreed that Marblehead could be separated, and the General Court confirmed this agreement on May 2, 1649.

26. These figures do not include sons of earlier residents who reached maturity in these years.

27. These figures do not include those who died.

28. These figures include ministers, tavernkeepers, merchants, etc.

29. The following discussion of neighborhoods is based on those who remained in Salem and lived until 1683 to appear on the tax lists of that date, plus those others who bought land and had it conveyed by deeds specific enough to indicate the location of the purchase.

30. Three artisans—a blacksmith, a fuller and a mason—moved to Salem Village, but the other 18 settled in the 4 quadrants of the peninsula.

31. Even by 1683, the new residents of Salem Village between 1650 and 1670 and their sons comprised only 18.1% of the taxpaying population in that district; their proportion of the population in 1670 would have been even less due to the higher death rate among earlier residents between 1670 and 1683.

32. J.B. Felt, vol. I, pp. 188-89. This difference between the Salem selectmen and the General Court reveals just how atypical Salem was by 1660 among the towns of Massachusetts Bay. The General Court, in which a majority of the deputies were from inland, agricultural towns agreed with Salem's commoners—who were trying to protect their rights of commonage from the consequences of population growth—while the merchant-selectman stood to gain by the influx of artisans and seamen, and therefore wished to allow these newcomers access to the common pens and pastures.

33. Boyer and Nissenbaum, *Salem Possessed,* pp. 120-22.

34. *Ibid.,* p. 197.

35. The immigrants of 1650-70 were not as acquisitive as either earlier residents or later arrivals; these mid-century immigrants accounted for only 14.8% of the deeds between 1670 and 1689. Both earlier residents and those who came after 1670 were far more active in the land market. The immigrants of 1650-70 usually acquired only enough land to house their families and accommodate their trades.

36. T.R. vol. I, p. 171.

37. Wenham, Manchester and Marblehead were all empowered to grant their own lands by 1650.

38. Few owners of land at Winter Island (fishermen) or Cape Ann (Old Planters) bought additional land. Jeffrey Massey, a West Country resident of the latter area, was the only large grantee of the 1650s who did not purchase additional land, but his behavior was typical among his neighbors.

39. There were 205 men who received land grants and purchased no other land; 116 received land from the town but also bought additional acreage; 416 men never received a grant but purchased land.

40. William Brown Sr. provides a good example. He bought 26 pieces of property in addition to his 4 grants, including upland, meadow, saltmarsh, town lots, house lots and houses. He made 17 separate sales. Overall, he was accumulating land; for example, he bought nine houses and sold six between 1652 and 1687.

41. Richard Hutchinson was granted 60 acres, and bought 626 more between 1644 and 1650.

42. Fully half of the taxpayers on the lists of 1683 were not landowners.

43. This change represents a *real* increase in the purchasing power of these buyers, since prices remained stable throughout the charter period. William I. Davisson, "Essex County Price Trends: Money and Markets in 17th Century Massachusetts." *Essex Institute Historical Collections,* vol. CIII (1967), pp. 148-51. Davisson's study covered the period from 1640 to 1682.

44. Between 1651 and 1660, 271 exchanges were made; in the next decade, there were 316.

Chapter Seven

1. T.R. vol. I, p. 200.

2. T.R. vol. II, p. 14.

3. T.R. vol. I, p. 201.

4. T.R. vol. II, p. 79. This duty of the selectmen was delegated to a subcommittee after 1667. E.g., T.R. vol. II, p. 78.

5. *Ibid.,* p. 27.

6. *Ibid.,* pp. 50, 61, 91.

7. *Ibid.,* p. 27.

8. *Ibid.,* p. 29. Another good example is the case of John Luff in 1644 (*Ibid,* p. 41).

9. *Ibid.,* pp. 48, 54.

10. *Ibid.,* p. 68.

11. *Ibid.,* p. 77.

12. *Ibid.,* p. 75.

13. *Ibid.*

14. Only a few payments were made through intermediaries, as in 1657 when the selectmen returned £1 16s. to Constable Nathaniel Putnam to pay workers on the bridge in the Village (T.R. vol. I, p. 208).

15. T.R. vol. I, p. 195.

16. T.R. vol. II, p. 39.

17. *Ibid.,* pp. 33, 43, 76, 81, 86.

18. *Ibid.,* p. 22.

19. *Ibid.,* p. 12.

20. *Ibid.,* pp. 24, 39, 41, 49, 73, 76, 86, 91, 97.

21. *Ibid.,* p. 24.

22. *Ibid.,* p. 74.

23. *Ibid.,* p. 13.

24. T.R. vol.I, p. 148; T.R. vol. II, pp. 28, 37, 48, 57, 69, 79, 92. The first rater was appointed by the selectmen in 1637 (T.R. vol. I, p. 59).

25. The group included two small merchants, two members of the Putnam family of Salem Village, and Jeffrey Massey, a farmer who lived on the North Neck (and eventually in Beverly) and served as selectman 17 of the years between 1637 and 1657.

26. T.R. vol. II, pp. 39-40.

27. *Ibid.,* p. 49.

28. *Ibid.,* p. 24.

29. T.R. vol. I, pp. 212-13; in 1661 the selectmen were "to have the same instructions as formerly." (T.R. vol. II, p. 12.)

30. T.R. vol. II, pp. 12, 13, 19, 23, 29, 35, 54, 67, 71, 81-82.

31. *Ibid.,* p. 24. In addition, Edmund Batter served as commissioner for votes in 1667 (T.R. vol. II, p. 78). Two special committees were set up by the town meeting in these years; one of the three men appointed to settle a land dispute in 1661 was a merchant-selectman, as were two of the four men appointed to settle a dispute over the Topsfield bounds (T.R. vol. II, pp. 19, 47).

32. Miller, p. 407; also pp. 398-431 *passim.*

33. The General Court made it equally clear that a town could not refuse to grant land because a man was not a member of the church, and ordered Watertown to correct past abuses: "Watertown freemen, promising to yield to every townsman his portion alike, without respect to freedom or not freedom, were dismissed." (*Mass. Bay Recs.*, vol. I, p. 310; December 1, 1640.)

34. T.R. vol. I, pp. 108-9.

35. T.R. vol.I, pp. 111, 156-57 (Marblehead); pp. 164-65 (Cape Ann Side); 168 (Ryal Side).

36. T.R. vol. II, p. 13.

37. *Ibid.*, p. 21.

38. *Ibid.*, p. 43. See Appendix B, Map 2.

39. *Ibid.*

40. *Ibid.*, pp. 68-69 (1666).

41. *Ibid.*, p. 54. The order was reiterated in 1666, 1667, and 1673. (*Ibid.*, pp. 68, 77, 163.)

42. *Ibid.*, pp. 88-90.

43. *Ibid.*, p. 31.

44. *Ibid.*, p. 45.

45. *Ibid.*, p. 54.

46. T.R. vol.I, p. 197.

47. T.R. vol. I, p. 20. Both of these rates were to repay selectmen for their expenses to date: £50 to George Corwin for the parsonage, and £50 to William Brown for the meetinghouse.

48. *Ibid.*, p. 210.

49. *Ibid.*

50. *Ibid.*, p. 215.

51. T.R. vol. I, pp. 223-24.

52. T.R. vol. II, p. 1.

53. *Ibid.*, pp. 2, 4.

54. *Ibid.*, p. 9.

55. *Ibid.,* pp. 24, 54.

56. *Ibid.,* p. 77.

57. *Ibid.,* pp. 79, 82.

58. *Ibid.,* pp. 82-84.

59. *Ibid.,* pp. 88-89.

60. *Ibid.*

61. *Ibid.*

62. *Contra* Gildrie, who sees these orders as new limits for the selectmen, imposed by a resurgent town meeting, pp. 153-54.

63. T.R. vol. II, pp. 30-31, 40.

64. *Ibid.,* p. 89.

65. *Ibid.,* p. 17.

Chapter Eight

1. Miller, pp. 418-19.

2. *Ibid.,* p. 420.

3. Bernard Bailyn, "Politics and Social Structure in Virginia," *Seventeenth Century America,* ed. James Morton Smith (Chapel Hill: University of North Carolina Press, 1959), p. 91.

4. For example, it was he who provided the funds for Higginson's house in 1659 (T.R. vol. II, p. 2). His wife was a church member.

5. Tables are not provided for this office as few men served more than once. The constabulary was the only office not dominated by early arrivals; over half were neither church members nor freemen, and there were proportionally fewer constables in the top tax bracket than any other office.

6. T.R. vol. II, p. 57. At the same meeting, Eleazer Hathorne and William Brown Jr.—sons of Salem's major leaders—were excused from election to this post, another indication of its undesirability.

7. Rev. William Bentley, "A Description and History of Salem," *Massachusetts Historical Collections,* ser. I, vol. VI (1799). (Reprinted: Boston: Charles C. Little and James Brown, 1846), p. 266.

Chapter Nine

1. *Mass. Bay Recs.*, vol. I, p. 161.

2. *Ibid.*, vol. I, p. 87.

3. Charles M. Andrews, *The Colonial Period of American History* (New Haven: Yale University Press, 1934), vol. I, p. 443.

4. T.R. vol. I, pp. 101-4.

5. Winthrop, *Journal*, vol. I, pp. 317-18.

6. Winthrop, *Journal*, vol. I, p. 83; T.R. vol. I, p. 131.

7. Thomas Hutchinson, *The History of Massachusetts, from the first settlement thereof in 1628, until the year 1750* (Salem: Thomas C. Cushing, for Thomas & Andrews, 1795), vol. I, pp. 493-95.

8. *Ibid.*, vol. I, p. 497.

9. Timothy Breen raises the question whether "some of the so-called 'nonfreemen' who broke the law by serving as selectmen before 1647 were actually freemen whose names were either lost or misrecorded." From "Town Franchise in Massachusetts," *William and Mary Quarterly*, vol. XXVII (July, 1970), p. 464.

10. *Mass. Bay Recs.*, vol. II, p. 41.

11. *Ibid.*, vol. II, p. 208.

12. *Ibid.*, vol. II, p. 197; see also Breen, pp. 466-67.

13. *Ibid.*, vol. II, pp. 57, 266.

14. T.R. vol. I, p. 179.

15. *Mass. Bay Recs.*, vol. II, p. 241.

16. T.R. vol. II, p. 37. The changes in colonial law in 1658 already enabled men over 24 with £20 of estate who had taken the oath of fidelity to vote in elections for local office (*Mass. Bay Recs.*, vol. IV, pt. I, p. 336), so this motion focussed on freemanship itself rather than being strictly a move to increase participation in town affairs. (See *infra*, "Consequences of Dispersion and Differentiation: The Town," pp. 153-56.)

17. Edmund Morgan, *Visible Saints*, pp. 125ff.

18. It must be remembered that nearly half of the church members in Salem before 1689 joined *before* the test of visibility was in effect; there may in fact have been less real "declension" between the first generation and the second than numbers of admissions alone indicate.

19. *Church Records,* p. 223.

20. *Ibid.*

21. *Ibid.,* p. 224.

22. *Ibid.*

23. *Ibid.,* p. 234.

24. *Ibid.*

25. *Ibid.,* p. 235.

26. *Ibid.,* p. 236.

27. *Ibid.*

28. *Ibid.,* p. 237.

29. John Cotton, "Plymouth Church Records," vol. I, part 2 (1667-1699), *Publications of the Colonial Society of Massachusetts,* vol. 22 (Boston: 1920), p. 145.

30. *Church Records,* p. 225.

31. For the duration of visibility elsewhere, see Lockridge, pp. 34-36; the Dedham church held out for the "pure" covenant until 1691. In 1671 the General Court endorsed the Half-Way Covenant, which was not widely practiced before that date. (*Mass. Bay Recs.,* vol. IV, pt. 2, p. 492.)

32. *Church Records,* pp. 240, 242.

33. *Ibid.,* pp. 221, 272, 273.

34. *Ibid.,* p. 238.

35. *Ibid.,* p. 239.

36. *Ibid.,* p. 241.

37. *Ibid.,* pp. 230-31.

38. Lockridge, pp. 31-34.

39. Some of these men were made freemen before the General Court decreed in 1631 that only church members could be freemen.

40. The date of arrival for the last two men made freemen without the requisite church membership is not known.

41. The residence of the remaining three men is unknown.

42. The failure of church members in Marblehead to become freemen was a particular problem, since there were so few freemen in Marblehead. By 1674, the leaders of that town asked for relief, and received the following answer from the General Court: "In answer to the petition of the selectmen of Marblehead, it is ordered that such persons as from time to time shall be approved of by the selectmen and County Court at Salem shall by the said Court [be] impowered to act in all affairs as if freemen in town affairs, until this Court shall take further order." *Mass. Bay Recs.* vol. V, p. 8 (May 27, 1674).

43. After 1650 those who joined only the church were from the areas east and west of the town center, while those who became freemen only were from the western sector of the town. Within each of these neighborhoods, moreover, no difference can be found in these patterns between native sons and new arrivals to Salem, indicating that the areas themselves were important in the decisions of individual men concerning which signs of status were worth pursuing.

44. The other colonial deputies after 1677 were John Putnam (two terms), and Bartholemew Gedney, John Price, John Hathorne, and John Ruck one term each. Also elected as Assistants were Bartholemew Gedney (1680-1683) and John Hathorne (1684-1686).

45. T.R. vol. III, pp. 104, 134, 153.

Chapter Ten

1. T.R. vol. II, pp. 87-89.

2. *Ibid.*

3. *Ibid.*, pp. 91-92.

4. *Ibid.*, pp. 99-100.

5. *Mass. Bay Recs.* vol. V, p. 22.

6. Perley, vol. III, pp. 57-58.

7. T.R. vol. II, pp. 109, 111.

8. *Ibid.*, p. 112.

9. *Records and Files of the Quarterly Courts of Essex County, Massachusetts*, George Francis Dow ed. (Salem: Essex Institute, 1911), vol. V (1672-1674), p. 173; hereafter cited as *EQCR*. Reprinted by Paul Boyer and Stephen Nissenbaum, eds., *Salem Village Witchcraft: A Documentary Record of Local Conflict in Colonial New England* (Belmont, California: Wadsworth Publishing Company, Inc., 1972), p. 233.

10. *EQCR*, vol. V, p. 274; testimony of John Putnam and Joseph Hutchinson, reprinted in Boyer and Nissenbaum, *Salem Village Witchcraft,* p. 233.

11. 10 *Mass. Arch.* p. 105; Boyer and Nissenbaum, *Salem Village Witchcraft,* pp. 233-34.

12. *Ibid.,* p. 234.

13. T.R. vol. II, p. 141.

14. *Salem Village Book of Record* (1672), excerpted in Boyer and Nissenbaum, *Salem Village Witchcraft,* p. 234. See also *Mass. Bay Recs.* vol. V, pp. 247-48.

15. T.R. vol. II, p. 141.

16. T.R. vol. III, pp. 64-65; 67-68, 161, 167, 211, 214.

17. Boyer and Nissenbaum, *Salem Village Witchcraft,* pp. 245-48.

18. *Church Records,* p. 264.

19. The conflict, which concerned the right of non-members to vote in church affairs, was carried to the General Court, which declared (in opposition to the advice of the Salem church) that non-members who met the civil voting requirements could participate fully in church votes.

20. *Church Records,* p. 268.

21. *Salem Village Church Records, 1689-96:* Manuscript volume in Samuel Parris's handwriting in the Library of the First Church of Danvers, Mass.; covenant and list of original members reprinted in Boyer and Nissenbaum, *Salem Village Witchcraft,* pp. 268-69.

22. *Salem Village Church Records,* First Church of Danvers.

23. *Ibid.* (Boyer and Nissenbaum, *Salem Village Witchcraft,* p. 270). Hannah Wilkins was admitted in this way in 1691. She was "called forth, and her relation read in the full assembly, and then it was propounded to the church, that, if they had just exceptions, or, on the other hand, had any thing further to encourage, they had opportunity and liberty to speak." (*Ibid.,* pp. 275-76.)

24. T.R. vol. II, pp. 87-88.

25. *Ibid.,* pp. 128-29.

26. *Ibid.,* pp. 99, 100, 128-29.

27. *Ibid.,* pp. 164, 261, 292, 251-54; T.R. vol. III, p. 65.

28. T.R. vol. II, p. 145.

29. T.R. vol. III, p. 110.

30. *Ibid.,* p. 31. (1681)

31. *Church Records*, p. 250. Higginson's health may have been poor at this time. In November of 1670 he had written a letter to the Quarterly Court in which he described himself as "being very crazy and ill that I cannot stir abroad." (Reprinted in Perley, vol. III, p. 79.) He was 56 years old at the time.

32. *Town Records*, vol. II, p. 158.

33. *Church Records*, p. 250. The town meeting referred to was held on Tuesday, May 6, 1673; the date of the church vote is not recorded, but was on a Sunday. It is impossible to determine whether the church vote preceded the town vote (which seems unlikely) or followed it, as Perley would have us believe. (Perley, vol. III, pp. 53-55.)

34. T.R. vol. II, pp. 144-45.

35. *Church Records*, p. 252.

36. T.R. vol. II, p. 186.

37. *Church Records*, p. 253.

38. *Ibid.*

39. T.R. vol. II, p. 195. He was also associated with another attempt to divide the Salem church that year, when two men who were not church members tried to form a church to include some residents of Lynn. The Salem church "did not approve of their sudden church gathering . . . [so] there was a forbearance of the church gathering for that time." (*Church Records*, pp. 251-52; see also Robert E. Moody's introduction to the published edition of the church records, xix.) While the Salem Villagers were permitted to maintain their own church after two decades of controversy spanning the end of the charter period, other attempts to separate the east end of the Town and the farms south of the Village were forestalled until the eighteenth century.

40. *Church Records*, p. 253.

41. *Ibid.*, p. 252.

42. *Ibid.*, p. 254.

43. T.R. vol. II, p. 199.

44. *Church Records*, p. 255. Higginson and others also wrote to the General Court requesting a resolution of the conflict. *Mass. Bay Recs.* vol. V, p. 34.

45. *Mass. Bay Recs.* vol. V, p. 67; note that the General Court opposed voting by those not officially allowed the franchise, but did not deny a vote in church matters to non-members who were enfranchised. Four years later the Salem church would oppose voting by non-members in the Salem Village dispute, while the General Court upheld it. The conflict concerned the right of non-members to join with church members in voting to call a minister to preach.

46. *Church Records*, p. 256.

47. Felt, vol. I, p. 626.

48. *EQCR*, vol. VII (1678-1680), pp. 402-4.

49. No names of women appear on either petition.

50. John Higginson, *The Cause of God and His People in New England* . . . (Cambridge: Printed by Samuel Green, 1663). Perry Miller described this sermon as the first jeremiad. (*New England Mind: The Seventeenth Century*, p. 36.)

51. These figures are for first-generation petitioners only; when second and third generation petitioners are added (using the dates of arrival of their fathers or grandfathers, not their own birth dates), 50% of those for and 9.1% of those against a new church arrived after 1660.

52. In 1689, 21.2% of the taxable population were seamen; thus they exceeded the statistically expected frequency of their signing by half.

53. Of six constables' wards in 1683, the two which include the east end contained 39.6% of the population. The division of the Salem foot companies in 1678 indicates that the population center had moved east, since 50 "seamen and fishermen that live in the lower part of the town, below [east of] the meetinghouse"—the traditional center of the town—were assigned to the western company of the peninsula for balance. *Mass. Bay Recs.*, vol. IV, p. 204 (October 7, 1678).

54. See *infra*, "The Glorious Revolution: Salem in 1689," pp. 176-78 for an extended analysis of occupational differentiation by neighborhood by 1689.

55. T.R. vol. II, p. 163. This joint responsibility was established at least as early as 1657, when the town meeting authorized the selectmen "for ordering the seats in the meetinghouse to continue during the town's pleasure." (T.R. vol. I, p. 201.)

56. Portions of 16 meetings of the selectmen between the completion of the new meetinghouse in 1673 and the conflict of 1680 were devoted to seating; in the former year, the town meeting "voted that the selectmen and the undertakers for the meetinghouse with Mr. Higginson are appointed and empowered to seat the people in the meetinghouse." (T.R. vol. II, p. 163.) See also T.R. vol. II, pp. 155-56, 161, 167, 173, 210, 219, 239, 242, 250, 256, 274, 294, 302, 308; T.R. vol. III, pp. 33, 38. This responsibility was taken seriously, as an entry for 1681 divulges: Jacob Manning was warned "not to sit any more in the fore gallery of the meetinghouse, thereby keeping out others unto whom the place belongs." (T.R. vol. III, p. 40.)

57. The other two, William Hathorne and George Corwin, served five terms each after 1670. William Hathorne was a selectman for 33 years between 1637 and 1676; George Corwin served 24 terms from 1646-1676. Both were merchants.

58. Israel Porter and John Turner, both sons of church members and selectmen, joined the church after they had been elected.

59. Despite repeal of a colonial law requiring freemen to be church members, the pattern in Salem was not broken until the 1670s. Church membership nearly always preceded the application for freemanship before 1670.

60. The property qualifications of 14 petitioners for the new church and 4 against cannot be determined since they do not appear on the first surviving colonial tax list of 1683.

61. The ages of 14 opponents and 62 proponents are known.

62. The petition of those who opposed a second church does not appear to have been circulated in the same way.

63. Only three men who arrived in Salem after 1660 served as selectmen before 1689. Nicholas Manning, a gunsmith, was elected for one term in 1675; Daniel Andrews, a mason, served in 1688; and Timothy Lindall, a merchant, was elected in 1686 and 1687.

64. The selectmen's endorsement appears in the Quarterly Court Records, vol. VII, pp. 402-3. Only one selectman in 1680 signed the opposing petition, while the majority wrote that it was "a matter of duty to declare it is our judgment . . . both for the glory of God and the good of this place" that a second meetinghouse be built. None of the petitions specify that the new meetinghouse would be in addition to, rather than a replacement for, the existing meetinghouse, but the conflict can only be understood in these terms—particularly since the opposing petition states that the proponents made "great endeavors in a private way to draw many of the freemen of this place to sign a writing for the approving of the building of a new meetinghouse, we conceiving such a practice to be illegal and tending to division and disturbance." The opponents also claimed that there was "no apparent necessity of it," and concluded their petition by "desiring that when there shall be need it may be done in a fair legal way by mutual concurrence without disturbance to the peace of church and town." The emphasis on "church and town" and "mutual concurrence" supports the view that two clearly defined groups existed, one of which placed little value in retaining coterminous boundaries for Salem's civil and ecclesiastical institutions.

65. Robert G. Pope, *The Half-Way Covenant: Church Membership in Puritan New England* (Princeton: Princeton University Press, 1969), pp. 247-48.

66. *Church Records*, p. 150. (Published version)

67. *Ibid.*, p. 161.

68. *Ibid.*

69. *Salem Church Covenant* (Boston: Printed . . . by J. F[oster], 1680; Evans Microcard no. 295.

70. *Ibid.*

Chapter Eleven

1. 112 *Mass. Arch.*, pp. 175-77; reprinted in Boyer and Nissenbaum, *Salem Village Witchcraft*, pp. 229-31.

2. *Ibid.*, pp. 231-32.

3. *Mass. Bay Recs.*, vol. V, p. 172.

4. Boyer and Nissenbaum, *Salem Possessed*, pp. 110-32.

5. T.R. vol. II, p. 57.

6. T.R. vol. III, p. 105.

7. J. B. Felt, vol. II, pp. 468, 586.

8. T.R. vol. I, pp. 182-83, 195, 203; T.R. vol. II, p. 3.

9. T.R. vol. II, p. 103.

10. *Ibid.*, p. 97.

11. *Ibid.*, pp. 107-8.

12. *Ibid.*, p. 92.

13. T.R. vol. I, p. 188.

14. T.R. vol. II, p. 92.

15. *Ibid.*, p. 93.

16. *Ibid.*, p. 187.

17. Perley, vol. III, pp. 75-76.

18. E.g., T.R. vol. II, p. 194.

19. *Ibid.*, p. 206. This was the third-largest tax among the 49 towns of the Bay colony, behind Boston (which was assessed twice as much) and Charlestown (which paid only slightly more). *Mass. Bay Recs.*, vol. V, p. 56.

20. *Ibid.*, p. 213.

21. *Ibid.*, pp. 241-42.

22. T.R. vol. I, pp. 223-24.

23. T.R. vol. II, p. 57.

24. *Ibid.*, p. 82.

25. *Ibid.*, p. 92.

26. *Ibid.*, pp. 173, 222.

27. *Ibid.*, p. 199.

28. *Mass. Bay Recs.*, vol. V, p. 80 (May 3, 1676).

29. T.R. vol. III, p. 31.

30. *Ibid.*, p. 207.

31. *Ibid.*, p. 158.

32. *Ibid.*, p. 161.

33. T.R. vol. II, p. 257.

34. *Ibid.*, p. 206.

35. T.R. vol. III, pp. 31-32; only once before 1676 was such action necessary; in 1657 John Stone Sr. was unable to collect the minister's rates and had an "attachment" taken out against him by the selectmen on orders of the town meeting (T.R. vol. I, pp. 206-8), again a sign of the town's troubles with Quakers.

36. T.R. vol. II, pp. 205, 207, 216, 222. See also *Mass. Bay Recs.*, vol. V, p. 343. In 1682, "in answer to the petition of Abraham Cole and Eleazer Giles, late constables of Salem, humbly desiring the favor of this Court to grant them some recompense, etc., for their great loss in collecting of their rates therein mentioned, the Court judgeth it meet to grant them forty pounds in county pay." Both men had served in 1676, during the height of taxation for the war.

37. *Ibid.*, p. 316.

38. *Ibid.*, pp. 290-91.

39. *Ibid.*, p. 292; T.R. vol. III, pp. 68, 109.

40. T.R. vol. III, pp. 114, 132-33.

41. *Ibid.*, pp. 141, 151.

42. *Ibid.*, pp. 144, 155, 163, 169.

43. E.g., *Ibid.*, pp. 68, 104, 121-31, 142-43, 149-50, 171-72, 174; T.R. vol. II, p. 250.

44. T.R. vol. II, pp. 123, 224.

45. *Ibid.,* p. 291. Also, in 1670 John Gardner was given 20s. for running a line and "attending the business of the town at Ipswich Court." T.R. vol. II, p. 109.

46. *Ibid.,* p. 88.

47. T.R. vol. I, pp. 120, 217-18. John Moore was also granted a ten acre plot in an attempt to help him gain self-sufficiency. (T.R. vol. I, p. 119; the land was "loaned" for 10 years.)

48. T.R. vol. I, pp. 136, 138. Mr. Andrews of London had sent £10 to the colony for the relief of the poor; the selectmen used the money to buy two cows, and then gave them away.

49. *Ibid.,* pp. 135, 144, 170, 197.

50. *Ibid.,* p. 173.

51. *Ibid.,* p. 195.

52. T.R. vol. II, p. 254; see also J.B. Felt, vol. I, pp. 299-301.

53. Felt vol. II, p. 397.

54. T.R. vol. II, pp. 246, 323-26; T.R. vol. III, p. 2.

55. T.R. vol. III, p. 61.

56. *Ibid.,* p. 88.

57. *Ibid.,* p. 112.

58. T.R. vol. I, p. 138. This transformation, while clear enough by the end of the charter period, was not complete. Inn licenses were still occasionally granted to the poor—as in the case of a war veteran in 1683 (T.R. vol. III, pp. 82-83)—and there were still some personal notes in the care of the poor. In 1680 the selectmen chose Walter Skinner as bellman and gave him in addition to this salary "jersey sufficient to make him a good coat." (*Ibid.,* p. 17.) In 1686, the selectmen provided a shirt for a poor man in addition to his keep. (*Ibid.,* p. 180).

59. Felt, vol. II, p. 398. Part of the Brown bequest was dispensed by his son on the advice of the selectmen in 1688 (T.R. vol. III, p. 199).

60. T.R. vol. III, p. 198.

61. T.R. vol. II, p. 24.

62. *Ibid.,* pp. 30, 31, 36, 37, 40.

63. *Ibid.,* p. 133.

64. *Ibid.*, p. 141. This measure did not fully meet the housing crisis, however; some continued to encroach on the common (T.R. vol. III, pp. 87, 91).

65. This was the criterion for serving on the constables' watch stipulated by the General Court; quoted in T.R. vol. III, p. 5.

66. T.R. vol. II, p. 164.

67. *Ibid.*, pp. 261-62. This money was to be repaid to the town's accounts when the minister's rate was collected.

68. *Ibid.*, p. 268.

69. *Ibid.*, p. 272.

70. *Ibid.*, p. 256.

71. *Ibid.*, pp. 251-54, 292; vol. III, pp. 56-57, 65.

72. T.R. vol. III, p. 200.

73. *Ibid.*, p. 109.

74. *Ibid.*, p. 135.

75. The term "overseer" is first used in 1688. *Ibid.*, p. 197.

76. Pope, p. 178.

77. T.R. vol. II, pp. 159, 185; *Mass. Bay Recs.*, vol. II, p. 197.

78. T.R. vol. II, p. 159.

79. T.R. vol. III, pp. 164-66; Perley, vol. III, pp. 116-19.

80. T.R. vol. II, pp. 130, 254.

81. *Ibid.*, pp. 6, 21. (1660, 1662)

82. T.R. vol. I, pp. 201-2.

83. T.R. vol. II, pp. 6, 50, 61.

84. *Ibid.*, p. 112.

85. *Ibid.*, pp. 101-2, 116, 123, 303, 306.

86. *Ibid.*, pp. 106, 316.

87. T.R. vol. III, p. 28.

88. *Ibid.,* p. 101.

89. *Ibid.,* p. 113.

90. E.g., T.R. vol. III, pp. 100, 102, 113, 145, 147, 148, 162.

91. T.R. vol. II, pp. 109, 195.

92. T.R. vol. III, p. 44.

93. T.R. vol. II, p. 195.

94. T.R. vol. I, p. 179.

95. T.R. vol. I, p. 204.

96. Between 1646 and 1657, attendance at town meetings was extensive enough to require separate meetings of the freemen to elect deputies (T.R. vol. I, pp. 142, 183, 192, 194, 198); however, between 1637 and 1645 and again from 1658 to 1660, deputies were elected at general town meetings, which may indicate that only freemen were present (T.R. vol. I, pp. 45, 48, 85, 121, 125, 136, 142, 183, 192, 194, 198).

97. *Mass. Bay Recs.,* vol. IV, pt. I, p. 336.

98. Wall, *Crucial Decade,* p. 304.

99. *Mass. Bay Recs.,* vol. IV, pt. I, p. 336.

100. *Ibid.*

101. William H. Whitmore, ed., *Book of the General Lawes and Libertyes Concerning the Inhabitants of the Massachusetts* (Cambridge, 1660; reprinted in facsimile, with supplements to 1672; Boston, 1889), p. 148. Hereafter cited as *Colonial Laws.*

102. These are the votes for men elected; the lowest votes cast in these years were 13 for Nathaniel Felton in 1683, 7 for William Brown Jr. in 1684, and 8 for Timothy Lindall in 1685. The names and votes for losing candidates were not recorded before 1683.

103. Taken by the constables on order of the colony ("country") treasurer. T.R. vol. III, pp. 42, 68-69, 88, 115, 139.

104. Votes and names of candidates for these years are recorded in the Town Records, vol. III, pp. 1, 29 83 104, 134.

105. Since negative votes were not recorded, the total number of voters cannot be determined with certainty.

106. T.R. vol. III, p. 28.

107. *Ibid.,* p. 83.

108. Michael Zuckerman, *Peaceable Kingdoms: New England Towns in the Eighteenth Century* (New York: Alfred Knopf, 1970), pp. 165-69.

109. T.R. vol. III, p. 134.

110. 1683: 197 of 494 total affirmative votes, or 39.9%; 1685: 72 of 191 affirmative votes, or 37.7%. *Ibid.*, pp. 83, 134.

111. T.R. vol. I, p. 231. Only five men were actually chosen in 1659 due to a successful attempt to eliminate the Quaker, Joseph Boyce, who received the sixth highest number of votes.

112. 19.1% of the Salem Village taxpayers were eligible to vote, comprising 29.3% of the eligible voters in 1683.

113. Even the estimated number of voters in Salem in 1659 was not large in comparison to other towns. Lockridge et al. claim that 90% of the adult males in Dedham were eligible to vote prior to 1670, a proportion which decreased to 60% by 1686. (Kenneth Lockridge and Alan Kreider, "The Evolution of Massachusetts Town Government, 1640-1740," *William and Mary Quarterly,* 3d Ser., vol. XXXIV (1967), pp. 393-94; Lockridge, Simmons and Foster, "Letter to the Editor," *W & MQ,* 3d Ser., vol. XXV (1968), p. 332.

114. E.g., T.R. vol. I, pp. 40, 84, 92, 106, 127, 132, 136, 192, 209.

115. *Ibid.*, p. 184.

116. T.R. vol. II, pp. 15, 56, 66, 90.

117. *Ibid.*, pp. 56, 91-92.

118. T.R. vol. I, pp. 131-32, 179.

119. T.R. vol. II, pp. 145, 167.

120. *Mass. Bay Recs.*, vol. V, p. 305 (1681). The Court limited Salem at Higginson's request to two wine taverns, four inns, and four retailers of wine and strong liquors." The total adult male population of the town (including Salem Village) was at that time approximately 550.

121. *Ibid.*, p. 180. Children from one more family were also placed out that year.

122. Cotton Mather, *Family Religion Urged* (Boston: Printed by B. Green, 1709), p. 1. See Morgan, *Puritan Family,* pp. 133-60 for an extended discussion of this topic.

123. T.R. vol. II, p. 210.

124. *Ibid.*

125. *Ibid.*

126. *Ibid.*, p. 238.

127. *Ibid.*, p. 239.

128. *Ibid.*, pp. 239-40. See also *Colonial Laws*, p. 235, and Morgan, *Puritan Family*, pp. 148-49.

129. T.R. vol. II, p. 270.

130. *Ibid.*, p. 311.

131. T.R. vol. III, p. 18-19. The number was reduced to two in each ward after 1681 (*Ibid.*, pp. 46, 94).

132. *Ibid.*, p. 55; this order was repeated verbatim in 1682 (*Ibid.*, p. 82).

133. *Church Records*, p. 5. (Published version)

134. T.R. vol. II, pp. 243, 304-5.

135. *Ibid.*, p. 304.

136. *Ibid.*, p. 303.

137. *Ibid.*, p. 308.

138. *Ibid.*, p. 305.

139. T.R. vol. III, p. 108.

140. *Ibid.*

141. *Ibid.*, p. 55.

142. *Ibid.*, p. 107.

143. *Ibid.*, p. 138; again in 1686, p. 164.

144. T.R. vol. II, p. 89.

145. *Ibid.*, p. 118.

146. T.R. vol. III, pp. 109, 135, 156.

147. *Ibid.*, p. 181.

148. *Ibid.*, p. 198.

149. *Ibid.*, p. 200.

150. T.R. vol. II, pp. 210, 238.

151. T.R. vol. III, p. 198.

Chapter Twelve

1. Perley, vol. III, p. 208. See Robert E. Wall, *Massachusetts Bay: The Crucial Decade,* for an extended discussion of colonial relations with England prior to 1650.

2. Perley, vol. III, p. 209.

3. Perley, vol. III, p. 210; Bailyn, *New England Merchants,* p. 132. A conciliatory letter was sent by men from Salem, Boston, Newbury and Ipswich, however, declaring their obeisance to the King (Massachusetts Historical Society, *Collections,* Ser. 2, vol. VIII, (Boston, 1814), pp. 103-7); 33 Salem men signed this letter, only two of whom were among the major leaders (Edmund Batter and William Brown). Bailyn notes that support for the Commission of 1665 came largely from newly arrived merchants who did not join the Boston church (*New England Merchants,* p. 124). Paul Lucas notes this division between a small number of merchants "half-hearted in covenant theology" and the majority of Bay leaders who desired independence over conciliation. ("Colony or Commonwealth: Massachusetts Bay 1661-1666," *W&MQ,* vol. XXIV (1967), pp. 88-107.) The General Court, in an attempt to appease the Royal Commissioners sent to the colony in 1665, did broaden the franchise requirements as ordered by the king in 1662 hoping thereby to protect other liberties enjoyed by the Bay Colony.

4. T.R. vol. III, p. 162.

5. See for example, Lockridge, p. 88.

6. Perley, vol. III, p. 211.

7. *Ibid.*

8. Gildrie, pp. 150-51.

9. Hathorne, Gedney and Brown had, in fact, been elevated to the Court of Assistants after 1680 due to their prior years of exemplary service as deputies.

10. T.R. vol. III, p. 198.

11. *Ibid.,* p. 199.

12. *Ibid.,* p. 209. This "overplus" was extraordinary. In 1683, for example, the extra tax for the town added to the colony rate was only £6 15s. 11d. (T.R. vol. III, p. 99)

13. *Ibid.,* pp. 200-201.

14. *Ibid.,* pp. 201-2.

15. *Ibid.*, pp. 200-1.

16. *Ibid.*, pp. 208, 210.

17. *Ibid.*, p. 208.

18. *Ibid.*, pp. 202-4, 209-10.

19. *Ibid.*, p. 211.

20. *Ibid.*, p. 214.

21. *Ibid.*, pp. 216, 224-25.

22. *Ibid.*, pp. 226, 228-29. Again in March in 1691 the town meeting approved new rates, this time for £180 (*Ibid.*, pp. 242-43).

23. The other three were Jonathan Corwin Jr., Timothy Lindall, and John Leach.

24. The policy of requiring the Villagers to pay half rates for the ministry of the peninsula is nowhere iterated, but in 1682 "George Hacker is abated half his rate to the minister this year upon consideration of his removal to live among the farmers." T.R. vol. III, p. 68. Since Village church members continued to use the Salem church on sacrament days, they were apparently required to assume a portion of the rate for the minister who administered the sacraments—in addition to their own minister in the Village.

25. See Boyer and Nissenbaum, *Salem Village Witchcraft.* pp. 237-39.

26. The fact that no Putnams appear on the lists of defeated candidates for the office in those years during the 1680s when votes were recorded suggests that they did not aspire to the office, since it would have been a simple matter to nominate each other.

27. T.R. vol. III, p. 206.

28. See *supra,* "The Consequences of Dispersion and Differentiation: The Church," p. 126.

29. T.R. vol. III, p. 211.

30. *Ibid.*, p. 214.

31. See *supra,* "The Consequences of Dispersion and Differentiation: The Town," pp. 141-42. Another factor in the Villagers' desire for separation may have been their decreasing wealth *per capita* as the second and third generations divided their fathers' lands. (See Boyer and Nissenbaum, *Salem Possessed,* pp. 89-91.) Meanwhile, the average wealth of the townsmen was increasing, according to probate statistics. (See Manfred Jonas, "The Wills of the Early Settlers of Essex County, Massachusetts," *EIHC,* vol. XCVI (1960). See also Gildrie, p. 167.)

32. The only other selectmen who arrived after 1640 and were elected prior to 1685 were Nicholas Manning, a gunsmith who arrived in 1663, and Dr. Weld, who arrived in 1669. They each served one term in 1675.

33. These extra-local ties signal a new phase of community organization according to Robert Redfield's theory (*Peasant Society and Culture*, Chicago: University of Chicago Press, 1956, pp. 24-34).

34. Perley, vol. III, pp. 102-3, 301. Gerrish married Hannah Ruck, daughter of one of Salem's rising merchants, and was a nephew by marriage of Walter Price.

35. Perley, vol. III, pp. 163-65, 216, 165. Stephen Sewall's brother Samuel also became well known as a leading citizen of Boston; this commercial family relationship, like extra-local marriage, was a new phenomenon in the late charter period, and is another example of the increasing incidence of "vertical" relationships (see *supra*, n. 33).

36. Bernard Bailyn (*New England Merchants in the Seventeenth Century*) brilliantly chronicled the emergence of men like Gerrish and Sewall, but has overestimated their political impact—at least in Salem—before the Glorious Revolution.

37. The discussion which follows is based on tax lists for 1683 and 1689. The original lists for 1689 are available (manuscript collections of the Essex Institute); however, only Philip English's list of rates is available in the original form for 1683 (Manuscript collections, County Clerk's Office, Salem), and the published version of that list (Perley, vol. III, pp. 419-22) is somewhat different; 5 of the names on the original do not appear in the printed version—which is the one Gildrie used—while 11 names appear in Perley's printed list but not on the original. Gildrie's results, and mine for the other five wards in 1683, must therefore be regarded as approximations.

38. Nathaniel Putnam and John Putnam Jr., both among the top taxpayers, were members of the original Village Church covenant in 1689; Joseph Putnam, also a top taxpayer, was not. The conflict between Joseph and his brothers after 1689 is a major chapter in the witchcraft episode; see Boyer and Nissenbaum, *Salem Possessed*, pp. 133-52.

39. Captain Samuel Gardner served 13 terms after 1689; Timothy Lindall, 5; John Pickering Jr., 7; Israel Porter, 10; John Hathorne did not serve after 1684, and Bartholemew Gedney's last term was in 1686; John Leach never served.

40. See Appendix A for complete list and categorization.

41. Even by 1678, the General Court recognized the increasing population of the eastern end of the peninsula and assigned 50 "fishermen and seamen" who lived there to the western company of the peninsula for balance [*Mass. Bay Recs.*, vol. V, p. 204 (October 7, 1678)]; Salem Village had separated into its own company the previous year (*Mass. Bay Recs.*, vol. V, p. 172). See Appendix B, Map 5.

42. T.R. vol. III, p. 205.

43. See Bailyn, *New England Merchants,* p. 96, for a discussion of the similar transformation of Boston.

44. Donald Warner Koch, "Income Distribution and Political Structure in 17th Century Salem, Massachusetts," *Essex Institute Historical Collections,* vol. CV (1969), p. 60. The tax distribution is based on my own computations.

45. *Ibid.,* pp. 55, 57-58.

46. Some of these men may in fact have inherited property by 1689.

47. This process is outlined by Boyer and Nissenbaum, *Salem Possessed,* pp. 90-91; the diminished resources of the third generation in the Village was a factor in the tensions which produced the accusations of witchcraft.

48. Bailyn, *New England Merchants,* pp. 102-3.

49. 48.8% of the light artisans were sons of Salem residents, compared to 37% of the seamen; average age at first purchase was 28.6 for artisans, 32.2 for seamen.

50. The crowded conditions in the east end can also be seen in the fact that all of the seamen who lived elsewhere in 1689 had arrived in Salem after 1670, by which time housing in the eastern wards had become scarce.

51. These figures are taken from several sources: English's list and the six lists for 1689 from the original manuscript at the Essex Institute; the other five lists for 1683 are from Perley, vol. III, pp. 419-22.

52. T.R. vol. III, pp. 99, 208-9. The town paid slightly more than the ½ rate required in 1683 (£32 18s 4d instead of £30) so these figures are not exactly equivalent.

53. The minutes of these meetings are in the manuscript collections of the Essex Institute. (South Field Proprietors' Records, Volume II, "Petitions and Lists"; includes records of 1668-1669, 1673-1690, and lists of proprietors for 1678, 1691, and 1701.) Of the proprietors of known occupation, 10.8% were yeomen or husbandmen, 13.5% were seamen, 18.9% were merchants, and 56.8% were artisans—again showing the persistance and stability of that group of the population. The South Field proprietorship lasted until 1742, and the North Field was dissolved around 1750. (Felt, vol. I, pp. 185-86)

54. T.R. vol. III, p. 204.

55. Jonas, "Wills," p. 234. 80% of the assets of the wealthiest farmers consisted of land. See also Koch, "Income Distribution," p. 58.

56. Bailyn, *New England Merchants,* p. 139.

57. *Ibid.,* p. 170.

58. Gildrie notes the rise of these merchants, but says they "did not threaten the political or social dominance of the older families." (pp. 168-69) By carrying the analysis forward just two years, this statement no longer holds.

59. Bailyn, *New England Merchants,* p. 144. Philip English epitomizes the wider commercial contacts which assured the success of these new merchants.

60. *Ibid.,* p. 155.

61. T.R. vol. III, p. 204.

62. Morgan, *Founding,* p. 454; *Church Records,* p. 3.

Appendix A

Occupations of Salem Heads of Households

Agriculture:
  Farmer
  Husbandman
  Planter
  Yeoman

Seamen:
  Fisherman
  Mariner
  Master mariner
  Salter
  Sea captain
  Seaman
  Shoreman

Merchants:
  Merchant
  Ordinary keeper
  Shipowner
  Shopkeeper
  Tavernkeeper

Sea Trades:
  Chandler
  Cooper
  Netmaker
  Ropemaker
  Sailmaker
  Shipbuilder
  Ship Carpenter

Building Trades:
  Brickmaker

Glassmaker
Glazier
House carpenter
Housewright
Joiner
Mason
Plasterer
Shingler
Turner

Laborer:
  Clerk
  Chimneysweep
  Ferryman
  Laborer
  Servant

Heavy Artisans:
  Blacksmith
  Brickmaker
  Calender
  Carter
  Currier
  Dryer
  Fellmonger
  Fuller
  Ironmonger
  Maltster
  Miller
  Millwright
  Pumpmaker
  Sadler
  Sawyer

Slaughterer
Soapboiler
Sowgelder
Tanner
Traymaker
Vintner
Wheelwright

Professional:
  Attorney
  Chirurgeon
  Pastor
  Physician
  Schoolmaster
  Teacher
  Translator

Light Artisans:
  Apothecary
  Baker
  Barber
  Candlemaker
  Cutler
  Glover
  Goldsmith
  Gunsmith
  Hatmaker
  Pewterer
  Potter
  Shoemaker
  Tailor
  Upholsterer
  Weaver

Appendix B

Maps

Map 1
Essex County in 1643

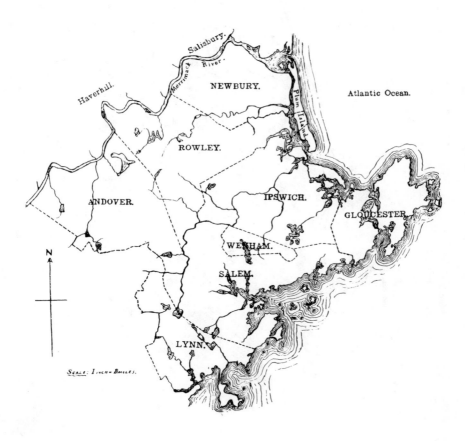

Map 2
Salem in 1629

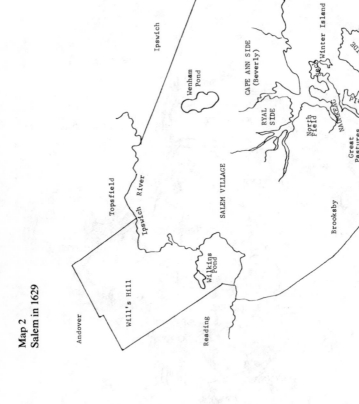

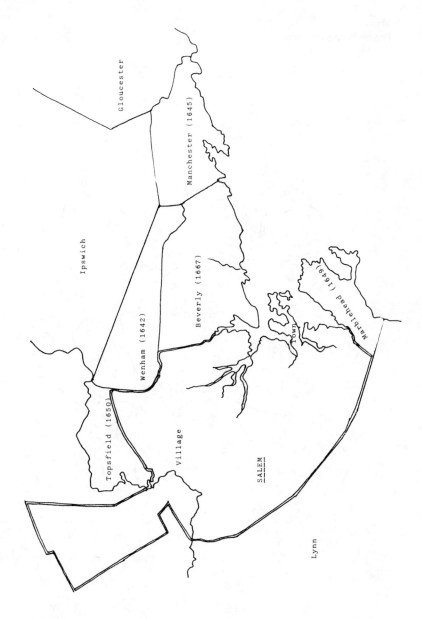

Map 3
Salem after 1668

Map 4
Peninsula and Environs

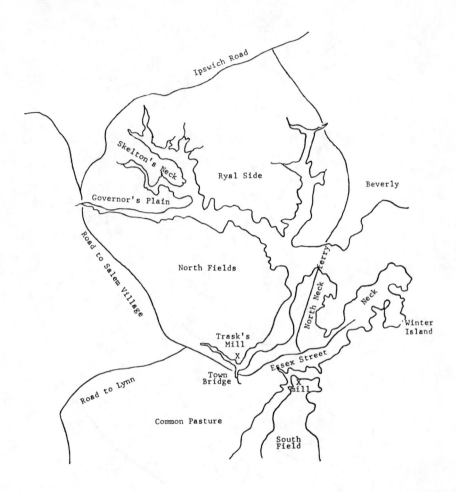

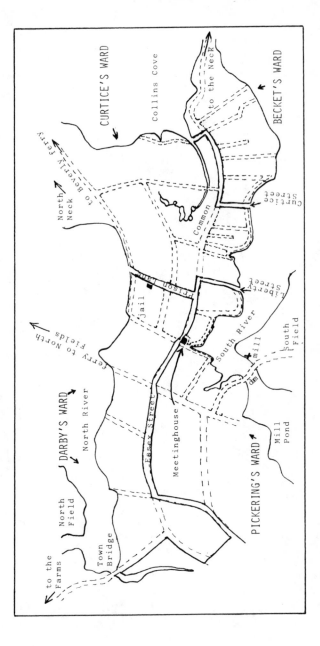

Map 5
The Peninsula in 1689

The Four Tax Wards of the Main Peninsula of Salem in 1689

William Becket—East of Curtice Street and south of Essex (Main) Street

William Curtice—East of Prison Lane and south of Essex Street to harbor

John Pickering—West of Liberty Street and south of Essex Street

Roger Darby—West of Prison Lane and north of Essex Street

(Based on a map from the researches of Sidney Perley, assembled by William W. K. Freeman; Copyright 1933 by James Duncan Phillips, Salem, Massachusetts. 1689 Tax Wards calculated by this author from tax lists and deeds.)

Appendix C

Tables

Table I
Distribution of Land in 1636

Minimal majority = 15.0% of population (22 of 147) who own 51.6% (4820 acres) of
the land in amounts of 150 acres or more apiece.

The lower half = 49.7% of population (73 of 147) who own 16.1% (1500 acres) of
the land in amounts of 30 acres or less apiece.

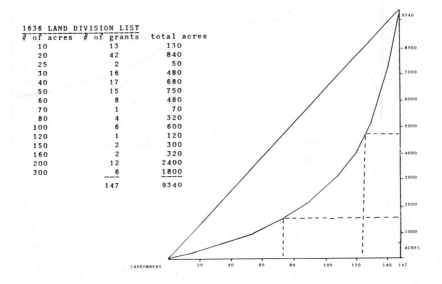

1636 LAND DIVISION LIST		
# of acres	# of grants	total acres
10	13	130
20	42	840
25	2	50
30	16	480
40	17	680
50	15	750
60	8	480
70	1	70
80	4	320
100	6	600
120	1	120
150	2	300
160	2	320
200	12	2400
300	6	1800
	147	9340

Table II
Church Membership Relative to
Population Size, 1636-1689
(heads of households only)

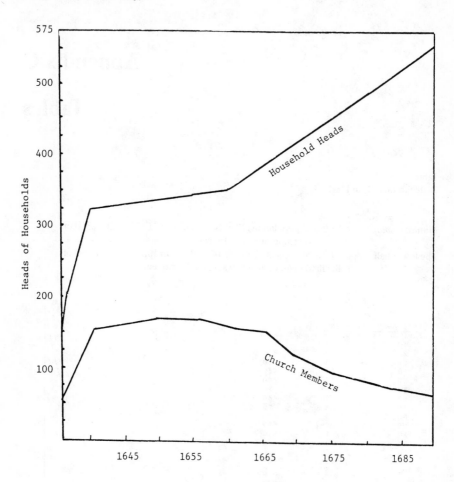

Table III
Number and Percentage of Church Members in Each Ward, 1683-1689

Tax list	of 1683 Church members		of 1689 Free & CM after 1650	of 1689 Church member only	of 1689 Free & CM before 1650	of 1689 Total members	
	#	%	#	#	#	#	%
East End							
English/Becket	16	= 11.7	5	6	1	12	= 10.2
Phelps/Curtice	12	= 14.5	5	3	1	9	= 10.7
West End							
Lambert/Derby	10	= 14.1	4	1	0	5	= 6.3
Hirst/Pickering	11	= 13.8	8	5	0	13	= 14.0
Beyond Bridge							
Hayward/Trask	15	= 22.7	6	4	1	11	= 10.2
Pope/Putnam	17	= 22.7	7	6	4	17	= 16.3
TOTALS	81	= 15.8	35	25	7	67	= 12.2

Bibliography

Primary Sources

Boyer, Paul and Nissenbaum, Stephen, eds. *Salem Village Witchcraft: A Documentary Record of Local Conflict in Colonial New England*. Belmont, California: Wadsworth Publishing Company, Inc., 1972.

Bradford, William. *Of Plymouth Plantation* . . . Notes and Introduction by Samuel Eliot Morison. New York: Knopf, 1966.

_____ . "Governor Bradford's Letter-Book," *Collections of the Massachusetts Historical Society*, ser. I, vol. 3, 1794. Reprinted by Munroe and Francis, no. 4 Cornhill, Boston, 1810, pp. 27-77.

Cotton, John. in "Plymouth Church Records (vol. I, pt. 2)," *Publications of the Colonial Society of Massachusetts*, vol. 22 (1920), pp. 142-89.

Essex County Deeds. Essex County Registry of Deeds, Salem, Massachusetts, 1638 to the present. Uncatalogued manuscripts filed chronologically; handwritten copies made in the nineteenth century available in bound volumes also at the Registry of Deeds.

Hall, David D. "John Cotton's Letter to Samuel Skelton," *William and Mary Quarterly*, ser. 3, vol. 22 (July, 1965), pp. 478-85.

Higginson, John. *The Cause of God and His People in New England* . . . Cambridge: Printed By Samuel Green, 1663.

Hubbard, William. *A General History of New England from the Discovery to 1680*. Second Edition. Boston: C.C. Little and J. Brown, 1878.

Johnson, Edward. *Wonder-Working Providence of Sion's Saviour in New England* (1654). Reprinted, Edward J. Gallagher, ed. Delmar, New York: Scholars' Facsimiles and Reprints, Inc., 1974.

Mather, Cotton. *Family Religion Urged: Or, some serious consideration offer'd to the reason and conscience of every prayerless householder* . . . Boston: Printed by B. Green, 1709.

_____ . *Magnalia Christi Americana: Or, the ecclesiastical history of New-England, from its first planting in the year 1620, unto the year of our Lord, 1698*. Book I, Chapter 4. (London, 1702). First American edition from the London edition of 1702. Hartford: S. Andrews, 1820.

Morgan, Edmund S., ed. *The Founding of Massachusetts: Historians and the Sources*. New York: The Bobbs-Merrill Company, Inc., 1964.

Morton, Nathaniel. *New England's Memorial; or, A Brief Relation of the Most Memorable and Remarkable Passages of the Providence of God, Manifested to the Planters of New England in America* (Cambridge; Printed by S.G. and M.J. for John Usher of Boston, 1669). Reprinted by Howard J. Hall, ed. New York: Scholars' Facsimiles and Reprints, 1937.

Morton, Thomas. *New English Canaan* (Amsterdam, 1637). Facsimile edition, Amsterdam, 1969.

Pierce, Richard D., ed. *Records of the First Church in Salem, 1629-1736*. Introduction by Robert E. Moody. Salem: Essex Institute, 1974.

Probate Records of Essex County, Massachusetts, 1635-1681. Vol. I (1635-1664), vol. II (1665-1674), vol. III (1675-1681). Salem: Essex Institute, 1916.

Records and Files of the Quarterly Courts of Essex County, Massachusetts. Vol. I (1636-1656), vol. II (1656-1662), vol. III (1662-1667), vol. IV (1667-1671), vol. V (1672-1674), vol. VI (1675-1678), vol. VII (1678-1680), vol. VIII (1680-1683). George Francis Dow, ed. Salem: Essex Institute, 1911.

Salem Church Covenants. A Copy of the Church-Covenants which Have Been Used in the Church of Salem both formerly and in their late renewing of their covenant on the day of the public fast, April 15, 1680. As a direction pointing to that covenant of God's grace in Christ made with his church and people in the holy scripture. Boston: Printed, at the desire and for the use of many in Salem, for themselves and their children, by J.F[oster], 1680. Evans Microcard no. 295.

Salem Church Records, 1629-1736. Typewritten copy of the manuscript. Salem, Massachusetts: Essex Institute.

Salem Village Church Records. Manuscript collections. First Church of Danvers, Massachusetts.

Shurtleff, Nathaniel B, ed. *Records of the Governor and Company of the Massachusetts Bay in New England, 1628-1686*. Five volumes. Boston: William White, 1853-1854.

South Field Proprietors' Records. Vol. II, Petitions and Lists. Includes records of 1668-1669, 1673-1690, and lists from 1678, 1691 and 1701. Uncatalogued manuscripts of the Essex Institute.

Tax List of Constable Philip English, 1683. Manuscript collections. County Clerk's Office, Salem, Massachusetts.

Tax Lists of 1689. Manuscript collections. Essex Institute, Salem, Massachusetts.

Town Account Book, 1679-1707/8. Records of constables' accounts and bills owed by the town. Uncatalogued manuscripts. Essex Institute, Salem, Massachusetts.

"Town Records of Salem, Massachusetts, 1634-1659," *Essex Institute Historical Collections*, vol. IX (1868), pp. 5-233. *Salem Town Records, 1659-1680*. Salem: Essex Institute, 1913. *Salem Town Records, 1681-1691*. Salem: Essex Institute, 1934.

Vital Records of Salem, Massachusetts, to the End of the Year 1849. Six volumes. Salem: Essex Institute, 1916.

White, John. *The Planter's Plea* (London, 1630). Reprinted in *Proceedings of the Massachusetts Historical Society*, ser. 3, vol. 62 (1929), pp. 365-425.

Whitmore, William H., ed. *Book of the General Lawes and Libertyes Concerning the Inhabitants of the Massachusetts* (Cambridge, 1660). Reprinted in facsimile, with supplements to 1672. Boston, 1889.

Winthrop, John. *Journal, 1630-1649*. Two volumes. James Kendall Hosmer, ed. New York: C. Scribner's Sons, 1908.

Wood, William. *New England's Prospect; a true, lively and experimental description . . .* London: Printed by T. Cotes for I. Bellamie, 1634; Boston: Printed for the Society, 1865.

Secondary Sources

Adams, Herbert B. *Salem Commons and Commoners*. Salem: Essex Institute, 1882.

Andrews, Charles M. *The Colonial Period of American History: The Settlements*. Volume I. New Haven: Yale University Press, 1934.

Bailyn, Bernard. *New England Merchants in the Seventeenth Century.* Cambridge: Harvard University Press, 1955.

_____ . "Politics and Social Structure in Virginia," in *Seventeenth Century America.* James Morton Smith, ed. Chapel Hill: University of North Carolina Press, 1959.

Banks, Charles Edward. *The Planters of the Commonwealth . . . 1620-1640.* Boston: Houghton, Mifflin Co., 1930.

_____ . *Topographical Dictionary of 2885 English Emigrants to New England, 1620-1650.* Edited, indexed and published by Elijah Ellsworth Brownell. Philadelphia, Pennsylvania: The Bertram Press, 1937.

_____ . "The 'West Country' Origin of Salem's Settlement," *Essex Institute Historical Collections.* Vol. 66 (1930), pp. 317-24.

Belknap, Henry W. *Trades and Tradesmen of Essex County, Chiefly of the Seventeenth Century.* Salem: Essex Institute, 1929.

Bentley, Rev. William. "A Description and History of Salem," *Massachusetts Historical Society Collections,* ser. I, vol. VI (1799). Reprinted, Charles C. Little & James Brown, 1846, pp. 212-88.

Blake, J.B. "The Early History of Vital Statistics in Massachusetts," *History of Medicine,* vol. 29 (1955), pp. 113-19.

Bodge, George Madison. *Soldiers in King Philips's War.* Reconstructed rosters of the Massachusetts companies. Leominster, Massachusetts: Printed for the author, 1896.

Boyer, Paul, and Nissenbaum, Stephen. *Salem Possessed: The Social Origins of Witchcraft.* Cambridge: Harvard University Press, 1974.

Breen, Timothy. "Who Governs: The Town Franchise in Massachusetts," *William and Mary Quarterly,* vol. XXVII (July, 1970), pp. 460-74.

Brown, B. Katherine. "The Controversy over the Franchise in Puritan Massachusetts, 1954-1974," *William and Mary Quarterly,* ser. 3, vol. XXXIII (1976), pp. 212-41.

Davisson, William I. "Essex County Price Trends: Money and Markets in 17th Century Massachusetts," *Essex Institute Historical Collections,* vol. CIII (1967), pp. 144-85.

_____ . "Essex County Wealth Trends: Wealth and Economic Growth in Seventeenth Century Massachusetts," *Essex Institute Historical Collections,* vol. CIII (1967), pp. 291-342.

Demos, John. *A Little Commonwealth: Family Life in Plymouth Colony.* New York: Oxford University Press, 1970.

_____ . "Notes on Life in Plymouth Colony," *William and Mary Quarterly,* ser. 3, vol. XXII (April, 1965), pp. 264-86.

Erikson, Kai. *Wayward Puritans: A Study in the Sociology of Deviance.* New York: John Wiley & Sons, Inc., 1966.

Felt, Joseph B. *Annals of Salem.* Two volumes. Salem: W. & S.B. Ives, 1845.

Foster, Stephen. "The Massachusetts Franchise in the 17th Century," *William and Mary Quarterly,* vol. XXIV (1967), pp. 613-23.

Gildrie, Richard P. *Salem, Massachusetts, 1626-1683: A Covenant Community.* Charlottesville: University Press of Virginia, 1975.

Ginsburg, Arlin I. "The Franchise in Seventeenth-Century Massachusetts: Ipswich," *William and Mary Quarterly,* ser. 3, vol. XXXIV (July, 1977), pp. 446-52.

Greven, Philip J., Jr. *Four Generations: Population, Land and Family in Colonial Andover, Massachusetts.* Ithaca: Cornell University Press, 1970.

_____ . "Historical Demography and Colonial America," *William and Mary Quarterly,* vol. XXIV (1967), pp. 438-54.

Gutman, Robert. "Birth and Death Registration in Massachusetts: The Colonial Background, 1639-1800," *The Milbank Memorial Fund Quarterly,* vol. 36 (1958), pp. 58-65.

Higgs, Robert and Stettler, H. Louis, III. "Colonial New England Demography: A Sampling Approach," *William and Mary Quarterly,* vol. XXVII (April, 1970), pp. 282-94.

Homans, George C. "The Explanation of English Regional Differences," *Past and Present,* no. 42 (1969), pp. 18-34.

Hurd, D. Hamilton. *History of Essex County.* Vol. I. Philadelphia: J.W. Lewis & Co., 1888.

Hutchinson, Thomas. *The History of Massachusetts, from the first settlement thereof in 1628, until the year 1750.* Salem: Thomas C. Cushing, for Thomas & Andrews, 1795.

Jonas, Manfred. "Wills of Early Settlers of Essex County, Massachusetts," *Essex Institute Historical Collections,* vol. XCVI (1960), pp. 228-35.

Koch, Donald Warner. "Income Distribution and Political Structure in 17th Century Salem, Massachusetts," *Essex Institute Historical Collections,* vol. CV (1969), pp. 50-69.

Kuczynski, R.R. "The Registration Laws in the Colonies of Massachusetts Bay and New Plymouth," *Journal of the American Statistical Association* (1900-1910), pp. 65-73.

Lapham, Alice Gertrude. *The Old Planters of Beverly in Massachusetts and the Thousand Acre Grant of 1635.* Cambridge: Riverside Press, 1930.

Laslett, Peter. "Mean Household Size in England since the Sixteenth Century," in *Household and Family in Past Time.* Edited with an analytic introduction on the history of the family by Peter Laslett and Richard Wall. London: Cambridge University Press, 1972, pp. 125-58.

Lockridge, Kenneth A. *A New England Town: The First Hundred Years.* New York: W.W. Norton & Co., 1970.

————, and Kreider, Alan. "The Evolution of Massachusetts Town Government, 1640-1740," *William and Mary Quarterly,* ser. 3, vol. XXIII (October, 1966), pp. 549-74.

Lockridge, Simmons, and Foster. "Letter to the Editor," *William and Mary Quarterly,* ser. 3, vol. XXV (1968), pp. 330-34.

Lucas, Paul R. "Colony or Commonwealth: Massachusetts Bay 1661-1666," *William and Mary Quarterly,* vol. XXIV (1967), pp. 88-107.

McGiffert, Michael. "American Puritan Studies in the 1960's," *William and Mary Quarterly,* vol. XXVII (January, 1970), pp. 36-67.

Miller, Perry. *The New England Mind: The Seventeenth Century.* New York: The Macmillan Company, 1939.

Morgan, Edmund. *The Puritan Family; Religion and Domestic Relations in Seventeenth Century New England.* New York: Harper and Row, Publishers, Inc., 1966.

————. *Roger Williams: The Church and the State.* New York: Harcourt, Brace & World, 1967.

————. *Visible Saints: The History of a Puritan Idea.* Ithaca: Cornell University Press, 1965.

Nellis, Eric Guest. "Labor and Community in Massachusetts Bay: 1630-1660," *Labor History,* vol. XVIII, no. 4 (Fall, 1977), pp. 525-44.

Norton, Susan L. "Marital Migration in Essex County, Massachusetts in the Colonial and Early Federal Periods," *Journal of Marriage and the Family,* vol. 35 (1973), pp. 406-16.

Perley, Sidney. *History of Salem, Massachusetts.* Three volumes. Salem: Sidney Perley, 1924.

Phillips, James Duncan. *Salem in the Seventeenth Century.* Boston: Houghton Mifflin Co., 1933.

Pope, Robert G. *The Half-Way Covenant: Church Membership in Puritan New England.* Princeton: Princeton University Press, 1969.

Powell, Sumner Chilton. *Puritan Village: The Formation of a New England Town.* Middletown: Wesleyan University Press, 1964.

Rutman, Darrett. *Husbandmen of Plymouth.* Boston: Beacon Press, 1967.

_____. *Winthrop's Boston: A Portrait of a Puritan Town, 1630-1649*. New York: W.W. Norton & Company, Inc., 1965.

Savage, James. *A Genealogical Dictionary of the First Settlers of New England, showing three generations of those who came before May, 1692, on the basis of Farmer's Register.* Boston: Little, Brown & Company, 1860-1862.

Shammas, Carole. "The Determinants of Personal Wealth in Seventeenth Century England and America," *Journal of Economic History,* vol. XXXVII (September, 1977), pp. 675-89.

Simmons, Richard C. "Freemanship in Early Massachusetts: Some Suggestions and a Case Study, *William and Mary Quarterly,* ser. 3, vol. XIX (July, 1962), pp. 422-28.

Tawney, R.H. *The Agrarian Problem in the Sixteenth Century.* London: Longmans, Green, and Co., 1912.

Thirsk, Joan, ed. *The Agrarian History of England and Wales, 1500-1640.* Cambridge: Cambridge University Press, 1967.

_____. "The Family," *Past and Present,* vol. XXVII (April, 1964), pp. 116-22.

Wall, Robert Emmet, Jr. "The Franchise in Seventeenth-Century Massachusetts: Dedham and Cambridge," *William and Mary Quarterly,* ser. 3, vol. XXXIV (July, 1977), pp. 453-58.

_____. "The Massachusetts Bay Colony Franchise in 1647," *William and Mary Quarterly,* vol. XXVII (January, 1970), pp. 136-44.

_____. *Massachusetts Bay: The Crucial Decade.* New Haven: Yale University Press, 1972.

_____. "A New Look at Cambridge," *Journal of American History,* vol. 52 (3) (1965), pp. 599-605.

Zuckerman, Michael. "The Fabrication of Identity in Early America," *William and Mary Quarterly,* ser. 3, vol. XXXIV (April, 1977), pp. 183-214.

_____. *Peaceable Kingdoms: New England Towns in the Eighteenth Century.* New York: Alfred Knopf, 1970.

_____. "The Social Context of Democracy in Massachusetts," *William and Mary Quarterly,* ser. 3, vol. XXV (October, 1968), pp. 523-44.

Methodological Sources

Alker, Hayward R., Jr. *Mathematics and Politics.* New York: The Macmillan Company, 1965.

Arensberg, Conrad M. and Kimball, Solon T. *Culture and Community.* Gloucester, Massachusetts: Peter Smith, 1972.

Beeman, Richard C. "The New Social History and the Search for 'Community' in Colonial America," *American Quarterly,* vol. XXIX (Fall, 1977), pp. 422-43.

Blumer, Herbert. *Symbolic Interaction: Perspective and Method.* Englewood Cliffs, N.J.: Prentice Hall, 1969.

Geertz, Clifford. "Thick Description: Toward an Interpretive Theory of Culture," in Geertz, *The Interpretation of Cultures.* New York: Basic Books, 1973, pp. 3-30.

Goist, Park D. " 'City' and 'Community': The Urban Theory of Robert Park," *American Quarterly,* vol. XXIII (1971), pp. 45-69.

Homans, George C. "A Conceptual Scheme for the Study of Social Organization," *American Sociological Review,* vol. XII, no. 1 (February, 1947), pp. 13-26.

Kaufman, Harold. "Toward an Interactional Concept of Community," *Social Forces,* vol. XXXVIII (1959), pp. 9-17.

Redfield, Robert. *The Little Community; Viewpoint for the Study of a Human Whole.* Chicago: University of Chicago Press, 1955.

————. *Peasant Society and Culture*. Chicago: University of Chicago Press, 1956.

Rutman, Darrett B. "The Social Web: A Prospectus for the Study of Early American Community," in William L. O'Neill, ed., *Insights and Parallels: Problems and Issues of American Social History*. Minneapolis: Burgess, 1973, pp. 57-89.

Tonnies, Ferdinand. *Community and Society (Gemeinschaft und Gesellschaft)*. Translated and edited by Charles P. Loomis. East Lansing: Michigan State University Press, 1957.

————. *Custom: An Essay on Social Codes*. Chicago: The Macmillan Company, 1961.

Turner, Victor. *Dramas, Fields, and Metaphors: Symbolic Action in Human Society*. Ithaca: Cornell University Press, 1974.

Weber, Max. *The City*. Translated and edited by Don Martindale and Gertrud Neuwirth. New York: The Free Press, 1958.

Wolf, E. "Aspects of Group Relations in a Complex Society," *American Anthropologist*, vol. LVIII (1956), pp. 549-54.

Wrong, Dennis H. "The Oversocialized Conception of Man in Modern Sociology," *American Sociological Review*, vol. XXVI (1961), pp. 183-93.

Index of Names

Alford, William, disarmed for supporting Anne Hutchinson, 38, 205n. 38; land grant to, 193n. 3
Andrews, Daniel, 75; as selectman, 74, 171, 174, 218n. 63; land purchased by, 74; marriage into Porter family, 74; mason, 218n. 63; refuses election as selectman, 172
Andros, Edmund, 165: administration of, 168, 174, 186; abolition of Quarterly Courts during, 168; and revocation of charter, 168; justices of peace established during, 168
Archard, Samuel: as selectman, 45; guarantees new resident, 2; house carpenter, 45
Arensberg, Conrad, 7; definition of community of, 7, 194n. 21

Bachelder, John, granted poor relief, 149
Bailey, Mr., as Salem Village minister, 125, 134
Baker, Robert, denied admission to town, 19
Balch, John, as selectman, 39; Old Planter, 39
Barney, Jacob, as deputy, 36; West Country origins, 36
Bartholemew, Henry, 82; as deputy, 36, 45, 69; as selectman, 39, 45, 91, 104, 143; East Anglian origins of, 36; land grants and officeholding of, 26-27, 46, 67; merchant, 46; service on jury, 46; service on Cape Ann committee, 49
Batter, Edmund, 83, 226n. 3; anti-Quaker activities, 50-51, 303n. 64; as deputy, 36, 69; as selectman, 45, 50, 63, 91, 104, 203; commissioner for votes, 209n. 31; duties as selectman, 47; in minimal majority of 1640, 46; merchant, 45; opposes second church, 170; on jury, 46

Becket, Constable, 181
Bishop, Townsend, elected as deputy, 35; sells land and removes from Salem, 5, 66
Blevin, John, 75
Boas, Franz, 6
Bockwith, Leonard, warned out, 152
Boyce, Joseph, as selectman, 50, 200n. 21, 203n. 63, 224n. 111; Quaker, 50
Bradford, Governor William, 54, 203n. 3
Bright, Francis, 167; Conformist associated with John White, 54; returns to England, 55, 167; sent by Company, 53-54
Britt, John, receives land grant, 29-31
Brown, William, 83, 226n. 3; as deputy, 69; as selectman, 46, 50, 68, 91, 203n. 63; bequest from, for poor, 149, 221n. 59; builds corn mill, 51-52; church membership, 29-30, 46; duties as selectman, 47, 51, 145-46, 210n. 47; family, 29-30, 46; land, 29-30, 46; land grants, 67; land purchases, 46, 202n. 45, 208n. 40; officeholding, 29-30, 46; service on jury, 46
Brown, William, Jr., 177; as deputy, 119; as selectman, 100, 102, 103-4, 119; defeated, 158, 223n. 102; excused from serving as constable, 144, 211n. 6; on Council, 168, 226n. 9; proponent of second church, 170; tax rate of, 102; urges withdrawal of charter, 186
Burroughs, George, as Salem Village minister, 125

Cantlebury, Mrs., 82
Champlin, John, 152
Chaplin, John, as constable, 145
Charles II, restoration of, to throne, 167
Chase, John, warned out, 152-53
Chichester, William, 148
Chickering, Henry, removes to Dedham, 22

Clark, William, arrived, 38; in minimal
    majority of 1636, 38
Cole, Abraham, as constable, 220n. 36
Clifford, John, 82; as constable, 145
Comyns, Mr., disarmed for supporting Anne
    Hutchinson, 205n. 38
Conant, Roger, 34, 38, 40; as Cape Ann
    representative, 88, 99, 103, 141; as
    deputy, 35; as selectman, 39-40, 48,
    50-51, 68, 99, 140; dissatisfied at Ply-
    mouth, 53; draws up 1637 list, 15, 105,
    204n. 32, 205n. 33; in minimal majority
    of 1640, 24; objects to Skelton's separa-
    tism, 56; settlement of Naumkeag, 9,
    53
Cook, John, receives land grant, 26
Corwin, George: arrival, 29-30, 46, 51; as
    deputy, 69; as selectman, 45-46, 50, 68,
    100, 104, 106-7, 203n. 63, 217n. 57;
    as supporter of second church, 217n. 57;
    builds corn mill, 51-52; church member-
    ship, 29-30, 46, 51; duties as selectman,
    47, 51, 143, 210n. 47, 211n. 4; land, 29-
    30, 46, 51; land grant, 67; land pur-
    chases, 46, 202n. 45; merchant, 45;
    occupation, 29-30, 46, 51; office hold-
    ings, 29-30, 46, 51; tax rate of, 102
Corwin, John: as commander of foot com-
    pany, 122, 141; as deputy, 119; as
    selectman, 100, 104, 119; defeated,
    158; tax rate of, 102
Corwin, Jonathan: as church member,
    227n. 23; as constable, 120; as deputy,
    168; as selectman, 102, 120; proponent
    of second church, 170, 172; refuses
    election as selectman, 172; tax rate of,
    102
Corwithen, David, purchases land, 65
Cory, Giles, land grants and purchases, 77
Cotton, John, 195n. 1; Samuel Skelton
    rebuked by, 56
Cradock, Matthew, letters to John Endicott
    from, 36, 54
Cromwell, Phillip: church membership,
    28-30; land grants, 28-30; officeholding
    28-30
Curtice, Constable, 181

Davenport, Richard, 5, 66; arrival, 38;
    land owned by, 38
Derby, Constable, 181
Dodge, William Sr., land purchases and
    grants, 66
Downing, Emmanuel, East Anglian origins,
    36; as deputy, 36

Endicott, John, 35, 38, 40; adapts Ply-
    mouth's covenant, 54; arrival with
    Massachusetts Bay Company charter,
    3, 5, 10; as magistrate, 12, 34; civil
    contract written by, 34, 199n. 3;
    contact with Plymouth church, 54; as
    governor, 201n. 26; as selectman, 40,
    42, 45; landholdings of, 38; power to
    grant land of, 12; principles of land
    distribution of, 14; receives orders
    from Company concerning government,
    33-34, 36
English, Philip, as constable, 146, 183,
    187, 228n. 37; extra-local ties of,
    230n. 59

Felton, Benjamin, as constable, 144
Felton, Nathaniel, 223n. 102
Fiske, John, gathers Wenham church, 22
Flint, Edward, as selectman, 172
Flint, Thomas, excused as constable, 151
Fogg, Ralph, enumerates families and
    acreage, 14, 30, 61, 204n. 32
Foot, Isaac, refuses election as constable,
    145
Fuller, Deacon Samuel, transmits Ply-
    mouth's covenant idea to Salem, 54

Gardner family, arrival of, 178; sons
    receive land grants, 26
Gardner, Ebenezer, bequest from, for
    poor, 149
Gardner, John, 221n. 45
Gardner, Joseph, as commander of foot
    company, 122
Gardner, Samuel as selectman, 172,
    228n. 39
Gardner, Thomas, as selectman, 172
Gardner, Thomas, Sr., 74; as selectman,
    39, 42, 45, 203n. 63; receives land
    grant, 26
Gedney, Bartholemew, 177; as Assistant,
    214n. 44, 226n. 9; as Deputy, 214n. 44;
    as selectman, 119, 228n. 39; joins
    church, 110-111; on Andros' Council,
    168; opposes second church, 170; urges
    withdrawal of charter, 186
Gerrish, Benjamin, 228n. 34, 228n. 36; as
    selectman, 174; colonial offices of,
    174; wealth of, 174
Gildre, Richard, 6
Giles, Eleazer, as constable, 146, 220n. 36
Goldthwaite, Thomas, 153
Goodale, Robert, land grants and purchases
    of, 77
Goose, Mrs. 82

Grafton, Joseph, Sr., as selectman, 102; tax rate of, 102

Graves, Richard, admitted by selectmen, 19; denied admission to town by freemen, 19

Guppy, Reuben, 62-63, 160

Hacker, George, rates of, abated, 227n. 24

Haines, William, sells land and removes from Salem, 5, 66

Hale, Mr., Cape Ann minister, 113

Hardy, John, as selectman, 45, 100; mariner, 45

Harwood, Henry, purchases land, 65

Hathorne, Eleazer, excused from serving as constable, 144, 211n. 6

Hathorne, John, 168, 177; as Assistant, 214n. 44, 226n. 9; as deputy, 119, 214n. 44; as justice of the peace, 165; as selectman, 102, 104, 119, 155-156; as supporter of second church, 134, 170; defeated, 158, 228n. 39; land purchases and grants, 66, 206n. 23; refuses election as elder, 137, 170; tax rate of, 102

Hathorne, William: anti-Quaker activities of, 50-51, 202n. 60, 303n. 64; as deputy, 36, 69; as selectman, 40, 42, 45-46, 50, 91, 104, 106, 143, 153, 217n. 57; as supporter of second church, 134, 217n. 57; church membership of, 2; duties as selectman, 47; immigrated from Berkshire, Midlands, 36, 40; in minimal majority of 1640, 46; land grant, 2; land purchases, 65, 67, 206n. 23; land sales, 66; on Court of Assistants, 36; service on Cape Ann committee, 49

Hayward, as constable, 183

Herrick, Henry, guarantees new resident, 3

Higginson, Francis: chosen as teacher, 55; death of, 56; sent by Company, 53-54; Separatist learnings of, 54

Higginson, John, Jr.: as selectmen, 172; opponent of second church, 170, 172; refuses election as selectman, 137, 170

Higginson, John: and Half-Way Covenant, 109-113, 126; anti-mercantilism of, 128, 130-32, 136-37, 186, 217n. 50; arrived in Salem, 56; attempts to accommodate, 189; boyhood of, in Salem, 188; called to Salem church, 49, 90, 124; conflict of, with Nicholet, 128-130, 137, 216m. 31, 216n. 44; extends baptism to non-members, 137; maintenance of, 83, 89-90, 92, 127, 150; petition to General Court concerning taverns, 159, 224n. 120;

preacher of jeremiads, 189-90; returns to Salem church, 49, 90, 124; urges renewal of covenant, 138

Higham, John, typology of New England town, 6, 195n. 25

Hirst, William, as constable, 183; as selectman, 103, 171, 174, 186

Holgrave, John: arrived from East Anglia, 35; chosen as overseer of munitions, 35; elected deputy, 35

Hollingworth, Widow, 82

Holmes, Obadiah, receives land grant, 26

Holton, Joseph, receives land grant, 29

Hooker, Thomas, 195n. 1

Horne, Brother John, as elder, 137

Humphries, John, 87; sells land and returns to England, 66

Hutchinson, Anne, 38

Hutchinson, Richard, purchases land, 66, 206n. 41

Ingersoll, Richard, land grants to, 66; land purchases by, 66

Jeggles, William, 77

Johnson, Francis, landholdings of, 38

Kenniston, Allan, receives land grant, 28

Kenny, Henry, 63-64

King, Daniel, land grants to, 66; land purchases by, 66

King, George, disarmed for support of Anne Hutchinson, 205n. 38

King, William, 82

Kirk, Henry, warned out, 2-3

Knight, William, admitted to Town, 20

Lambert, Sarah, 82

Lambert, as constable, 183

Lathrop, Thomas, Cape Ann planter, 50; elected as selectman, 50, 51, 52

Launder, John, 149

Leach, John, as church member, 227n. 23; as selectman, 132, 228n. 39

Leach, Lawrence, elected as selectman, 40; Old Planter, 39-40

Leach, Lt. Richard, as lieutenant of foot company, 141; as selectman, 132

Lindall, Timothy, 74; as church member, 227n. 23; as selectman, 103, 171, 174, 186, 218n. 63, 228n. 39; defeated, 223n. 102; merchant, 218n. 63; opposes second church, 172; refuses election as selectman, 172

Lockwood, Sergeant, request for land refused, 20

Lord, William: as church member, 106; as
    selectman, 45, 106; iron monger, 45;
    West Country origins of, 45
Lord, Mrs. William, 82
Lyford, John: expelled from Plymouth, 53,
    203n. 3; removal to Virginia, 9, 53;
    settled at Naumkeag, 53

Manning, Nicholas: as constable, 145; as
    selectman, 74, 100, 218n. 63, 228n. 32;
    gunsmith, 145
Massey, Jeffrey: as rater, 209n. 25; as
    selectman, 40, 42, 45; land grants to,
    76, 207n. 38; removed to Cape Ann, 49;
    service on Cape Ann committee, 49;
    West Country origins, 40
Maule, Thomas: land purchases, 73;
    Quaker, 73, 152; residents fined for
    harboring, 152
Meachum, Jeremiah, 64-65
Miller, Perry, 95
Moore, John, 148, 221n. 47
Morton, Nathaniel, ix; describes ministry,
    203n. 8; on Lyford, 203n. 3; witnesses
    church-gathering, 55
Morton, Thomas, 199n. 3
Moulton, Robert: arrival of, 27-28; as
    deputy, 27-28, 35; as selectman, 106;
    church membership of, 27-28, 106;
    excommunication of, 27-28, 205n. 38;
    freemanship of, 106; land grants to,
    27-28; office holding by, 27-28

Nicholet, Reverend Charles: arrival of,
    127-128; conflict of, with Higginson,
    128-130, 216n. 39; maintenance of,
    127; support for, 127, 129-130
Normon, John, 82
Norris, Edward, Jr., as schoolteacher, 147
Norris, Edward, as minister, 58
Noyes, Nicholas, 109

Oliver, Thomas: chosen to warn strangers
    out, 3, 147, 152; requests land grant,
    32; warns meeting of commoners, 73

Palfrey, Peter, elected as selectman, 40,
    45; Old Planter, 39-40
Parminter, Benjamin, receives land grant,
    20
Pease, John, sold land and moved to Marble-
    head, 66
Peter, Hugh: adopts new covenant, 57;
    arrival in Salem, 56-57; attitude toward
    seamen, 15; departure for England, 44;
    increases church membership, 58, 108;

receives land grant, 14; reduces dissen-
    sion, 58-59
Phelps, as constable, 183
Phillips, John, 22
Pickering, John, Jr., 186; as constable,
    180-181; as selectman, 228n. 39
Pope, Constable, 63, 183
Porter family, 125; in conflict over Village
    church, 125; in conflict with Putnams,
    141-142, 172
Porter, Israel: as church member, 171,
    217n. 58; as selectman, 102, 171, 217n.
    58, 228n. 39; defeated, 158; from
    Village, 102; refuses election as select-
    man, 172; tax rate of, 102
Porter, John, Jr.: as deputy, 119; as select-
    man, 118, 119; land purchases of, 66
Porter, John, Sr.: as deputy, 69, 119; as
    selectman, 45-46, 66, 68, 81, 91, 99,
    104, 139, 203n. 63; land grants, 46;
    land purchases of, 46, 66, 76, 79, 202n.
    45; on jury, 46; Salem Village farmer,
    45
Price, John: as deputy, 168, 214n. 44;
    as selectman, 102, 103, 119, 171, 172;
    proponent of second church, 170, 172;
    tax rate of, 102
Price, Matthew, 86
Price, Walter: as deputy, 119; as selectman,
    46, 50, 91, 103, 139, 203n. 63; builds
    corn mill, 51-52; church membership,
    28-29, 30; duties as selectman, 51; land
    grants, 28-29, 30; land purchases, 46,
    202n. 45; merchant, 46; officeholdings,
    28-29, 30; as constable, 46
Putnam, family, 125, 171; as Salem Village
    selectmen, 121, 141, 227n. 26; conflict
    within, 228n. 38; in conflict over
    Village church, 125; in conflict with
    Porters, 141-142, 172; pursue autono-
    my for Village, 172, 184, 186
Putnam, John, Jr.: as selectman, 88, 171-
    172, 173; joins Salem Village church
    covenant, 228n. 38; supervises Salem
    Village tithingmen, 163
Putnam, John, Sr., 63; as deputy, 68-69,
    214n. 44; land purchases of, 66
Putnam, Joseph, 228n. 38
Putnam, Nathaniel: as constable, 175, 181,
    209n. 14; as selectman, 88, 99, 171-
    172; defeated, 173; land grants and
    purchases of, 76; opposes second
    church, 170; signs Salem Village church
    covenant, 228n. 38
Putnam, Thomas, as constable, 143; as
    selectman, 88, 140, 171

Ray, Daniel: as selectman, 66; land grants, 67; land purchases, 66-67, 206n. 23
Redfield, Robert, 6; definition of community of, 6; diachronic theory of, 6, 195n. 25
Rich, Obadiah, as constable, 147
Ropes, George, denied land grant, 20
Ruck, John, as deputy, 214n. 44; as selectman, 103, 119

Sampson, John, admitted to town, 2
Scruggs, Thomas, disarmed for support of Anne Hutchinson, 38, 205n. 38; in minimal majority of 1640, 38
Sergeant, William, admission to town, 3
Sewall, Stephen, 228n. 35, 228n. 36; as selectman, 174; colonial offices of, 174; wealth of, 174
Sharp, Samuel: as elder of church, 38; dies, 66; East Anglian origins of, 56; land holdings of, 38; sells land, 66; Separatism of, 56
Shipley, John, admitted to town, 19
Silsby, Nathaniel, refuses election as constable, 145
Skelton, Samuel: chosen as pastor, 55; initiates Separatist practices, 56; sent by company, 54; Separatist leanings of, 54
Skerry, Henry, as constable, 144; guarantees new resident, 2
Skinner, Walter, receives poor relief, 221n. 58
Smith, Ralph, Separatist, 54
Stackhouse, Richard, ferryman, 148
Stacy, Hugh, returns to Marblehead, 22
Starr, Robert, 64
Stevens, Samuel, 152

Stileman, Elias, sells land, 66
Stone, John, Sr., as constable, 220n. 35

Thurston, John, removes to Newbury, 22
Trask, William: as constable, 181; as deputy, 35-36, 39, 52; as selectman, 102; North River mill owner, 51-52; tax rate of, 102; West Country origins of, 35, 52
Turner, John: as church member, 217n. 58; as constable, 145; as selectman, 217n. 58

Veren, Hilliard, as elder, 137

Wakefield, Samuel, admitted to town, 2
Walton, William (Marblehead teacher), 112
Weld, Dr. Daniel, as selectman, 74, 100, 228n. 32
West, Henry, 149
Weston, Francis, elected as deputy, 35
White, Reverend John, 54; and Dorchester Company, 9
Wilkins, Bray, 75; land purchases, 77
Williams, Roger, 57; banished, 35-36, 56, 200n. 9; dismissed from Plymouth church, 204n. 21; doctrinal tests of, 46; elected as Skelton's assistant, 56
Winthrop, John: arrival of, 12, 34; defines indivisibility of status, 108; delegation of powers to towns, 37; is denied communion with Salem church
Woodbury, John: and Dorchester Company, 9; elected as selectman, 39; Old Planter, 39
Woodbury, Nicholas, receives land grant, 30

Index

Accommodation: behavioral standards for, 19; failure of, 70, 72-74, 76, 79-80; and family composition, 16-17; as basis of good order, 131, 158-59, 188, 191-29; and mobility, 15-16, 197n. 42; principles of, 10, 12, 49-50, 61-62, 131, 188, 191-92; symbols of, 73. *See also* Good order

Accommodation in church, 57, 108-12, 113-14, 121, 137, 151-52, 175-189; standards of, eased, 121. *See also* Covenant, Half-Way

Accommodation into federal covenant, 105-8, 113-14, 121, 151-52; standards for, eased, 121; threatens unity, 135. *See also* Covenant, Federal

Accommodation in land system, 61, 86, 188, 191-92; by arrival date, 17, 23, 26-27; as cause of differentiation of neighborhoods, 32, 61, 173-74, 176; as cause of dispersion, 173-74, 176; of diverse immigrants, 9, 22-23, 198n. 19; and family composition, 16-17; fishermen excluded from, 15; according to hierarchical principles, 61-62; inclusiveness of, 14; landless outside of, 64-65; limits of, 19-32, 70, 72-74, 76, 79-80, 151-52, 156, 180-82; attempts to expand limits of, 23, 151; and mobility, 15-16, 197n. 42; related to occupation, 17-18; of Old Planters, 10; of open-field farmers, 11; purchasers outside of, 65-67; after 1640, 27, 29, 31; after 1660, 92. *See also* Good order; Differentiation; Dispersion

Admission to town: behavior required for,

152; by colony, 153; by freemen, 2; of laborers, 3, 194n. 12; controlled by land grants, 2; requirements for, 2; restrictions on, 152; by selectmen, 19, 82; based on self-sufficiency, 152

Agricultural occupations: acreage received by, 18; house lots received by, 21; immigration of, 16, 70-71; in leadership positions, 68-70; neighborhoods of, 177, 180; as percentage of population, 16; residence patterns of, 71-73; wealth of, 180

Anglicanism, 128, 186

Annales school, 6

Anti-mercantilism of Higginson, 128, 130-32, 136-37, 186, 217n. 50

Antinomians, 58

Apprentices, 20

Arminianism, 95

Arrival, date of: of proponents of second church, 131, 135-36, 217n. 51; of opponents of second church, 131, 135-36, 217n. 51; of church members, 97-98, 115-16; of freemen, 97-98, 114-16; related to land grants, 17; by neighborhood, 132; by occupational distribution, 183; and office-holding, 97; of selectmen, 218n. 63

Artisans: rate of immigration of, 16, 70-71; land grants to, 17-18, 64, 182-83, 229n. 49; mobility of, 183; numbers of, 178; persistence of, 183, 229n. 53; as percentage of population, 16, 69; residence of, 71-73, 178; wealth of, 180

Assistants, Court of: chosen by freemen; 34; Hathorne elected to, 36; assume legislative rights, 34; major leaders on,

118-19; and Salem Village church petition, 124; sons of major leaders on, 119, 214n. 44; strangers reported to, 19

Baptism: of adopted children, 112; of children of non-members, 137, 151; of older children, 112; as preparation for conversion, 109-10. *See also* Covenant, Half-Way

Bass River, Old Planters' grants at 24, 32, 61. *See also* Beverly

Beaver Dam, 63

Behavior, individual: regulation of, by constables 159-63; in 1680 covenant, 138; deviance of, controlled, 159-63; as basis of good order, 158; control of, requires new officers, 161-65; control of, to protect property, 159; control of, by tithingmen, 161

Beverly: church gathered in, 112-13; commons enlargment refused, 123; commons reserved, 31, 48; constable for, 49, 84; establishment of, as town, 94, 122, 173, 189; enclosed farms of, 13, 31, 69; highway surveyor named for, 49; separate ministry maintained by, 49; poor maintained by, 49; and Quaker crisis, 51; selectmen from, 50, 99, 102-3; separate services provided by, 84; settlement of, 25; exempted from taxation by Town, 143

Boston: Anne Hutchinson's supporters in, 205n. 38; church of, 56; removal of government to, 36

Boundaries, property: disputes over, 193n. 2; to be marked, 13; of town, 85

Boundaries, social: concern for, 151-53. *See also* Strangers; Warning Out

Bridge, town, 144

Brooksby: grants at, 87; farmers at, 177; location of enclosed farms, 31, 69

Burial grounds: in Glass House Field, 122; near Ipswich River, 122; in Salem Village, 49

Cape Ann. *See* Beverly

Cedar Pond, location of enclosed farms at, 13

Census: of 1637, 15-18; of 1636, 14-18; for country rates, 156

Centralization: of town arsenal, 44; of funerals, 44; limits to, in 1650, 40, 69-70; through nucleated settlement, 13, 180, 188; through public works on peninsula, 91, 122-23, 149, 189-90; as function of merchant-selectmen, 51-

52, 81, 85, 103-4, 158; of weights and measures, 44. *See also* Burial grounds, Funerals, Militia, Public Works, Town meeting

Charter: confirmed by Charles II, 167; conflict over, 139, 168; leaders' views of 170, 186; during Restoration, 167; restoration of, 168, 170; revocation of, 119, 168; of 1629, 167; suspension of, 158, 164

Church: admission to, 44, 58-59, 62, 73-74, 108, 110-111, 212n. 18; attendance of, 43, 49, 49, 62, 160; behavior in, enforcement of, 62-62, 160-61; dissension within, 58-59; 128-38 (*see also* Second church, controversy over); financial support of, 59; gathering of, in Beverly, 112-13, 124, gathering of, in Marblehead, 112; gathering of, in Salem, 54-56; gathering of, in Salem Village, 112-13, 123-24, 215n. 23; gathering of, in Topsfield, 113; gathering of, in Wenham, 113; numbers admitted to, 111-16; relation of town meeting to, 128; size of, 58-59, 73-74, 113, 137, 205n. 33, 205n. 36, 240-41

Church membership: related to arrival date, 97-98, 115-16, 132; of constables, 96, 98; decline in, 132-33, 137, 175, 240-41; related to freemanship, 34, 96, 98, 241; required for freemanship, 105, 108, 114-15, 218n. 59; Half-Way, 110; of jurors, 96, 98; related to landowning, 26-30, 59, 62, 65, 198n. 24; related to leadership, 57-59, 115-17, 175-76; of major leaders, 96; related to neighborhood, 115-16, 132, 140, 214n. 43; preparation for, 55, 58, 109-11; rates of, 96; requirements for, 108-11, 167, 215n. 23; of Second Church petititoners, 130, 132, 134-35, 137; of selectmen, 96, 98, 100-101, 171, 174; related to tax ward, 241; related to wealth, 132-33, 175-76

Church seating, 217n. 55, 217n. 56; by selectmen, 81-83; and status patterns, 133, 187

Cohesion: conditions for, 140, 188; through control of behavior, 159-65, 190-91; achieved by merchant-selectmen, 51-52, 81, 85-86, 103-4, 158; of neighborhoods, 31, 173; disrupted by Quakers, 139, 189

Collins Cove, house lots located on, 21

Colonial officers, relation of to town offiicers, 164-65, 171, 174

Commerce: growth of, after 1660, 121,
    168; related to landowning, 180-81,
    185; related to leadership, 174-75;
    and Puritan social theory, 95. *See also*
    Higginson, John; anti-mercantile views of
Commissioners, role of, in taxation, 168-69
Common: encroachment on, 149-50, 64n.
    222; house lots located around, 21;
    house lots sold on, 149-50
Commons: of Beverly reserved, 31, 48, 86;
    cattle, reserved, 42-43, 86; of Marble-
    head reserved, 42-43, 86; of peninsula
    reserved, 72-73, 86, 207n. 32; of
    Ryal Side reserved, 48, 86
Conformists, 54-55
Consensus: loss of, on board of selectmen,
    142; loss of, among electorate, 155-56;
    politics of, in church, 128-30, 137-38,
    185; politics of, in town, 137; among
    South Field proprietors, 185
Constables: arrival dates of 74, 97, 211n. 5,
    211n. 6; attributes of, 144-45; audited
    by selectmen 41, 161, 164; rate of
    church membership among, 96-98,
    211 n. 5; duties of, 50, 143, 145, 151;
    elections of, 45; enforcement of Sab-
    bath by, 160; established by General
    Court, 37; established for Salem Village
    and Beverly, 49; rate of freemanship
    among, 96-98, 211n. 5; instructions
    to, regarding curfew, 162; instructions
    to, regarding strangers, 162; instructions
    to, regarding watch, 161-62; liability of,
    145-47, 220n. 35; neighborhoods of,
    121; number of, 145, 163; payments
    for services by, 163; payments to, for
    service, 143-45, 220n. 36; refusals of
    office as, 144-45; suits against, 169;
    supervision of, by selectmen, 163-64;
    status of 97, 120, 211n. 6; and resistance
    to taxation, 143-44, 147; wealth of,
    97, 211n. 5
Council of New England, deputies ap-
    pointed to, 168
Court of Assistants. *See* Assistants, Court of
Court of Common Pleas, 174
Covenant: federal, 9, 93-95, 195n. 1 (*see
    also* Freemanship); of Grace, 95, 133;
    Half-Way, 108-113; of 1680, 138,
    165; of 1659, 138; of 1636, 57-138;
    of 1629, 54-56, 138; of Works, 54,
    95, 128, 133
Covenants, seals of: adoption of, by post-
    1660 immigrants, 121; relation be-
    tween church and federal, 105-6, 115;
    inseparability of, 105-6, 108-9, 113-15;

    numbers holding, 96, 100, 104, 111-14,
    116-18, 175; during Restoration, 167-
    68; separability of, 108, 114-17, 120,
    131, 190
Covenant theology: anti-Separatist views of,
    54; Conant's views of, 53; conditions of,
    6; Massachusetts Bay Company's views
    of, 54-55; at Plymouth, 53-54; as basis
    of social theory, 9, 195n. 1; as basis of
    voluntarism, 54, 59, 147. *See also*
    Good order; Voluntarism
Cowkeeps: appointed by selectmen, 45,
    48-49; hired by precincts, 48-49
Curfew, established, 162

Darby's Fort. *See* Marblehead
Deacons: minister's maintenance managed
    by, 164; poor relieved by, 163; refusal of
    election as, 137-38; role of, in church
    seating, 133
Dedham, 22
Deeds, 77-79
Deputies: views of charter among, 168;
    elections of, 153; establishment of,
    34-35; major leaders as, 118-19; origins
    of, 36, 200n. 9; accept Salem Village
    petition, 124; qualifications for voting
    for, 154; sons of major leaders as, 119,
    214n. 44
Differentiation of neighborhoods, 48-52,
    69-70, 80, 122, 131, 138-42, 158,
    188-92; increased by immigrants, 70-76,
    80; and use of land for income, 151;
    and leadership, 91; in second church
    conflict, 136. *See also* Accommoda-
    tion in land system; Dispersion
Dispersion: acceleration of, 94; conse-
    quence of accommodation, 121; conse-
    quences of, for church, 111-13; concern
    over, 44; consequences of, for town, 85-
    86, 120; by occupations, 61. *See also*
    Accommodation in land system, Cen-
    tralization, Differentiation
Dorchester Company, 9
Drunkenness: concern about, 159; punish-
    ment for, 162

East Anglia: differences from West Country,
    36; open field farmers of, 9, 11; promi-
    nent clergy from, 9
East Anglians: and principles of accommo-
    dation, 39; and covenant of 1636, 58;
    elected as deputies, 35-36, 45, 200n. 9;
    open fields established for, 13; elected
    as selectmen, 39, 45-46; separatism
    of, 56-57, Elder Samuel Sharp as leader

of, 56; Roger Williams as leader of, 35, 45-46

East Church, 137

East End (of Town): arrival dates of residents of, 132; foot company established for, 122; franchise in, 157; officeholders residing in, 157-58; population of, 157, 217n. 53; seamen residing in, 131, 176-77, 228n. 21; second church opponents in, 131-32; second church proponents in, 131-32; watch augmented in, 177

Elders: Maintenance of, 43, 45, 143; prohibited from officeholding, 105; care of poor by, 148; role of, in preparation for conversion, 109-11

Elections: of constables, 120; of deputies, 153; methods used in, 155-56; numbers of candidates for, 156, 224n. 110; of selectmen, 107, 120, 153-58, 173; votes in, 155, 223n. 102

Enclosed field farming: in Beverly, 31; commercial nature of, 23; established in Salem, 13; favored over open-fields, 23-24; located outside peninsula, 21, 31; religious implications of, 11; in Salem Village, 31; social implications of, 11

Essex County, map of, in 1643, 233

Extra-local relationships, 228n. 33; economic, 174, 230n. 59; marriages as form of, 7, 194n. 19; political, 174, 187

Family: composition of, among immigrants to 1636, 16; composition of, among immigrants of 1636-37, 16; composition of, as factor in admission, 19; control of, 160; inspection of, 161-62; removal of children from, 160; role in conversion of, 108-9, 138

Fence surveyors, 81, 187

Ferry, use of income from, 148

Franchise, church: condemnation of use of, by non-freemen, 130; extension of, to non-church members in Salem, 128, 216n. 45; extension of, to non-church members of Salem Village, 125, 215n. 19, 216n. 45

Franchise, colony: availability of, to petitioners against second church, 134, 218n. 60; availability of, to petitioners for second church, 134, 210n. 60; decline in, 154-58; exercise of, 153-58; limited to freemen, 105; impact of Half-Way Covenant on, 111; importance of,

in second church conflict, 133-35; by neighborhood, 156-58; opened to nonchurch members, 167; extended to nonfreemen, 106-8, 114, 121, 132, 212n. 16; requirements for, 153-55; size of, 155, 168, 223n. 102, 224n. 112, 224n. 113

Freemanship: and date of arrival, 97-98, 114-115; and position on second church, 132, 134-35, 137; and church membership, 96, 98, 114-15, 117, 241; preceded by church membership, 218n. 59; restricted to church members, 105, 114; defined by colony, 212n. 16; of constables, 96, 98; as seal of federal covenant, 95; decline in rate of, 96, 132, 175; of jurors, 96, 98, 107-8; and leadership, 175-76; of major leaders, 96; and neighborhood, 115-17; and occupational distribution, 115-17; of selectmen, 96, 98, 100-101, 107-8, 174; and tax wards, 241; related to wealth, 175-176

Freemen: change policy and practice of accommodation, 19-20; control admission, 2; views of charter among, 168; power of, to grant lands, 13, 34; Massachusetts Bay Company limits franchise to, 105; members of, 105-8, 114, 116; powers of, to extend franchise, 106; decline in voluntarism among, 49-50

Funerals, private ceremonies banned, 44. See also Burial grounds

General Court: appointments made by, 174; Beverly petition received by, 49; boundaries of towns determined by, 1; deportation required by, 14; deputies elected to, 34-36, 168, 170; restricts deputy elections to freemen, 37; franchise policies established by, 105-8, 134-35; fine for refusal of office increased by, 145; freemanship limited to church members by, 34; jury membership defined by, 105-8; land policies of, 2, 12-13, 37, 86; markets established by, 36-37; Oath of Fidelity required by, 151; Quakerism suppressed by, 50; Restoration policies of, 167-68; Salem Village petitions received by, 124, 140-41; second church petition received by, 129-30; separatism opposed by, 36, 56; concern of, about strangers, 19; tithingmen established by, 161; town government established by, 2, 37

Glass House Field, 26; burial ground

established for, 122; selectmen from, 99

Glorious Revolution, 168; consequences of, 174, 187, 191; conflicts within leadership during, 168; extra-local marriage patterns after, 7, 194n. 19

Good order, 93, 187; based on accommodation, 11-12, 158, 188; basis of, in second generation, 121; basis of, by 1680, 138; basis of, in 1629, 158-59, 188; behavioral standards of, 158, 163, 188; requires colonial authority, 165; and family governance, 160; hierarchical principle of, 158, 188; and mid-century immigrants, 73-75; and land distribution, 12-13, 24, 30, 61-62, 77-79; strained by land sales, 76; based on voluntarism, 158. See also Accommodation; Voluntarism

Governor: appointments made by, 174, 187; Endicott as, 201n. 26; elected by freemen, 34; after Glorious Revolution, 170; during Restoration, 167-68, 174; second church conflict appealed to, 129-30

Governor, deputy: elected by freemen, 34

Grand jurors: appointment of, 45; arrival dates of, 97; and church membership, 96, 98-99; and freemanship, 96, 98-99

Highways, repair of, 143, 147, 169; taxation for, 169. See also Services to towns

Historical population, 224n. 120; rates of arrival among, 97-98; church membership among, 96; definition of, 5, 194n. 22; freemanship among, 96; increase in, 137; size of, 5, 70, 153-54, 156-58, 206n. 21, 207n. 26, 207n. 27, 240; in 1650, 199n. 26, 205n. 36; in 1640, 25, 194n. 22; stability of, after 1640

Householders: desirability of maintaining, 86-87, 149-51; goal of full settlement of, 15

House lots: universal distribution of, 12; locations of, 13, 21; as percentage of grants, 21; purchases of, 21; shortage of, 20; reductions in size of, 21

Immigrants, after 1660: Anglicanism among, 128; heterogeneity of, 9, 36; mercantilism of, 142; neighborhoods of, 142; non-Puritans among, 140, 168

Immigration: heterogeneity of, consistent with good order, 12; rates of, 34, 194n. 15; rates of, by occupation, 176, 182-83, 207n. 31, 229n. 50; reduction of after 1640, 25, 30, 62, 70; after 1660,

65, 70, 92, 113, 121; sources of, 35

Inclusion. See Accommodation

Indians, fear of, 122, 141, 159, 162

Ipswich, boundary run, 85

Ipswich Road, 141

Ipswich River, 31

Jeffries Creek. See Manchester

Jeremiads, 187-88, 190

Jurors: arrival dates of, 97; church membership among, 96, 98-99, 107-8; freemanship among, 96, 98-99, 107-8; non-freemen serve as, 106-7; number of, 106; qualifications for service as, 106-7, 154; selection of, 45

Justices of the peace: established, 168; role of, in taxation, 169

King, authority of, 167-68

King Philip's War, 94, 189; expenses of, 122, 140, 144, 146; fear of Indians due to, 162; refugees from, 3, 152; selectmen during, 100; taxation for, 170

Land: and principles of accommodation, 14, 173-74; related to civic appointments, 62-65; as commodity, 173-74; distribution of, in 1689, 180-82; distribution of, in 1636, 239; managed by town for income, 127, 149-51, 163, 169; related to leadership, 26-30, 62; meaning of, 173-74, 185

Land grants: availability of, 20-21, 25, 30-32, 197n. 11; cessation of, 2, 32, 63; and church membership, 2, 26-30, 62, 86, 210n. 33; conditions of, 30-31, 48, 193n. 3; according to egalitarian principles, 14; inclusiveness of, 14, 20, 62; location of, 13-14, 20, 25-27, 31-32, 86-88; decreasing number of, 25, 30-32, 48; by occupation, 15, 17, 32, 61; and officeholding, 26-30; to Old Planters, 26; residency required for, 2; relative to sales, 62, 65-66, 77-78, 206n. 22, 208n. 39; decreasing size of, 17, 25-26; and status patterns, 14, 28-32, 61; to supplement former grants, 23, 26-27, 29-31; types of, 27

Landless men: by date of arrival, 181; by church membership, 65, by civic participation, 65; by neighborhood, 180-81; numbers of, 62, 65, 180; occupations of, 69-70; in 1683, 208n. 42; in 1650, 62-65

Land, sales of, 65-68; by date of arrival of buyers, 76-79, 207n. 35; conditions of,

78-79; frequency of, 79; to mid-century
immigrants, 74-76; to non-residents, 2,
193n. 5; occupational distinctions in,
77-78; limited by residency requirement,
1
Leadership: and dates of arrival, 38; attributes of, 35, 95, 99, 140, 148, 150-51,
156-59, 170, 175-76, 187, 192; church
membership among, 38-39, 69, 95-96,
101, 211n. 4; and seals of covenants,
105-8, 116-18, 120; disjunction of, 131-
36; of mid-century immigrants, 73-74;
land-owning among, 37-39, 66-67, 70,
76, 79-80, 95; of merchants, 68-69;
by neighborhood, 68-69, 140, 157-58;
by occupation, 45-48, 50-52, 68; origins
of, 35-36, 39-40; persistence and, 38-39;
after 1670, 100-103; submission to,
required for good order, 158; and
wealth, 46-47, 50, 62, 185-87. See also
Good order; Voluntarism
Leaders, major: ages of, 118; age at election
of, 100-101; arrival dates of, 98; as
Assistants, 118-20; church membership
of, 97-98, 103; as deputies, 118-20;
differences from minor leaders, 99-103;
divisions among sons of, 186; freemanship among, 97-98, 103; as jurors, 99;
land-owning among, 97, 99; length of
service by, 118; occupations of, 99,
103; residence of, 99-103; retirement of,
103-4, 119, 229n. 58; and seals of covenants, 118, 120; on board of selectmen,
95-104, 122; sons of, as selectmen,
158-59; sons of, 101-4, 118-20, 139-40,
171; as unifiers of town, 134-40, 158-59;
wealth of, 97-102
Leaders, minor, as selectmen: attributes of,
99-103; definition of, 99; differences
from major leaders, 99-103
Leyden community. See Plymouth
London, fire of, 167
Lynn, 87

Magistrates, duties of, 37, 42, 59, 106
Major leaders. See Leaders, major
Manchester: established for West Country
farmers, 21, 25, 43, 61, 69; farmlands
surveyed at, 13; empowered to grant
lands at, 207n. 37
Marblehead: church members of, 214n. 42;
confirmed as part of Salem, 56; established as town, 48, 69, 207n. 25;
reserved for fishermen, 15, 32, 61;
freemen of, 214n. 42; empowered to
grant land, 207n. 37; meetinghouse in,

112; nonfreeman as constable in, 107;
reserved for seamen, 176
Marriage: as definition of community, 7;
and economic ties, 174, 228n. 34,
228n. 35; extra-local, 5, 7, 194n. 18,
194n. 19; local, 5
Massachusetts Bay, characteristics of towns
in, 1
Massachusetts Bay Company: criteria for
adventurers in, 1, 14, 196-97n. 35;
charter granted to, 10; ties freemanship to church membership, 105-6,
213n. 39; instructions to governor of,
10, 33-34, 188; land distribution principles of, 12; recruitment of settlers by,
11
Massachusetts Bay, Council of: organization
of, 34; removal of, to Boston, 36
Meadow, division of in 1637, 15
Meetinghouse: house lots located near, 13,
21, 237; new, in 1670, 123; rates for,
144; repairs to, 143, 169; size of, 130-
31; as town center, 187. See also church
seating
Mercantilism: and Covenant of Works, 128;
of post-1660 immigrants, 131-32. See
also Higginson, John
Merchants: arrival dates of, 180; views of
charter among, 168, 171, 226n. 3;
church membership among, 51; as deputies, 36, 68-69; extra-local relationships
of, 5; diversified economic interests of,
79-80; as landowners, 17, 182-83, 185,
229n. 55; marriages of, 5; residence of,
51, 177-78; relations with seamen, 177;
as selectmen, 45-48, 50-52, 68, 81-94,
119-20, 139-40, 171, 186-87; wealth of,
51, 119-20, 178-80, 182, 184-86; as
unifying force for town, 7, 33, 50-52
Militia: costs of, 143; within neighborhoods, 122, 228n. 41; in Salem Village,
141. See also Primary interactions
Minimal majority: church membership
among, of 1650, 175; church membership among, of 1640, 175; freemanship
among, of 1650, 175; freemanship
among, of 1640, 175; leaders, major,
among, 95, 102; leadership among, 175;
in selected Massachusetts towns, 200n.
22; of 1650, 28-30, 61, 65-67; of 1640,
24, 38, 61, 66-67, 198n. 21, 198n. 25;
of 1636, 14, 239
Ministry: deacons manage maintenance of,
164; housing of, 47, 49, 51, 143; land
grants to, 17; maintenance of, 43, 49,
89-90, 122, 126-27, 143-44, 146, 150,

164, 169; maintenance of in Salem
Village, 171, 227n. 24; sent by Massachusetts Bay Company, 53-54; role of,
in church seating, 133; role of, in preparation for conversion, 108-11; in
1629, 55. *See also* Higginson, Francis;
Higginson, John; Norris, Edward;
Skelton, Samuel; Voluntarism
Mobility, economic, 76-77, 179-82, 186-87;
limited by land distribution, 62-65
Money, as basis of civic interactions, 147-
51, 164, 173-74. *See also* Primary interactions; Selectmen

Nantasket, Conant and other Particulars
in, 53
Navigation Acts of 1682, enforcement of,
174
Navy, King's, 167
Neck, fishing and shipbuilding lots laid out
on, 21; grazing, reserved for, 13
Neighborhoods: church members in 115-17;
franchise eligibility in, 157; freemen in,
114-17; land-owning patterns in, 180-82;
leadership within, 102-3; mobility of,
183; occupational distribution in, 68,
131-32, 176-78, 207n. 30; occupational specialization in, 121, 131-32,
176-78; persistence in, 183; population
of, 217n. 53, 241; second church
opponents in, 131-32; 136; second
church proponents in, 131-32, 135-36;
of selectmen, 102-3; tax rates within,
184; wealth in, 185. *See also* Dispersion;
Differentiation
Neighborhood cohesion, 188-92; in
Beverly, 31, 140; churches augment,
112-13; and seals of covenants, 114-17,
214n. 43; results in disunity, 122-38;
in harbor area, 142; and post-1660 immigrants, 142; based on primary interaction, 112; in Salem Village, 86-88,
140-42, 150-51; choice of selectmen
based on, 88-89; precinct services augment, 87, 142, 163-64; tithingmen
augment, 161, 163. *See also* Dispersion;
Differentiation; Primary Interaction
New England Company. *See* Massachusetts
Bay Company
New England towns, typology of, 1, 5
New Farmers, 67-68
New Merchants, 67-68
Nonfreemen: as constables, 107; granted
local franchise, 106; as jurors, 106-8;
as selectmen, 107
Non-Separatism, principles of, 53-58

Non-Separatist ministry, arrival of, 11
North Field: establishment of, 13; independence of proprietors of, 185; location of, 13; management of, 142;
reserved for yeomen, 61, 69
North Neck: farming on, 177; selectmen
from, 99, 103; watch established for,
159; watch maintained by, 122
Nucleated settlement, patterns of, 13, 178,
180, 188; fragmentation of, 40, 69-70

Oath of Fidelity, 106; as tool of accommodation, 151; required for franchise, 154;
required by General Court, 151;
numbers sworn to, 151
Occupational distribution, 228n. 40; by
date of arrival, 4, 182-83; of church
members, 115-17; of freemen, 115-17;
of immigrants, 70, 113, 132; and land-
owning, 180-82; list of, 231; by mobility, 183; by neighborhood, 32, 68, 176-
78, 182; within peninsula, 176-78; by
persistence, 70, 183; among second
church opponents, 131-32, 137; among
second church proponents, 131-32, 137;
in 1680, 130; in 1689, 176; in 1637,
16, 176; and wealth, 179-80, 186
Officeholding, 198n. 23; and landholding,
26-30, 46-47, 198n. 24; among second
church opponents, 135; among second
church proponents, 135
Old Merchants, 67-68
Old Planters: accommodation of, in government, 33-34; accommodation of, in land
system, 10; included in Covenant of
1629, 56; elected as deputies, 35, 68-69;
lands of, at Bass River, 32; inactive in
land market, 207n. 38; withdraw from
leadership, 39-40, 62; in minimal majority of 1640, 38; removal of, to
Cape Ann, 188; elected as selectmen, 39-
40, 68-69; as surveyors in Beverly, 42
Open field farming: size of grants for, 23;
lands for, allotted, 22, 31; residence of
those engaged in, 21, 184-85; occupations of those engaged in, 23, 185,
229n. 53; social and religious implications of, 11

Partible inheritance and enclosed field
farming, 11
Particulars of Plymouth, 53
Peninsula. *See* Town
Pennycook, 85
Persistence by occupational distribution,
176, 183. *See also* Mobility, geographic

Plymouth: Conant in, 53; homogeneity of, 9; Leyden community in, 53

Poor: abatements of taxes of, 147; admission to town of, 2-3, 152; care of, 148-50, 160, 221n. 47-48, 58-59; as separate class, 149, 185; employment of, 148-49; rates for support of, 148-49, 169; settlement of, as householders, 149-50

Poor Relief, 143; managed by deacons, 163; of Reuben Guppy, 62-63; by selectmen, 82; of Robert Starr's widow, 64

Population. See Historical population

Port, Collector of, 174

Pound, house lots located around, 21

Precincts. See Neighborhood

Primary interactions: funerals as locus of, 122-23; replaced by managerial interactions, 150, 163-65; militia as locus of, 122-23; within neighborhoods, 87, 121-25, 163, 177, 184; required by Puritan social theory, 86; as basis of cohesion, 189-90; between selectmen and townspeople, 82-83, 171, 189-90, 209n. 14; lack of, between Village and Town, 124. See also Neighborhood cohesion

Primogeniture and open field farming, 11

Public works: fort, 87; jail, 142-43; meetinghouse, 142-44; increase neighborhood cohesion, 124; rates for maintenance of, 149; town house, 142-44; warrants for, 63, 121

Puritanism, social theory of, 9, 57, 93-95, 104, 131, 136-38, 190-92, 218n. 64; and church polity, 111, 125, 127-28, 130, 138, 211n. 31; and church seating, 133; and qualifications for leadership, 114, 118, 131. See also Good Order; Covenants; Accommodation; Voluntarism

Quakers, 44; arrival of, 3, 50, 58; cohesion destroyed by, 139, 189; conflicts with, 50-51, 73, 86, 202n. 60; persecution of, 51, 107, 142-43, 200n. 21; as selectmen, 50, 203n. 63; exempted from taxation, 89-90. See also Warning out

Quarterly Court: abolished during Andros administration, 168; orders from, about canoes, 13; establishes fine for fighting, 64; enforces religious unity, 59; receives Salem Village petition, 150; in second church controversy, 135, 137; regulation of tithingmen by, 165; regulation of watch by, 165. See also Extra-local relationships

Raters: establishment of, 209n. 24; names of, 209n. 25; powers of, 84

Rates: abatement of, 62, 144, 147; amount of, 143-44, 147-50, 219n. 19; established by magistrates, 164-65; established by selectmen, 164; established by town meeting, 122, 164; for meetinghouse, 123; for ministry, 126-27

Removals, 25, 33; consequences of, to land system, 66-67

Residency: required for land grants, 1-2; average length of, 4

Ryal Side: commons of, reserved, 48; farmers on, 177; immigration to, 71

Sabbath, enforcement of, 105, 160

Saints, visible, 108-9, 111, 212n. 18, 212n. 31

Salem: as closed community, 1; as port of entry, 1, 4, 194n. 16; boundaries of, 1; in relation to central government, 1; location of, 1; maps of, 234, 235, 236; naming of, 11, 195n. 11

Salem Village: as agricultural precinct, 141, 117; attempts to establish church in, 112-13, 123-26; attempts to form town, 124; attempts to separate from Town, 75, 140-42, 172-73; average wealth in, 227n. 31; burial ground established, 122; church established, 175; commercial farming in, 32, 61, 69, 71-72; conflict within, 112-13, 141-42, 228n. 38; constable of, 84; enlargements to commons refused, 123; farms of minimal majority of 1640 located in, 24; franchise in church controversy of, 134-35; growth of, 157; immigration to, 71-72; land granted in, 87; land-owning in, 184; land policies in, 86-88; large grants of 1640s located in, 29; lobbies for separation, 86, 94; location of land sold by 1650 in, 66; merchants' farms in, 66; merchants' farms in, 141; opponents of second church in, 131-32; pattern of settlement in, 141; population of, 173, 184, 217n. 53; proponents of second church in, 131-32, 136; relations with Town, 87-89, 94; relieved from Town watch, 141, 151; representative to selectmen, 88-89; resistance to new meetinghouse, 123; resists Town land policies, 88; selectmen from, 99, 102-3, 119; support for ministry of, 150-51; taxation of, 171, 184; use of commons in, 150-51; voters within, 157

Salem Village church, conflict within over
    ministry, 125; conflict within over
    polity, 126
Salt marsh, division of 1637, 15
School, support of, 147, 150
Seamen, 64; accommodation not fully
    extended to, 15, 20; behavior of, 177;
    rate of immigration by, 70-71; and land
    system, 64, 182-83, 207n. 38, 229n. 49;
    mobility of, 183; neighborhood of,
    15, 21, 61, 71-73, 177-78, 217n. 53;
    persistence of, 183; as percentage of
    population, 16; as proponents of second
    church, 131, 217n. 52; as supporters
    of mercantilism, 131-32, 135-36;
    wealth of, 179-80. See also Occupa-
    tional distribution
Second church, controversy over, 128-38,
    218n. 64; by ages of petitioners, 135-36,
    218n. 61. See also Church member-
    ship; Franchise; Selectmen; Office-
    holding; Neighborhood; Occupational
    distribution; Arrival; Freemanship
Selectmen, 174; arrival dates of, 97, 100,
    171, 174, 218n. 63, 228n. 32; church-
    membership of, 96, 98-101, 103, 106,
    108, 118, 171; colonial offices held
    by, 118-19; seals of covenants held by,
    132-33; experience of, 118; extra-local
    ties of, 171, 174, 187; freemanship of,
    96, 98, 100-101, 103, 106-8, 118; as
    jurors, 98-99; major leaders as, 141;
    neighborhoods of, 88-89, 132-33, 157-
    58; occupational distribution of, 45-46,
    132-33; as opponents of second church,
    134, 218n. 64; as proponents of second
    church, 134-35, 218n. 64; qualifications
    of, 46-47; Salem Village farmers as, 94,
    141-42, 171-72, 227n. 26; wealth of,
    97, 174. See also Leadership
Selectmen, Board of: challenges to author-
    ity of, 41-42, 44; as bankers, 47, 82-84,
    150-51, 164, 171, 210n. 47; views of
    charter within, 168, 170, 226n. 3; rela-
    tion of, to colonial officers, 164-65;
    composition of, 38-40, 42, 45, 50-51,
    201n. 24; divisions within, 137, 170,
    172, 174; elections to, 153-56, 203n.
    63; establishment of, 37; as managers
    of behavior, 159-64, 170-71; as managers
    of land, 150-51, 170-71; as managers of
    other officers, 161-65, 170-71; meetings
    of, 40-42, 44-45, 81-82; penalty for
    refusal of election to, 153; primary rela-
    tions of, with townspeople, 171; qualifi-
    cations for, 46-47; quorum for, 42-43,
    51; refusal of election to, 137-38;
    rewards for service on, 28-30, 51-52;
    size of, 37, 50, 200n. 21, 201n. 25,
    224n. 111; subcommittee of, 84-85,
    209n. 31; as unifying institution, 170
Selectmen, Powers of, 1, 37, 41-45, 47-48,
    81, 85; admission to town, 2, 19, 82,
    152; appointments to other offices,
    45, 48; as bankers, 47, 82-84, 150-51,
    164, 171, 210 n. 47; to set boundaries,
    83, 85; to settle disputes, 82; to grant
    land, 2, 27-28, 30-31, 42-43, 81, 86-88;
    to manage land, 150; as managers,
    150-51, 159-65, 170-71; in meeting-
    house seating, 81-82, 133, 217n. 56;
    poor relief, 82, 148, 150; to abate rates,
    82; to approve rates, 82, 84, 93, 143,
    169; to audit rates, 83-84; to collect
    rates, 143; to enforce Sabbath, 105; to
    sue constables, 146-47, 150; to call
    town meetings, 83; in relation to town
    meeting, 81, 83-88, 91-94, 164, 209n.
    29, 210n. 41, 211n. 62; to warn out
    strangers, 3, 82, 152-53
Separatism, 53; East Anglians and, 56;
    of Francis Higginson, 54; practices of,
    56; and establishment of Rhode Island
    colony, 56; and other schisms, 58; of
    Samuel Skelton, 54; of Ralph Smith,
    54; of Roger Williams, 56. See also
    Non-Separatism, principles of
Services to town: fine for failure to provide,
    153; during Glorious Revolution, 169-
    70; payment for, 147-48, 174, 221n. 45;
    as form of poor relief, 148; voluntary,
    173. See also Voluntarism
Sheffield patent and Dorchester Company,
    9
Skelton's Neck, location of enclosed farms
    on, 13
South Field, established, 13; reserved for
    yeoman, 61, 69
South Field proprietors, 184-85, 229n.
    53; date of arrival of, 185; occupations
    of, 185, 229n. 53; residence of, 184-85
South River, mill located on, 102
South River districts, immigration of
    artisans and seamen to, 71
Status: inverse relationship of ascribed, to
    achieved, 67-68; and church member-
    ship, 72, 79-80; in church and town
    disjunct, 132-33, 135; and church seat-
    ing, 133; divisibility of signs of, 105-20,
    132-33, 135, 171; single hierarchy of,
    140, 171, 188-89, 191; and land
    purchases, 65-68, 76-79; and leadership,

70, 73, 79-80; signs of, 95-96, 101,
103-4, 120, 171. *See also* Accommodation, principles of; Covenants, seals of
Strangers: fine for harboring, 3, 152; search-
ing out, 3, 147, 152; giving security for,
2, 152; warned out, 152-53
Surveyors established by General Court, 37;
established for Cape Ann, 49
Synod of 1662, 109. *See also* Half-Way
Covenant

Taverns: numbers of, restricted, 159,
224n. 120
Taxation: age limits for, 154; Beverly
exempted from, 143; and poverty,
142-48; power of, 45; for public works,
142-43; rates of, 84, 89-91, 226n. 12;
resistance to, 92-93, 122, 127, 143-47,
169-70, 172; role of commissioner in,
168-69; role of selectmen in, 81-84,
93, 143, 149, 169; of Salem Village,
141, 171; for services to town, 147
Tax lists, 154, 156-57; of 1689, 97, 241; of
1683, 102, 156, 241; sources of, 228n.
37; validity of, as economic indicators,
178-79
Tax wards: church members in, 241; freemen in, 241; map of, 237
Tithingmen, 206n.15; established by
General Court, 161; by neighborhood,
161, 163; numbers of, 161, 225n. 131;
purposes of, 161, 163; report to Quarterly Court, 165; regulation of, by selectmen, 163. *See also* Extra-local relationships; Behavior
Town: constable of, 84; location of open-
field farmers and artisans on, 25; map of,
236, 237; selectmen from, 99, 102
Town bridge, 13-14; house lots located near,
21; repairs to, 44-45; settling of farmers
beyond, 43, 48
Town meeting: attendance at, 41, 50, 107,
153-56; fine for not attending, 107;
frequency of, 43-44; powers of, 1, 37,
41, 43-45, 48, 84, 91-93, 127, 143, 164,
168-70, 227n. 22; role of, in church
affairs, 128-29; Salem Village petitions
to, 123-24, 169, 172-73; in relation to
selectmen, 41-45, 47-48; of 1668, 122;
warning of, 41. *See also* Selectmen,
Board of; Selectmen, power of

Voluntarism: covenants based on, 54;
decline in, 49-50, 59, 91-94, 103, 139;
and exercise of franchise, 153-56; as
condition of good order, 158; and

inclusion, 62; in subjection to leaders,
85; and support of ministry, 89-90,
126-27, 147; and officeholding, 153;
reassertion of, 121-22; and services
provided to town, 147, 153; and taxation, 91, 143-44, 146-47; and town
meeting attendance, 153-54. *See also*
Good order

Warning out: frequency, 152-53; monthly
inspection for, 3; standards for, 2-3
Watch, 91-92; increased in East End, 177;
established for North Neck, 122; purposes of, 159, 161-63; regulation of,
163; Salem Village released from, 141;
size of, 162-63, 65
Wealth: and church membership, 132-33,
175; and Covenant of Grace, 133;
and Covenant of Works, 128; distribution of, 79, 179; of immigrants after
1660, 128; and leadership, 185-87;
meaning of, 185, 187; measurement of,
208n. 43; by neighborhood, 186-87,
227n. 31
Wenham, 69; attempt to establish, 22, 43;
empowered to grant lands, 207n. 37;
establishment of, 173; yeomen in,
61
West Country: origin of Manchester settlers,
21-23; origin of original Naumkeag
settlers, 9. *See also* East Anglia
West Countrymen: and covenant of 1636,
58; elected as deputies, 35-36, 52, 57-
58; elected as selectmen, 39-40, 45-46,
57-58
West End (of peninsula): officeholders
from, 157-58; opponents of second
church in, 131-32; population of, 157,
217n. 53; proponents of second church
in, 131-32; voters within, 157
Wills, 178-79
Winter Harbor, reserved for fisherman, 15
Winter Island: fishing and shipbuilding lots
laid out on, 21; reserved for fishermen,
32, 43, 61; seamen on, 176; use of,
for shipyards, 151
Witchcraft, sources of, 191-92, 228n. 38,
229n. 47
Wolf bounty, 88, 143
Wrentham, 22